THE NEW PRACTICAL HANDYMAN'S ENCYCLOPEDIA

BUSTER CRABBE POOLS by CASCADE

THE NEW PRACTICAL HANDYMAN'S ENCYCLOPEDIA
VOLUME 14

THE COMPLETE ILLUSTRATED

(DO IT YOURSELF)

LIBRARY FOR HOME & OUTDOORS

GREYSTONE PRESS/NEW YORK · TORONTO · LONDON

COPYRIGHT © MCMLXV, MCMLXVIII, MCMLXXI, MCMLXXV, MCMLXXVI BY GREYSTONE PRESS
225 Park Avenue South
New York, N.Y. 10013

All rights reserved under the
PAN-AMERICAN COPYRIGHT CONVENTION
and the **INTERNATIONAL COPYRIGHT CONVENTION**

No part of the text or illustrations in this work may
be used without written permission from Greystone Press

Cover and layout design by Silvio Lembo

Printed in the United States of America

•

Tools pictured on Endpapers by SEARS

CONTENTS OF VOLUME FOURTEEN

	Page
PLAY AREA	2084
PLAYHOUSE, Child's Take-Down	2090
PLUMBING, Basic Facts About	2094
PLUMBING, Tools	2100
PLUMBING, Water Supply	2106
PLUMBING, Running Pipe	2122
PLUMBING, Sewage Disposal	2128
PLUMBING, Service and Repair	2138
PLUMBING, Wells	2150
POOL, In-Ground Liner	2158
POOL, Raised Deck	2172
POSTS, Putting Up	2180
POTTER'S WHEEL, Build A	2184
POWER BOATS, Shipshape	2188
POWER BOATS, Hotie	2196
POWER BOATS, Ski Tow	2206
POWER BOATS, Ring-A-Ding	2210
POWER BOATS, Snapper	2214
POWER BOATS, Pakedo	2220
POWER LAWN MOWER, Equipment	2226
POWER LAWN MOWER, Repair	2230
ENERGY/MONEY SAVER IDEAS All About Fireplaces	2240

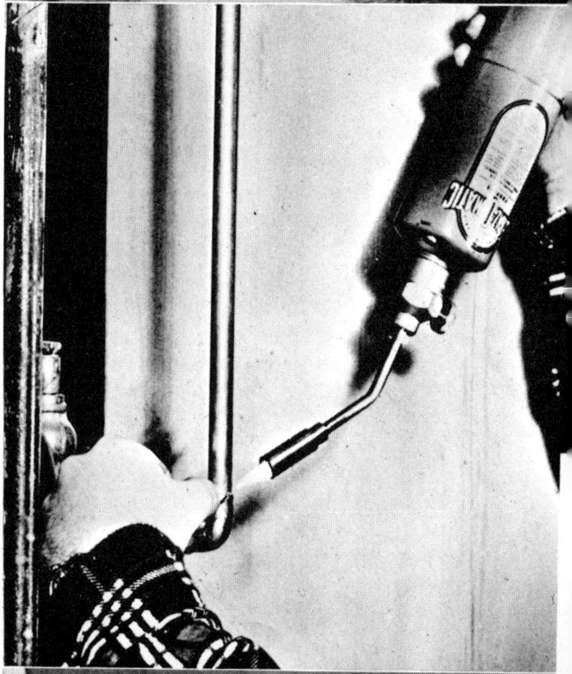

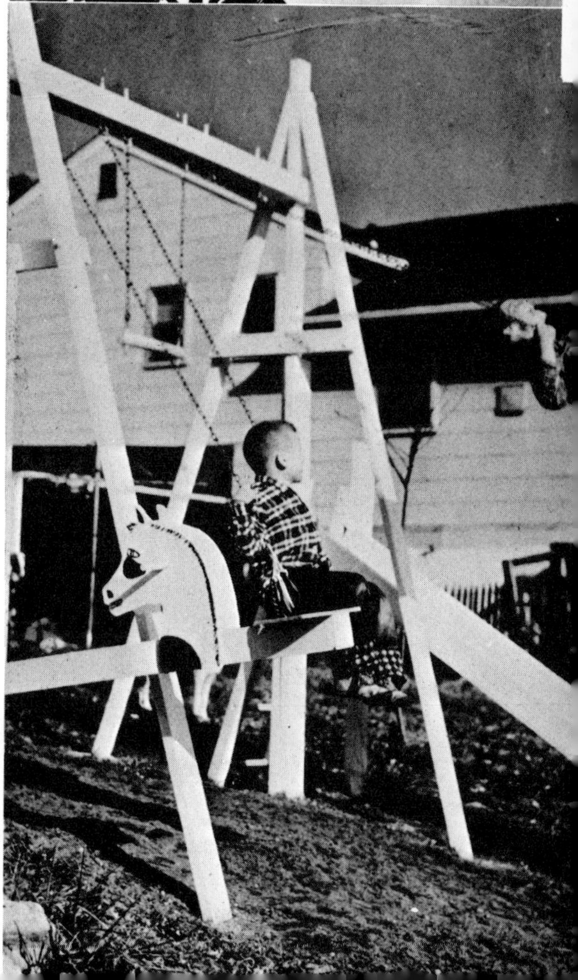

Growing Play Area

Keeping ahead of the kids is no small chore . . . this does it for you. Everything in the unit is adjustable to your own particular family needs

BUILDING a play area that can be adjusted to the growth of the children using it is not a difficult chore. The simple changes necessary to make a basic play unit larger will take no longer than a weekend and cost little more than a few dollars. With these adjustments to growing conditions, the kids will be happier, you will be ahead on the budget and the wife will have few worries about where the children are.

Careful weatherproofing and painting will keep the unit looking good and you can rest assured that structural weakness has been minimized. If sturdy materials are used at the outset, no amount of roughhousing will substantially shorten the life of a play area designed for ten years use.

This unit is also designed to allow changes in number and types of equipment contained within the unit. Instead of flying rings, another swing can be substituted. A chinning bar can be added as well as a rope ladder. If your imagination seems to grow delinquent just when you need it most, leave the changes to the kids. •——*by Emil Brodbeck*

Here is the final play area which has been updated from the basic unit at top of next page. Center crossbar was raised and rebraced. New paint added new life to the old unit. Basic sturdiness remains.

PLAY AREA • 2085

Note the strength in the old timbers used to brace this basic unit together. There is a more rugged look overall plus all of the advantages of the new unit. Trapeze, swings, teeterboard are all good.

Using 2 x 6 planks for basic uprights, fasten together as shown here and in drawing on next page. Smear creosote on the bases of the posts and area that will come in contact with ground.

After digging holes two feet deep, mix enough cement to fill around posts. Place flat stone at bottom of hole and pour in cement. Then set uprights, shimming with some stones until straight.

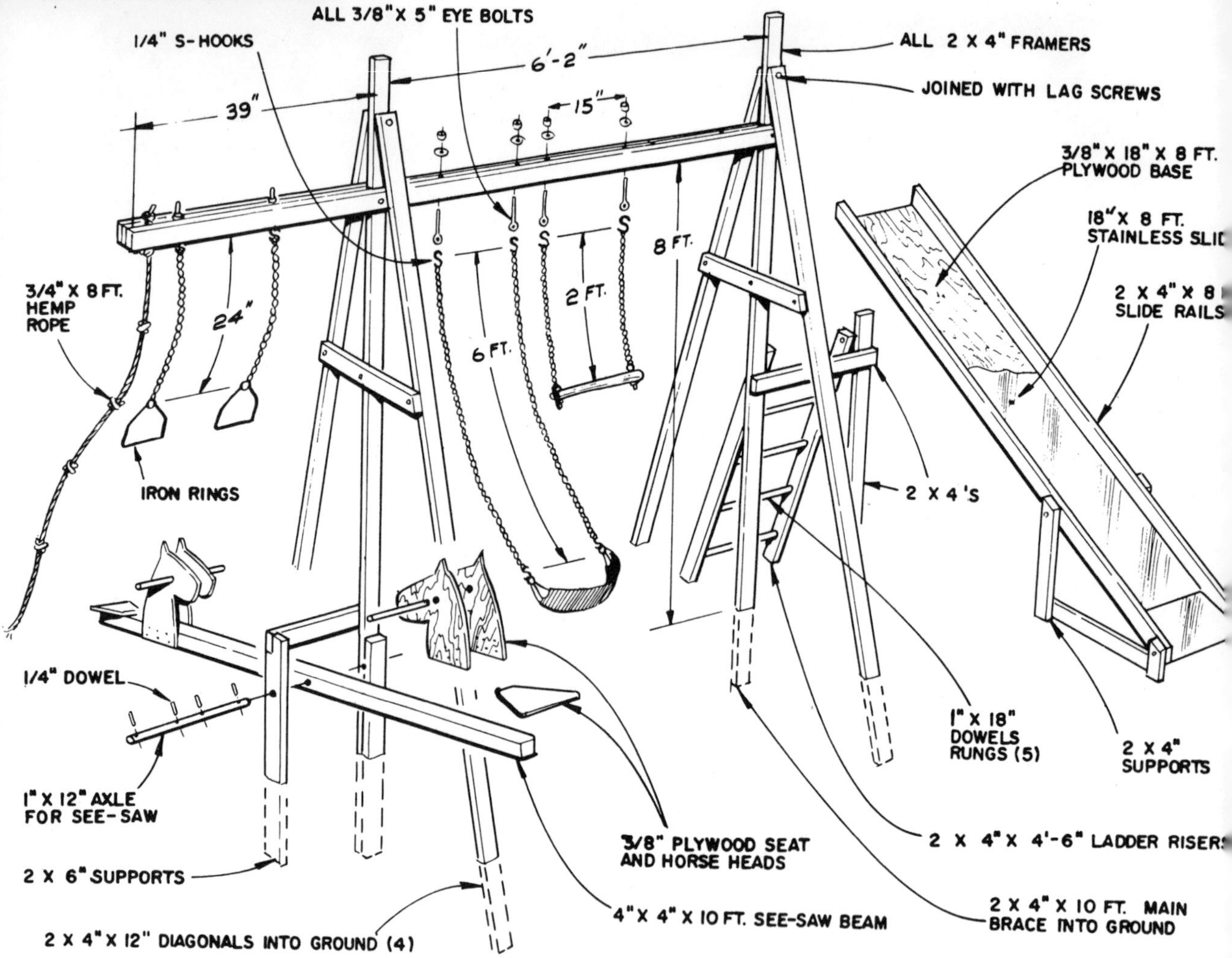

2086 • PLAY AREA

Diagram labels:

- 1/4" S-HOOKS
- ALL 3/8" X 5" EYE BOLTS
- 6'-2"
- 39"
- 15"
- ALL 2 X 4" FRAMERS
- JOINED WITH LAG SCREWS
- 3/8" X 18" X 8 FT. PLYWOOD BASE
- 18" X 8 FT. STAINLESS SLIDE
- 3/4" X 8 FT. HEMP ROPE
- 24"
- 2 X 4" X 8' SLIDE RAILS
- 8 FT.
- 2 FT.
- 6 FT.
- IRON RINGS
- 2 X 4'S
- 1/4" DOWEL
- 1" X 12" AXLE FOR SEE-SAW
- 2 X 6" SUPPORTS
- 2 X 4" X 12" DIAGONALS INTO GROUND (4)
- 3/8" PLYWOOD SEAT AND HORSE HEADS
- 4" X 4" X 10 FT. SEE-SAW BEAM
- 1" X 18" DOWELS RUNGS (5)
- 2 X 4" SUPPORTS
- 2 X 4" X 4'-6" LADDER RISERS
- 2 X 4" X 10 FT. MAIN BRACE INTO GROUND

Bolt two more 2 x 6's to main crosspiece for additional support. Ladder sides are 2 x 4's sunk into the ground. Use 1 x 18-inch dowels and drill holes in the sides to fit. Place dowels, then cut off.

Sides of the ladder should be finished at least to the extent that no splinters will catch in children's hands and clothes. A quick sanding does the job. Use a plane to remove sharp edges.

PLAY AREA • 2087

Finished basic area includes swing, trapeze, rope climb, slide and seesaw. Rope may be substituted for chain hangers but chain is much safer. Weatherproof the whole unit completely.

The growth process from the basic area starts by removing crosspiece and raising the 2x4 uprights. Use heavy bolts throughout. Side braces are buried and bolted in place as shown in art.

Seesaw has been reinforced and modified to a more refined styling. Brace with top crosspiece. Use 4x4 for teeterboard and cut horse heads from new or scrap plywood. The dowel is held with key.

Crossbrace and handles between horses' heads are held in place with keys hammered into predrilled holes. Seat and heads can best be made from templates on a jig shaw. Paint to suit your fancy.

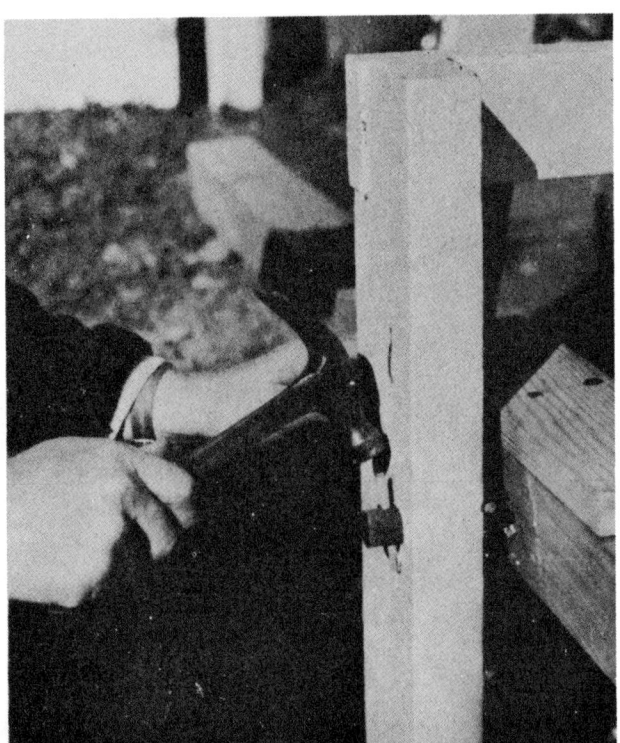

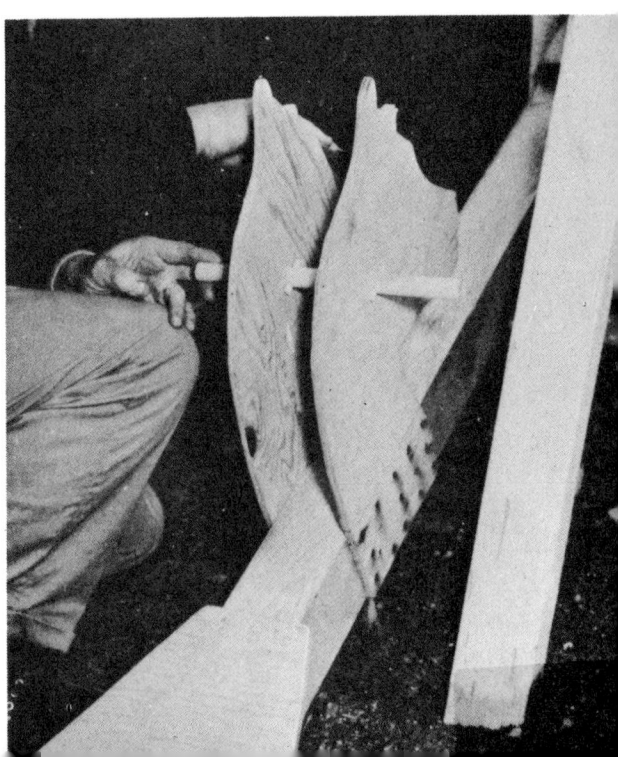

2088 • PLAY AREA

Extending the slide is liable to be tricky. The first brace is built up from the old. A crosspiece ties 2x4's together and gives added height. Height here is optional; second brace is set.

Second brace establishes height of bottom of slide. Be sure slide will rest on both braces evenly. Tie the two braces together with 2x4's and trim off excess. Now drop slide in place.

Stainless steel plate is fastened on top of all-weather plywood. This is attached to 2x4 crosspiece and fastened to bottom braces. Now side bar is installed to extend the old sidepieces and the brace.

PLAY AREA • 2089

Measure and cut piece of scrap wood to fill in exposed area beneath sidepiece. Once fitted, nail in securely using sidepiece for anchor. It may be wise to sand all areas that might come in contact with children's hands to be safe.

All end-of-slide construction is covered by plywood sheet. This is glued and screwed in place and acts as a protective shield over all piecework inside. Painted, you can be sure of your weatherproofing. You can sand smooth.

This time it would be wise to use chain for swing and trapeze rigging since it is assumed that this will be the last change in the play unit. If you like, you can again change arrangement of devices or add different ones to suit kids.

CHILD'S TAKE-DOWN PLAYHOUSE

It's a jungle trade post . . . a space station on the perilous moon route. And, for anxious parents, it's assurance they're safe and happy in their own yard.

HERE is a play house to renew any child's interest in his own back yard. Its 4 x 8-ft. "floor plan" will shelter several children and their toys. The cheery front windows are unbreakable, safe, and the ventilation via the louvered rear window is never forgotten, never left open to a rain.

Best of all, this play house need never become musty or old. It is fully take-down; the six sections and two roof beams can be stored away through the winter season. Or, with its mere 5½-ft. overall height, the play house can be set up in your basement during the cold months.

This is really a house-building project,

PLAY HOUSE • 2091

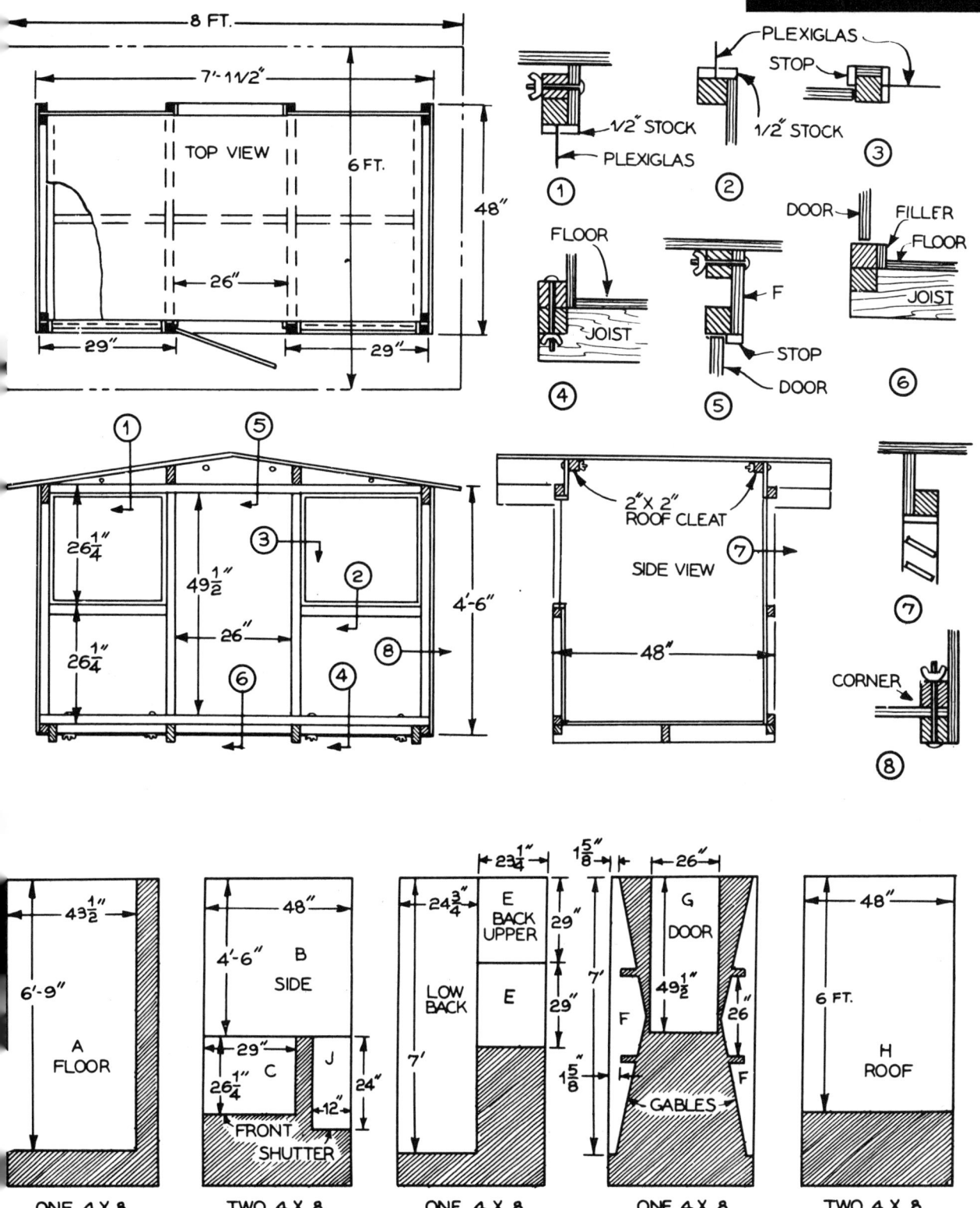

though far from difficult, as your multi-purpose tool will handle every cut required. For the plywood, ordinary rotary-cut fir panels of any exterior grade and in either ½, ⅝ or ¾-inch thickness is used throughout. There is no need to purchase a "marine" grade of exterior plywood. Though such plywood has no blemishes on either side, it is no more waterproof than a less-expensive A-C grade of exterior plywood and the small blemishes of the latter do not detract from the appearance or strength of this construction. The floor joists, 2 x 2 framing and the roof beams should be of No. 1 or No. 2 common structural lumber.

2092 • PLAY HOUSE

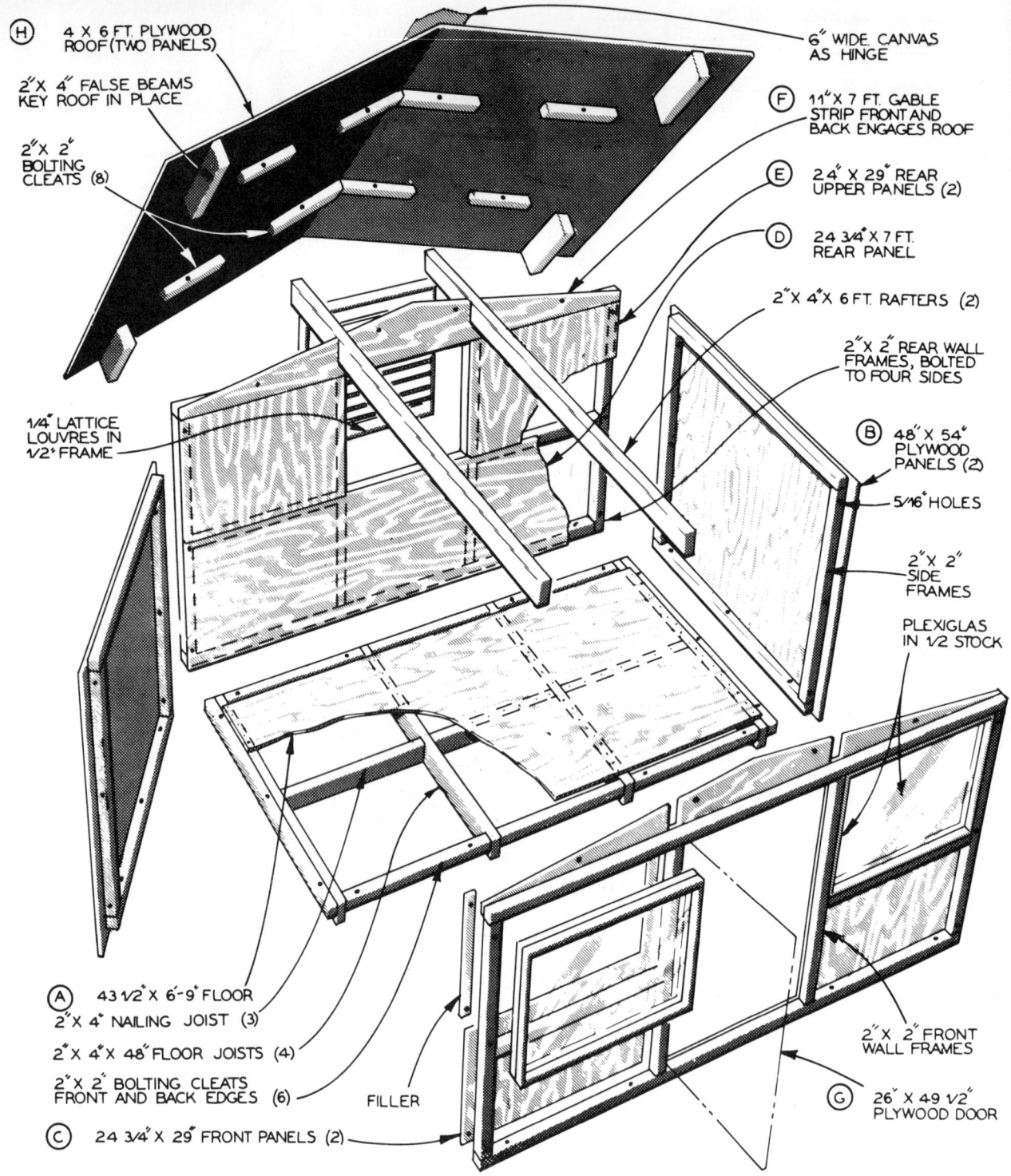

As shown by the drawings, the major sections of the house are its floor, four sides and the roof. All sides bolt together and to the floor section. Use 8d casing or finish nails to attach the floor to its 2 x 4 joists. Use 6d casing or finish nails to attach the 2 x 2 framing to the sides and to the two gable strips.

Throughout the entire construction, it is preferable to use galvanized nails to prevent rust spots under paint and to use galvanized bolts and wing nuts for easy assembly. When cutting the larger pieces of plywood on your table saw, make full use of its extension table and, if alone in your workshop, use some homemade extension stand to provide support for the opposite end of the 8-ft. panels.

The roof anchors to the front and rear sides of the play house by bolts through the gable strips and through the 2 x 2 bolting cleats on the underside of the roof. Use glue and 6d nails to secure the bolting cleats to the roof; use glue and 8d nails to secure the 2 x 4 false beams to the roof. Any fairly heavy canvas can be utilized for the hinge of the two roof sections. Use galvanized tacks and any waterproof glue or cement on hand to secure the canvas, and it is best to use a tent preservative or a paste floor wax, thinned with turpentine and well soaked in, on the canvas. If painted, the canvas will crack under repeated folding.

Windows of 1/8-in. plexiglas or other rigid plastic are preferable, but for economy, they can be of translucent plastic cloth, the inexpensive type with a fly screen bonded into the middle. In a warm climate, the windows can be left open, if desired, or simply covered with aluminum, galvanized or plastic fly screen. The rear louvered window can be the same.

The plywood front door is best hung with a full length of piano hinge, or at least four 3 x 1½-in. butt hinges—to prevent warping and because children will not be able to resist swinging on it. The door latch should be one made for a closet or cabinet, of a type that cannot be locked from the inside. If a keyed lock is desired it is best to use a separate cabinet or desk drawer lock.

To finish, first give the entire house, inside and out, a coat of white resin sealer. This both protects the wood against moisture and prevents undue grain rise in the plywood. Finish the outside with two coats of any good exterior paint. Inside, an attractive and simple modern finish is obtained by brushing a fairly thin coat of paint of the desired color, over the white resin sealer, wiping it off with rags while still wet, and, finally, applying a coat of wax, thinned shellac or wallpaper lacquer. Best to try a sample of scrap plywood first, to find how much to wipe your particular paint for the desired toning. This gives a toned or stained "natural" finish—the grain shows through the thin coats but without overly accenting the plywood's rotary grain. The finish has the definite advantage of not showing bumps and scratches as would any enamel or other solid coloring. •

MATERIALS REQUIRED

7 pcs.—4' x 8' x ½", ⅝", or ¾" ext. plywd.
40 lin. ft.—2" x 4" studs
122 lin. ft.—2" x 2"
32 lin. ft.—½" x 1"
40 lin. ft.—½" x 2½"
8 metal hinges
3 metal door handles
36 ¼" x 4" carriage bolts with wing nuts
3 cupboard catches

All pieces needed for the play house can be cut to the size required on the multi-purpose power tool.

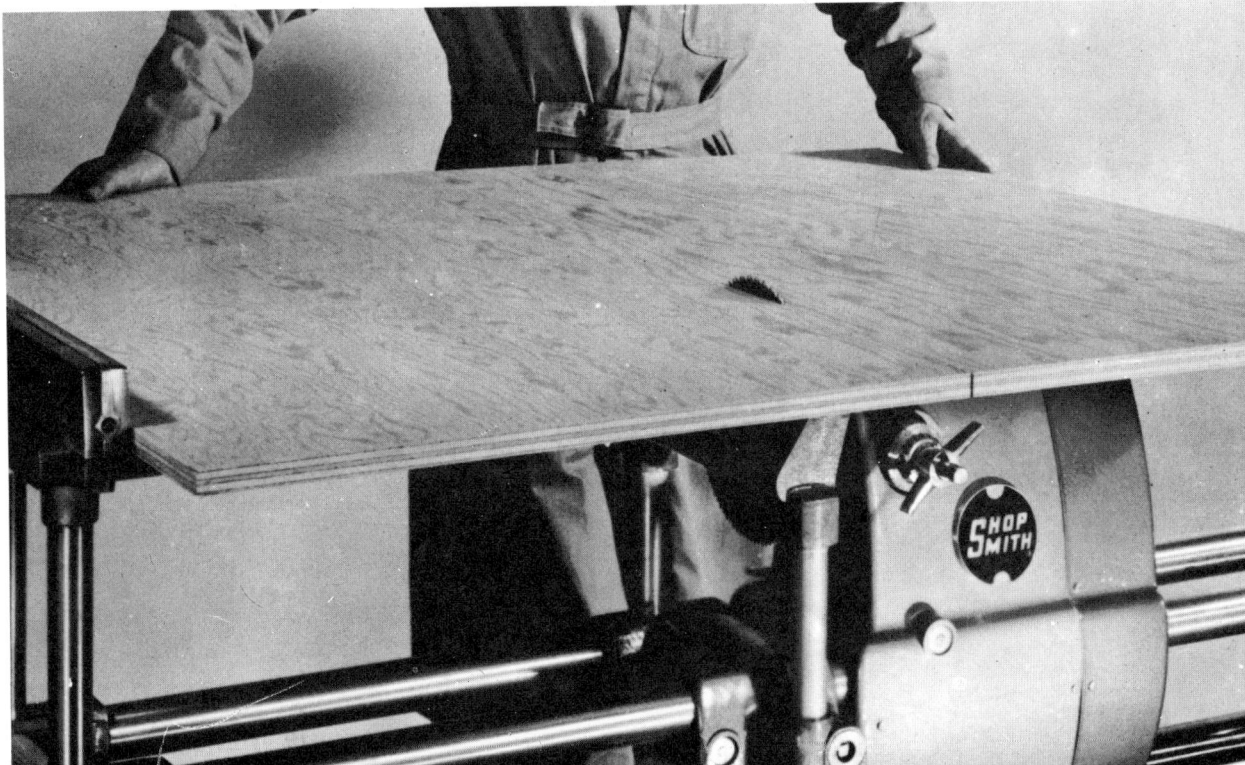

A drab, dull bathroom can be made colorful by the addition of moisture-resistant wallpaper by Stockwell Wallpaper Co. The windowless room is made light and cheerful with floral stenciled fixtures by the Rheem Mfg. Co. Tile enclosure, by American Olean Co., allows the toilet to be recessed in a niche of its own.

BASIC FACTS ABOUT PLUMBING

THE PLUMBING in your house is not the mystery many people think it is. Nor is it so technically impossible that the do-it-yourselfer cannot attempt almost any kind of plumbing, whether it be an addition, repair or new work.

Plumbing is a straightforward thing. Its sole purpose is to get water where you want it, and to get rid of water and waste when you are through with it. Nothing complicated at all.

In early days each manufacturer made his own fittings and attachments to suit his own design. Many of them were not interchangeable with those of other manufacturers. If you had a water closet from one company in your house, and it failed for some reason or other, unless you could get parts from the people who made it in the beginning, a repair was almost impossible to do, and you were forced to rely on professional men to help out, or replace the fixture.

Today, however, plumbing fixtures, pipes, fittings and attachments have been standardized to the point that, up to the final fixture, any make and any source of pipe and fittings can be used for the installation. The fittings themselves may vary greatly in appearance, size and operation, but they will all fit into or onto the plumbing installation. Furthermore, most of them will fit with no alteration of distances, centers of supply feeders, etc.

PLUMBING • 2095

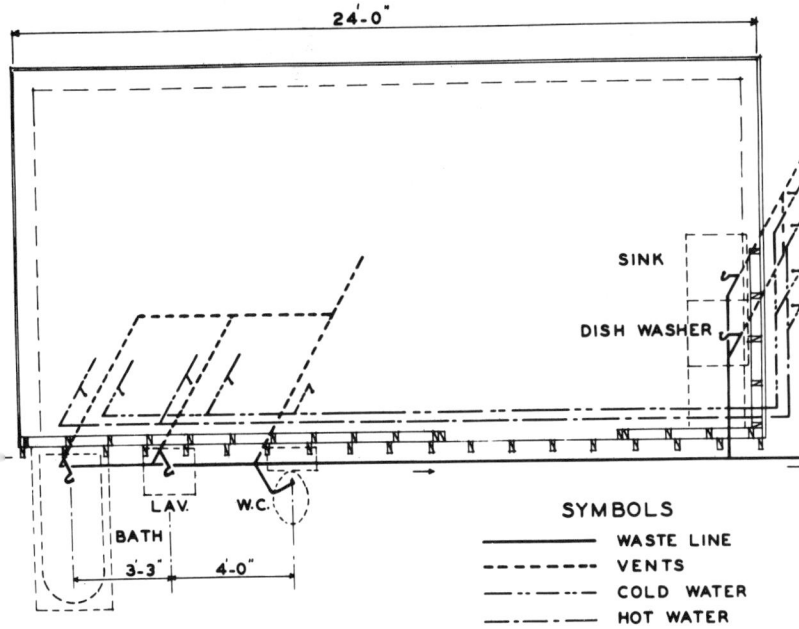

Installation plans for plumbing are usually shown in a schematic drawing like this. You may find it helpful to use these symbols in planning your plumbing project.

Chase Brass and Copper

This makes it easy for the homeowner or home builder who wants to do his own work for several reasons. It can be from a point of economy—you can save up to 50% or more by doing your own work—or it can be because you like to do your own work for the immense satisfaction of accomplishing something with your own hands.

The only drawback, indeed, for the person who wants to undertake his own plumbing installation is that of local codes. Perhaps you live in a neighborhood which has a regulation that no work may be done by other than licensed plumbers, electricians, carpenters, etc. This is, to my way of thinking, an unfortunate area to live in.

Your local town hall, courthouse or records bureau can tell you about the local building restrictions. If there are none, you need have no qualms about diving right into the job yourself. Really, there is nothing much to plumbing except a number of fundamentals which are apparent to anyone who can figure out a few things for himself. For instance, it should be understood that all supply lines must be continuous and closed systems. That is to say, the hot water lines are all one continuous system and the cold water lines are another. The two come together only at one point—the cold water supply to the hot water heater.

The next fundamental is that all drains and soil lines be pitched at an angle downward from the fixture it is supposed to drain. It would be evident even to a person who knew nothing of mechanics and plumbing that a drain would not work uphill.

The third fundamental is that all drains

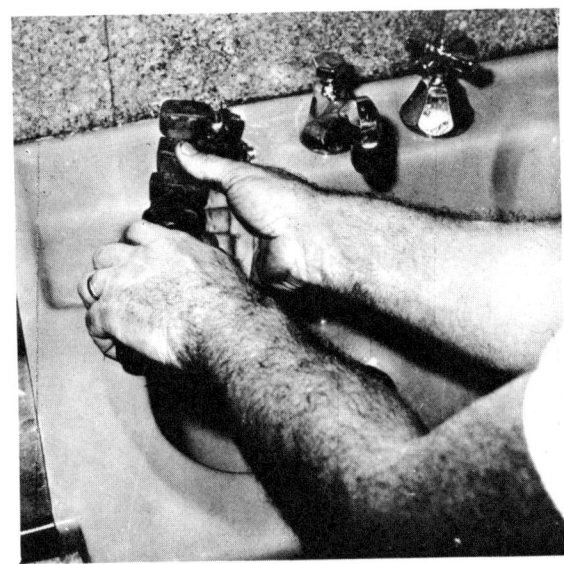

A knowledge of how to make plumbing repairs will not only save you money, but is great convenience. When emergency arises, there will be no need to phone, then wait helplessly for plumber.

should be vented to the open air. This may be news to a lot of people, because it deals with a concept of optimum operation rather than fundamental operation. The purpose of venting is to avoid suction-locking in a drain and to allow water and waste to run through the drain as freely as possible. Besides consideration of the pitch of the pipe, venting also helps water to pass slight obstructions, bends, sags—and whatever may occur after installation such as ground settlement and foundation cracking.

Vents are a very important part of plumbing, even though they do not carry water or waste. They carry sewer gases

2096 • PLUMBING

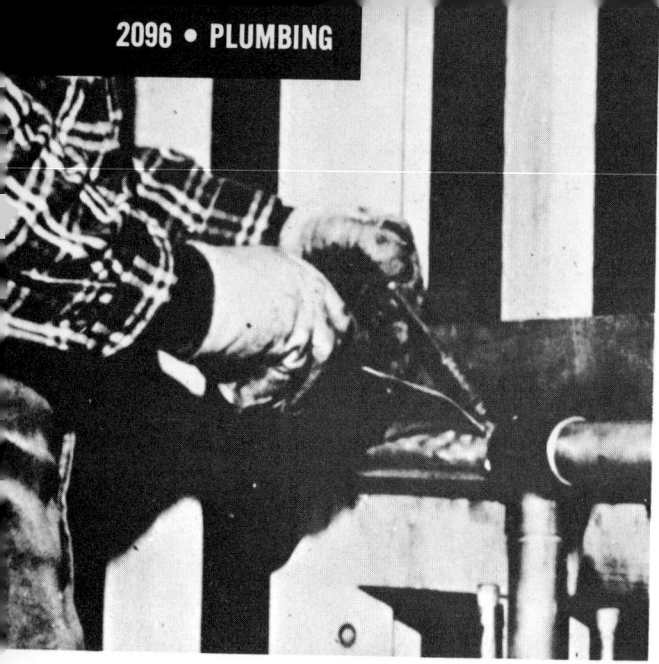

Vent flashing makes leakproof joint between vent and roof. Tuck flashing under the roofing felt.

Vents provide air needed for free flow of sewage down the drains. Here several branch vent lines are connected to stack which extends to the roof.

and direct them up above the roof of the house instead of allowing them to leak inside. They release back pressure so that fixtures do not gurgle when drained and waste does not back up into the lower floor fixtures when the upper floor fixtures are operated. Each vent pipe has its lower end tied into the soil drain, and its upper end free to the air above the roof.

The vents from individual fixtures can all be tied into the main vent stack by 1½- or 2-inch pipes, and the stack itself be made 3- or 4-inch pipe of many different compositions. Galvanized steel or copper pipe may be used, or the newer plastic pipes. The main point to keep in mind is that each individual fixture has a line running to the vent stack and thence to the drain, with a trap in between the fixture and the stack. This trap serves to block sewer gases and prevent them from coming into the room. These gases can be a serious health hazard, possibly even fatal. The traps must therefore be installed with tight joints, as should all soil and waste lines. A leak in a water line merely means a loss of water, and possibly some water damage to the house or its furnishings. A leak in a soil line can mean the health or life of some member of the family.

As to the technical requirements in plumbing installations, these, too, are few and practical. A certain minimum is required of all installations. A minimum size is needed for sufficient water flow. A certain minimum is required for a drain to allow it to take not only the fixture immediately in use, but two or more fixtures simultaneously, for instance when two toilets in the house are draining at the same time, or perhaps a bath and kitchen sink, or any combination all draining together. A minimum pitch is also needed for drain pipes to accelerate the flow of waste to the sewer line, cesspool or septic tank, whatever the method of disposal be.

All these minimums can be found in plumbing code books, generally available from dealers and supply houses. There is nothing against using better than the minimum in size, quality, or in installation methods. The better your work, the longer the installation will last, and the easier it

If your bathroom looks antiquated, modernize it by installing new fixtures where old ones stood, using the existing water supply and waste lines.

Because of its light weight, copper lends itself to "shop fabrication." Entire assemblies can be made and then placed into position in structure.

will give trouble-free operation. This is so up to a point. You certainly would not install 1½-inch supply lines, for example, when a ½-inch pipe is enough to supply a line that is used only occasionally, or that supplies a small fixture. You might very well, however, go to a ¾-inch supply line. This would have a certain advantage, e.g., the water flow would not drop to a trickle when someone turned on a tap somewhere else in the immediate line. The pressure with the ¾-inch pipe would be greater at the faucet, so the tub, basin or sink could be filled more quickly.

Many plumbing supply houses do not like to sell to individuals. This because they feel they have an obligation to their larger customers, the professional plumber who buys many times the amount an individual would need, and this as a long term repeat customer. The supplies feels that he is taking part of the living away from the professional.

Other suppliers are very happy to help with information, advice and even know-how when you tell them your problems. Many of them will, if you outline your job, rough out the system and determine the exact number of fittings, amount of pipe required, etc. Large mail-order houses, such as Montgomery Ward, Sears Roebuck and a few others, have a design service. You tell them what you want to install, sending a floor plan of your house, and they will not only make the parts list for you, but rough in a drawing of all the plumbing installation. Furthermore, they will rent you, for a minimal fee, or free, the tools you will need to do the job, obviating the necessity of investing a sizable amount in tools and equipment you may never need again.

Of course, if you intend to make repairs and alterations yourself, it is a good idea to buy a minimal set of plumbing tools—a couple of good wrenches, a cutter and a threading die with the two most-used sized of cutters (½ inch and ¾ inch), together with a good solid pipe vise. With these few simple and inexpensive tools you will be surprised at the amount of work you can do.

In new construction, if you are building a house, the most economical method is to locate all rooms using water and waste lines either directly above each other or back to back. This is good planning since, by having two or more rooms using the supply lines within the same wall, a single feeder can be run and the individual fixtures tapped off with short risers.

Whatever installation you perform, and however your fixtures are located, you start with the same thing—a cold water intake for the entire house. If it is from a city water source located out in the street, you generally cannot tie into this line yourself, but must, after all the installation is completed and inspected, have the city tie in for you. Also, if you are using city water, a water meter must be put into the supply feeder between the street source and the first used tap of the water in the house. Often the meter is located in a sunken pit with a metal cover out near the front of the property. In this case the tie-in from the street enters the pit from the main side, and the feeder line leaves on the opposite side to enter your home. All this is underground, of course, and well below the frost level to keep the pipes from freezing in the winter. Frost levels vary according to the mean lowest temperature your area endures, and the local inspectors or plumbing supplies can tell you the depth if you do not know it already.

If you are supplied from the city, the chances are that you will also tie into the city sewer line. If this is the case, the same trench can be used for the supply pipes and the sail pipes to avoid cutting two trenches in the street.

If your water supply is from your own well, then a meter is note needed, unless you are curious as to how much water you are drawing, or whether you intend to rent the place and charge for water. When the source is a well, you will either have a well-house or pump-house, or locate the well in the basement of the house itself. This last is not so good, if work is ever necesary on the well, because the well driller cannot get a rig into the basement very easily. Quite often, if you are building from scratch, the location for the foundations can be laid out, and the well drilled alongside one wall. Then, when the foundations are poured,'or built up with small bay can be built to enclose the well block or whatever you are going to use, a pipe, with an access to the crawl space are having one. If the walls of the bay are under the house, or the basement if you insulated, you should have no worry about the supply freezing in the winter. However, provide a shed roof or other removable covering for the bay. Should the well ever need to be reworked, for any of a number of reasons, the simple removal of the cover will allow the driller to back his rig right up to the wall and drop his drill down the well without having to tear the house down to get at it. Often, a well might need some such service, and, if you provide for this when you drill, it will save a lot of headaches and trouble later on.

It will save a lot of trouble, also, if, when you design the layout in the beginning you take into consideration all the appliances you might want to install in the future and provide for them, even if you do not install them immediately. For instance, you can provide supply lines and drains, capped off if not put into immediate use, for a dishwasher, clothes washer, garbage disposal, water softener, a photographic darkroom if you are a camera bug, laundry trays, even an extra bath or half-bath in some out-of-the-way nook.

You need not run pipes to all these places. Merely include a tee in the line at the most convenient location for future tie-ins, and then plug the takeoff leg of the tee, or, cap a short nipple in it. The same with the drains. Tees or wyes located at a convenient spot, for tying in at a later date, cost only the price of the tee or wye fitting at the time of installation. It costs a lot more in time, labor and frayed tempers, cutting out the line and installing a new fitting at a future time.

Cleanouts should be planned for, and installed, at strategic points in the drains. Remember that you may never open them for the life of the building. But there is the chance that you may have to get to them, so position them in such a manner that the openings are of easy access with a snake or other cleanout device. Individual traps on each fixture should also be located so they are of easy access for cleaning and draining. Most traps have a drain plug located on the bottom of the bend, and enough space should be allowed under the bend to put a bucket or deep pan big enough to hold the contents of the trap plus a good quantity of water standing in the fixture. Very often a trap will plug up in the kitchen sink, or the bathroom lavatory. In the former instance the stoppage is usually right in the trap and is caused by the accumulation of particles of food packing up. When this happens, the sink is often full of water, and the only way you can get rid of it is to dip it out from the top, or let it run out through the trap drain. The bathroom lavatories will clog up if much hair-washing is done in it, and the popup drain is not periodically removed for cleaning. The loose hairs mat up into a surprisingly tight, waterproof mat and the trap must be disassembled for cleaning. •

When planning your plumbing lines, consider all appliances you may install, such as water softener, requiring supply and drainage connections.

Sears, Roebuck

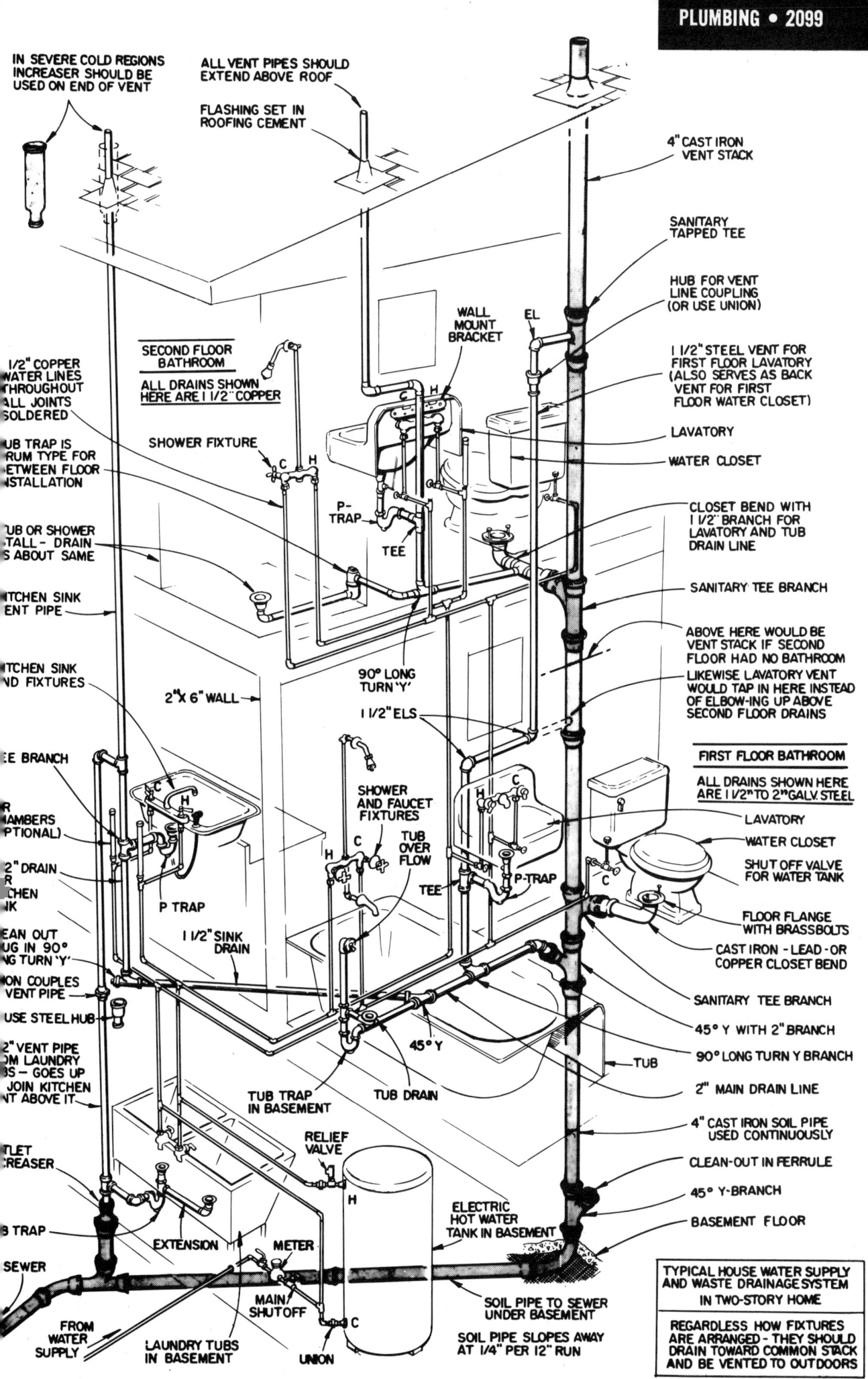

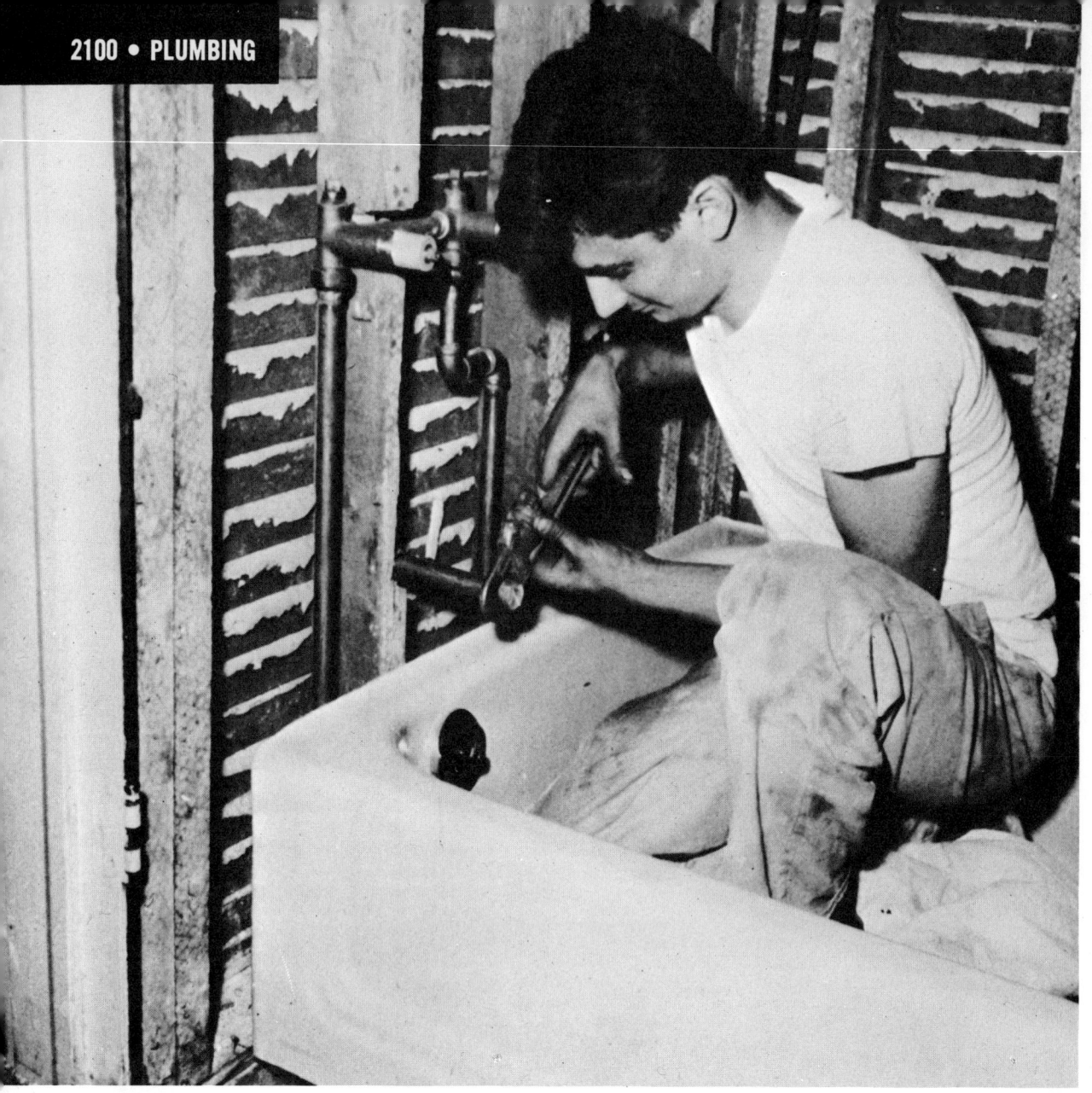

Wrenches are a plumber's most used tool. Here he hooks up water pipe connections after tub was put in place. Until chrome fittings are ready for installation he covers pipe ends for protection.

PLUMBING TOOLS

PLUMBING AND PIPE tools are made to fit almost every conceivable situation. A good set of such tools is a valuable asset to any homeowner, and more especially to one who undertakes his own installation or repair work.

Pipe Wrenches come in sizes from six inch, which will take the smallest work, up to sixty inch, for enormous drain systems seldom, if ever, encountered in the home. The Ridge Tool Company makes these wrenches in two styles—straight, and end. The end wrenches have offset heads which make the tool invaluable for working in tight places where the pipe is close to a wall or other obstruction.

Hex Wrenches and *End Hex Wrenches* are for use on the flanges of ground-joint unions, the bonnets of valves, etc.

Offset Hex Wrenches are made for the express purpose of operating the drain nuts on the fittings under sinks, tubs, lavatories, etc.

Strap Wrenches have a hard canvas belt attached to a handle so shaped that when the strap is wrapped around the pipe and

PLUMBING • 2101

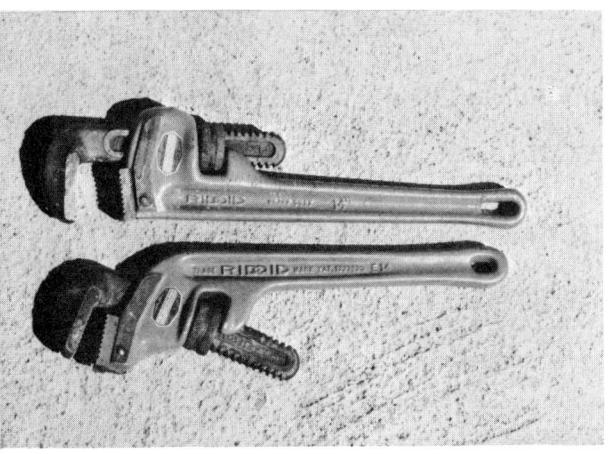

A standard and an offset Rigid pipe wrench. The offset or end wrench is useful for tight corners. Both types of wrenches come in different sizes.

Rigid hex wrenches are used to tighten ground joint unions, nuts on basins, sinks, etc. They come in 6 sizes, in offset and end wrench styles.

For the plumber this compound leverage wrench is a blessing. It is capable of exerting many times the force of a plain wrench of same size.

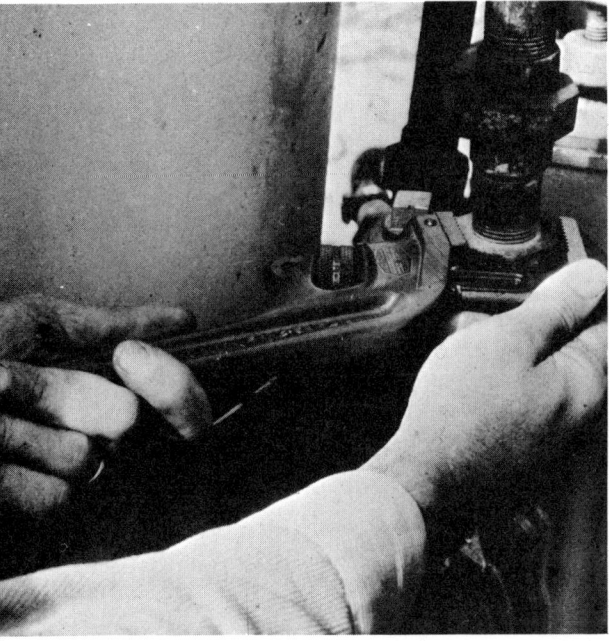

End pattern pipe wrench makes work easier when pipe is close to wall, or quarters are cramped. The offset is its only difference. Its operation is the same way as any straight pipe wrench.

Ratchet pipe threaders come in many styles and sizes. This one has cutters for pipes from ⅛ inch to 1¼ inches. Each cutter has a built-in pipe guide so threads at pipe ends start square.

pressure put on the handle, the strap tightens up and turns the work by the friction of the belt. They are used on fancy fittings, chrome-plated shower pipes, etc. They do not mar the finish on the work.

Chain Wrenches are a variation of the strap wrench, in that a chain is substituted for the strap. They are for use in tight places, or for irregularly shaped objects in extra close quarters. They will not crush the work, since the pressure of the chain is distributed all around the object.

One of the most valuable types of tools for the person plumbing his own house or doing much work with pipe is the *Compound Leverage Wrench*. These wrenches give many times the turning power of a standard wrench. When fittings are frozen or rusted in place, a compound leverage wrench will turn them out easily and with practically no exertion. They are invaluable for disassembling fittings or pipes that have been in use long enough to let the threads rust tightly together. The tool will allow easy removal of the fittings without damaging them so they may be used over again in future installations.

Pipe Threaders are available in many different styles, from the simple die-in-a-stock kind to ratchet back-geared compound types for large pipes, and to electrically driven ones for production threading.

Each size of pipe threader has a matching size of *Pipe Tap*. These are useful for chasing rusted or worn threads in female fittings.

Pipe Cutters are also made in several styles. The standard one is the one the homeowner will find most useful for his work. There is also a four-wheeled cutter which will cut a pipe in a trench or other tight quarters with short quarter-turns of the handle.

Tubing Cutters, for working copper pipe or tubing, are made the same way and in the same styles as the regular pipe cutters.

Reamers are supplied for clearing the burrs out of the ends of pipe after it has been cut. This is a real must in any plumb-

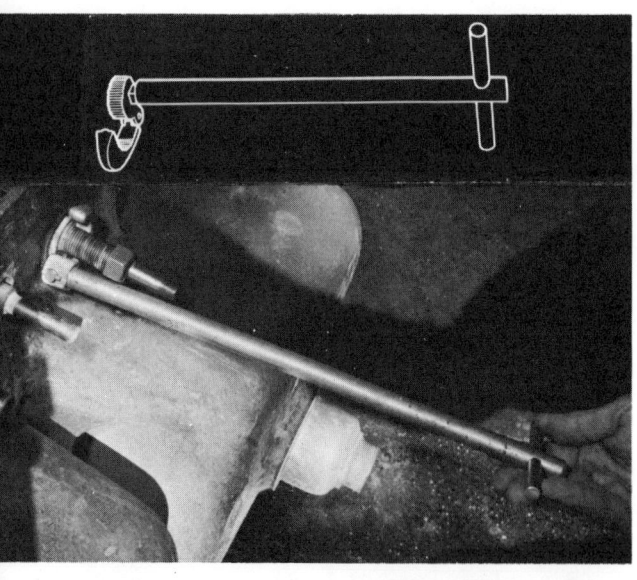

A basin wrench is designed to get at nuts in close quarters or hard-to-reach spots, such as flush valves, traps and basin nuts. The jaw is reversible, so that it can tighten or loosen.

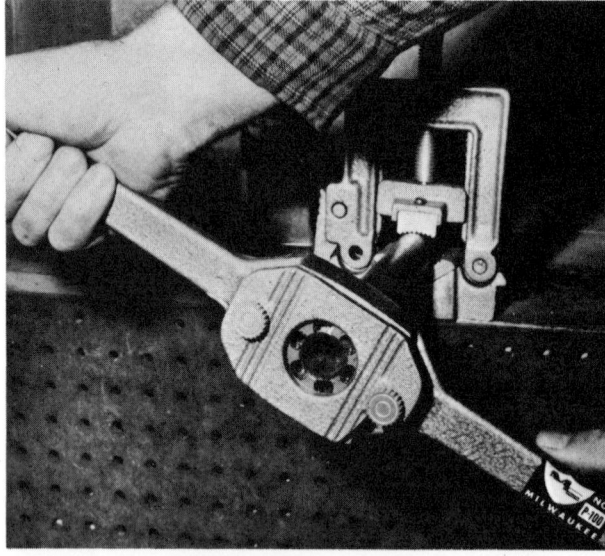

In starting thread, stock is turned clockwise on pipe end until the die takes hold. The stock is then turned half a turn forward, back a quarter turn, until the cutting of thread is completed.

Before and during cutting of thread, cutting oil must be liberally applied to the die and the threads. The oil lubricates and cools the die, prolongs its life by preventing loss of temper.

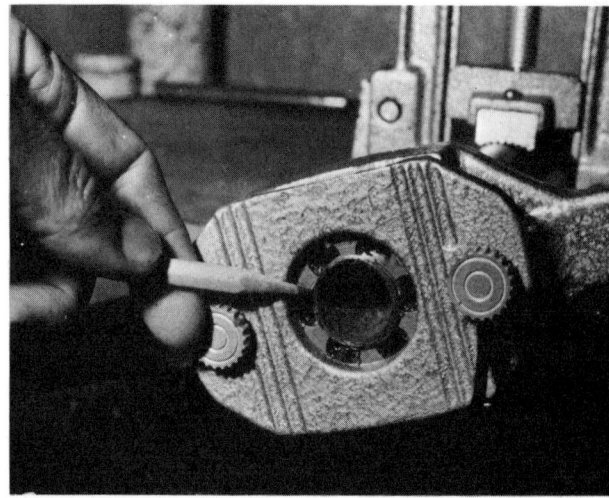

Thread is cut until pipe's end projects half a turn beyond the end of the die. Threader is then removed by turning it counterclockwise. Wipe away surplus oil, chips, and job is done.

ing installation to avoid cutting down the flow of water. Drains should also be reamed to eliminate catching-spots for waste. You can get reamers with square shanks to use in an ordinary carpenter's brace; ratchet reamers which can be fitted right in the pipe-threader handle; straight or spirally-cut reamers and reamers for use on motor-driven threaders.

Benders, for making bends in copper pipe or tubing, as well as step-on benders for galvanized pipe and thick or thin-wall electrical conduit, are to be had from any plumbing supply house.

Flaring Tools are made for putting the flares on the ends of copper tubing when flare fittings are to be used. Be sure to remember to put the nut on the tube before flaring the end.

Pipe Vises are a must if you are going to do any amount of cutting and threading. They are made in many different styles, from small ones that are bolted to the edge of a workbench for occasional small hold-

A standard pipe cutter is a must for anyone doing much plumbing or repair. Takes pipe up to 2 inches in size and makes perfectly square cuts.

When cutting flexible copper tubing, work carefully to avoid squeezing tube out of round. Turn hand screw to tighten cutter half turn at a time.

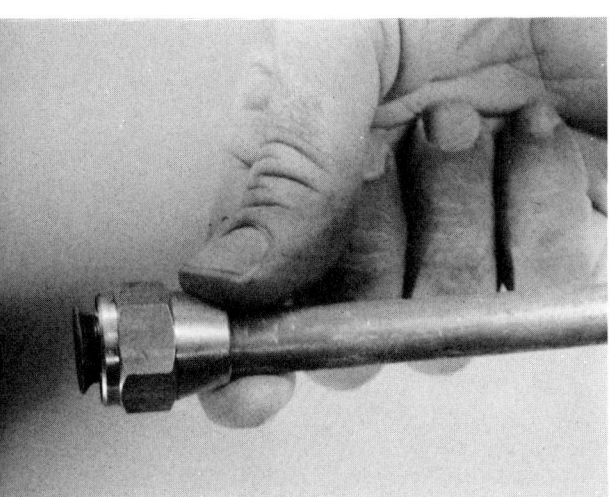

After tube end has been flared, slide flanged retaining nut back up to tube end. This nut was placed over tubing before the flaring operation. Now the nut will fit snugly over the flared end.

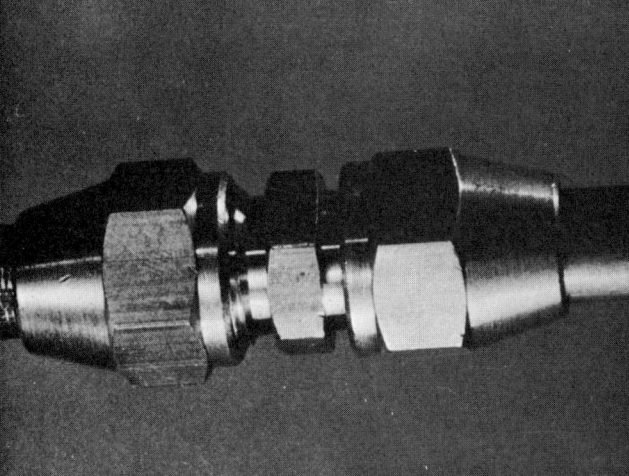

The flared coupling joint is assembled with two wrenches. One wrench is used to hold nut on one side, while other side is tightened. However, be careful. Too much force may destroy flange.

2104 • PLUMBING

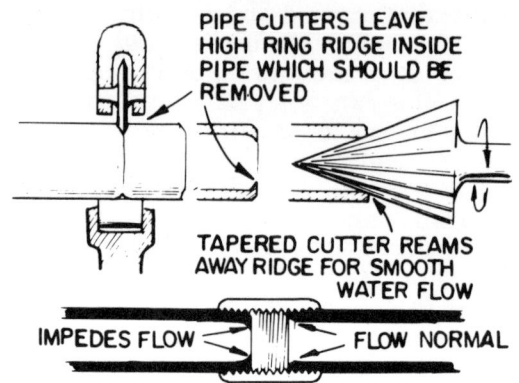

Chain wrench is useful in tight corners and for those jobs where piping runs tight up against a wall. On installations of this kind you may not have clearance for jaws of standard pipe wrench.

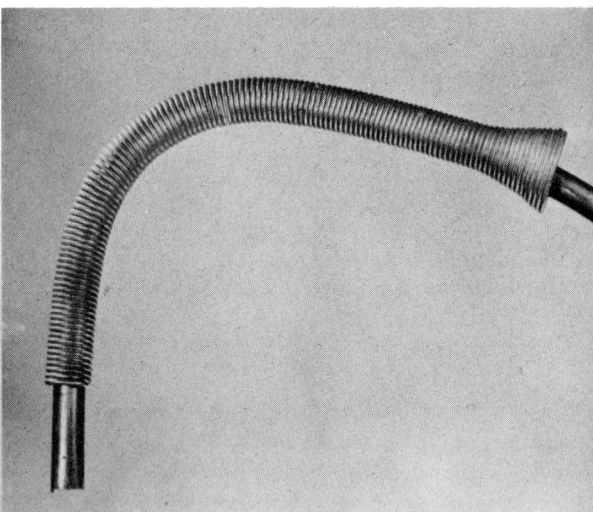

To make smooth bends in flexible copper tubing use a spring-type tubing bender. Tight spring covers the tube and prevents it from collapsing.

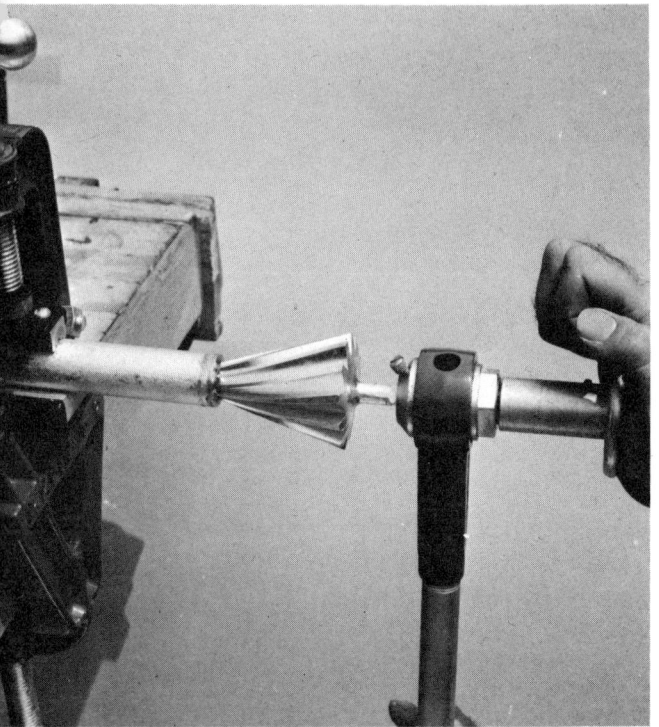

After end of pipe is cut, use reaming tool to clean burrs prior to threading. Make sure vise is tightly locked before starting pipe threading.

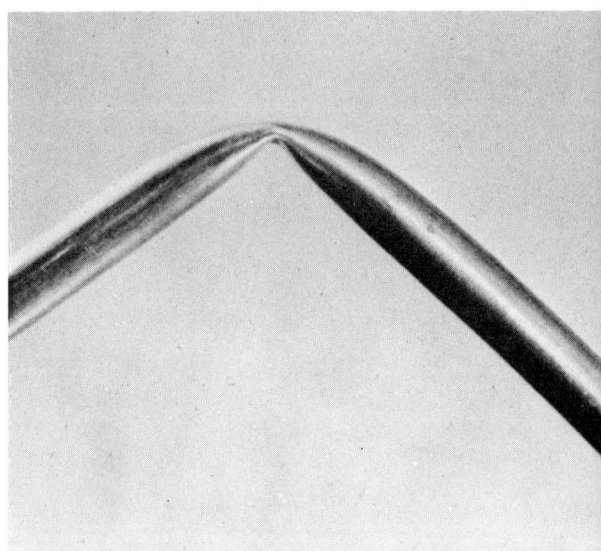

Failure to use tubing bender may cause pipe to kink at center of bend. To prevent this, don't try tight bends, and always use a bending tool.

PLUMBING • 2105

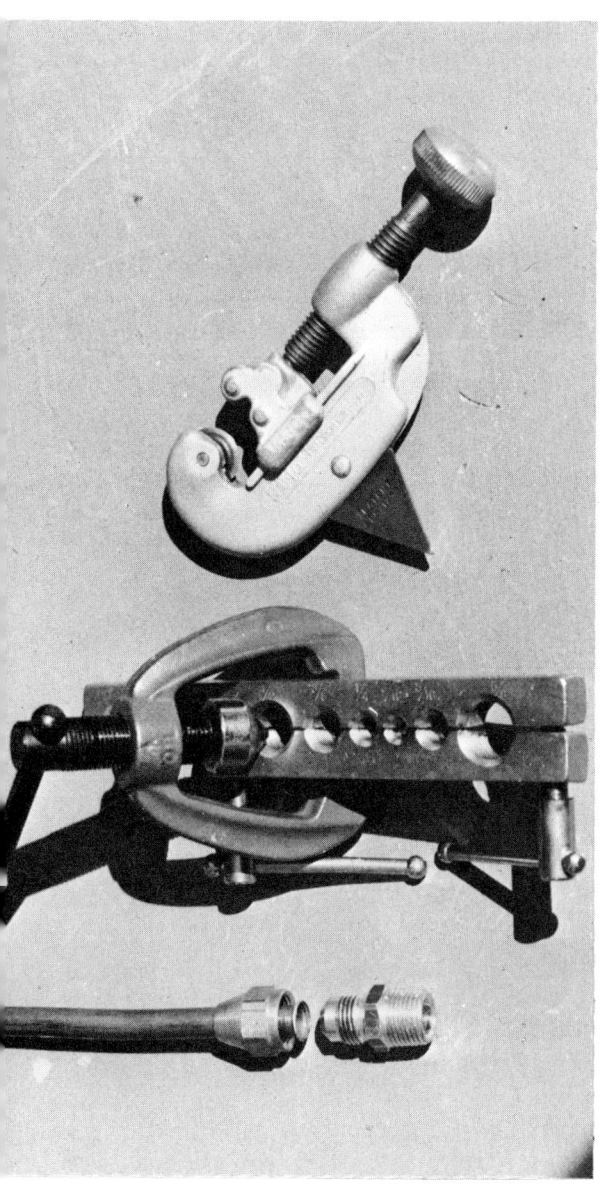

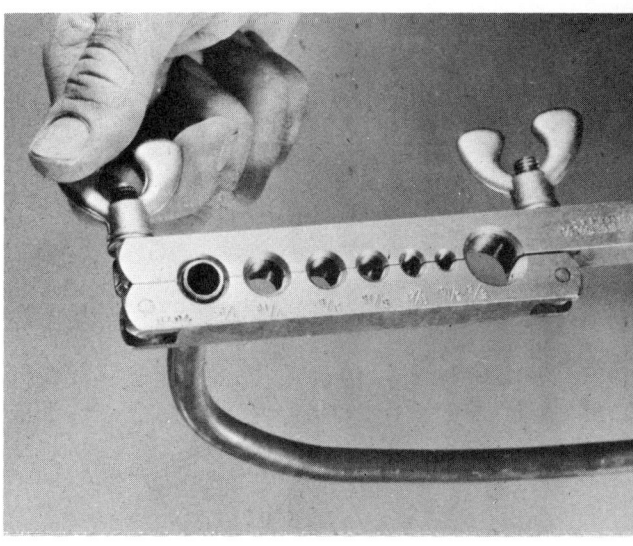

To flare the tubing with a flanging tool, clamp the tube end in appropriate size hole in the die and turn wing nut on the side to lock it tight.

Above is a flaring outfit. The tubing cutter carries its own built-in burring blade, and the flaring set accommodates tubing of several sizes.

Flaring tool is now clamped into place over the die so that tapered point is in line with tube end. Turn of hand screw will flare tube neatly.

ing jobs, to the kind that attach to the lally columns in your basement. Perhaps the handiest type of pipe vise for the homeowner is the *Tristand Vise*. This has its own collapsible stand of three sturdy legs, with a locking platform in between that turns into a handy shelf for fittings or tools. When the Tristand is set up it is very stable and rigid, and pipe, up to two-inch size, is easily handled in it. The Tristand comes with either a yoke-type or a chain vise.

Pipe Extractors are offered in all the standard pipe sizes, and are invaluable when removing broken ends of threaded pipe from fittings.

A tool which lightens labor and preserves tempers is the *Basin Wrench*. This is a peculiar looking affair which has an adjustable head that flips over to tighten or loosen, as the case may require. It is the only tool which will reach up in behind a basin or sink, after installation, to fasten the supply-tube nuts, or to remove them when taking the fixture down. Many other kinds of special tools are available from various manufacturers. Many of them are just gadgets, rather than tools for serious work, but also, many of them will fill a real need and do a job that otherwise would be very cumbersome. •

Plastic, flexible polyethylene, copper and steel are the types of pipe and fittings available for installing water supply lines.

WATER SUPPLY PIPES AND FITTINGS

Plastic pipes cost little and are also easy to use

You have a wide choice of materials to use in a home water supply system. Each one comes with its own way of joining the different pieces together to make runs of pipe. To some extent the materials you can use are limited by local code. Check yours before picking a pipe type.

Water supply pipes are made in plastic, copper and steel. Lead too, but forget it. Too hard to work with. Plastic pipe is the easiest to handle. Its smooth, almost frictionless walls pass water better than any other material. In use it has a few limitations. More about them later. Copper pipe is easy to handle and almost all codes okay it. Neither copper nor plastic pipe will corrode even in very hard water. Steel pipe, because of its serviceability and low cost, is still the standby of many plumbers. It costs more than the others if you figure the time it takes to cut and fit the threaded joints. While you can work with steel pipe successfully, and it's a challenge, there are easier materials to use.

Hot and cold plastic water pipe is the newest thing in plumbing. The standby polyvinyl chloride (PVC) pipe has been chemically toughened to the point where it can be used for both cold and hot water supply lines. The new pipe is called *chlorinated polyvinyl chloride,* CPVC for short. Part of the family of rigid PVC materials, its sister pipes have seen years of service in cold water and drainage-waste-vent installations. CPVC is an improved version of what used to be termed *PVDC*, polyvinyl dichloride. The older material, with threaded joints, was used for hot and cold water supply in houses as early as 1960. The recent improvements should make it the plumbing of the future. More than 100,000 installations are now in service. CPVC pipe is rated to take 100 pounds per square inch (psi.) pressure at 180 degrees.

CAN YOU USE IT?

Plumbing and codes are synonymous, practically. And plastic pipe isn't mentioned in most codes. The reasons vary from "let's wait and see what the others do" to "we've never done it that way before." In any case you are left to interpret your code's provisions relating to plastic piping. Since, good or bad, you are bound by local codes, check yours before going ahead.

I know a man and his teen-age son who installed CPVC piping throughout their

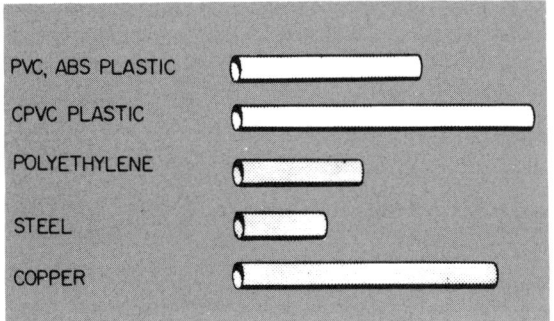

Water supply valve engineering

new home a few years ago. Upon completion, the system was pressurized to 100 psi. and the pipes left under pressure overnight. In the morning the pressure gauge still showed the original 100 psi. No leaks. After three years of use, there still are no leaks and no other problems either, they report.

A remodeling contractor I know will use no other piping material because of the ease of working with plastic. In three years of using CPVC, he has never had a problem or complaint.

I interviewed other handymen who have used the new plastic pipe in home plumbing additions and modernization work. All are completely sold on it; none reported any troubles with it.

Plastic pipe weighs only 1/20th of what galvanized pipe of the same size does. It's lighter than the lightest copper pipe, weather-resistant, too. You can use it outdoors. You need no flame, no flux, no hot solder. Another advantage, plastic pipe doesn't sweat as readily as metal pipes. Neither does it feel blistering hot when carrying hot water. The self-insulating benefits of plastic will help you save on hot water costs by cutting heat loss in pipes.

No taste or odor is passed into the water. Plastic pipe is available with all the fittings you'll need for a complete installation. These include transition fittings, elbows, tees, wyes, couplings, reducing fittings, traps, saddle connections and caps.

DRAWBACKS

Anything this good must have some drawbacks. CPVC pipe is no exception. You'll have to be careful with your plastic pipe installation. Proper installation is no different for plastic pipe than it is for any other. It's just more important to the success of the system. The secret is to design the system to avoid temperatures of more than 180 degrees and pressures of more than 100 psi.

See that your water heater has a temperature-pressure relief valve on it. Its temp-relief setting may be as high as 210 degrees, but plastic pipe will take tem-

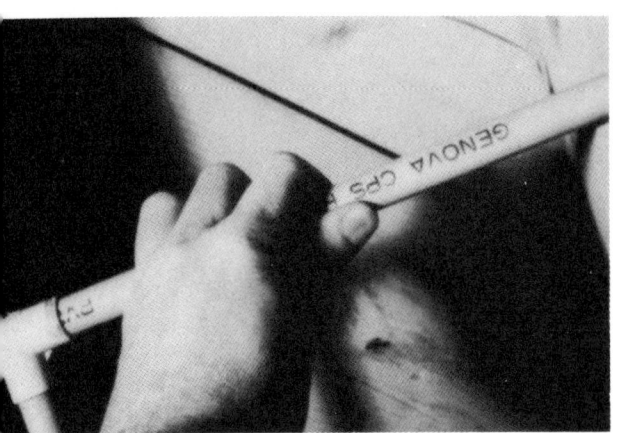

The type of plastic pipe in the above photo can carry cold water because it's self-insulating. It doesn't sweat like metal pipe.

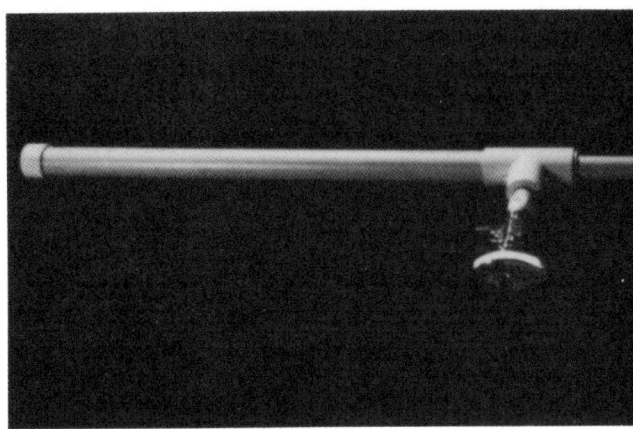

Keep pressures in plastic pipe down. This ¾" x 18" air chamber provides air cushion for quick-acting auto washer shutoff valve.

A 10 foot run of plastic hot water pipe can expand ½" when it gets hot. Plastic pipe hangers are specifically designed to allow back and forth movement of pipe.

As shown in photo, flexible polyethylene pipe is held to fittings with screw-type clamps. Poly pipe is good for use in both wells and underground sprinkler systems.

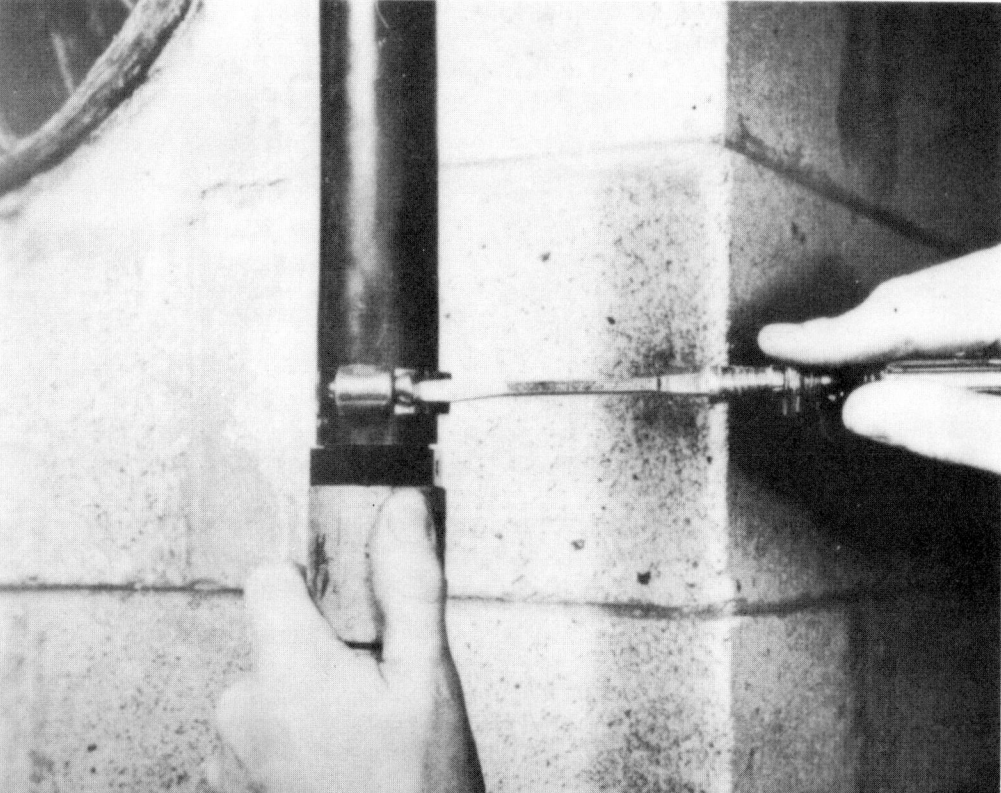

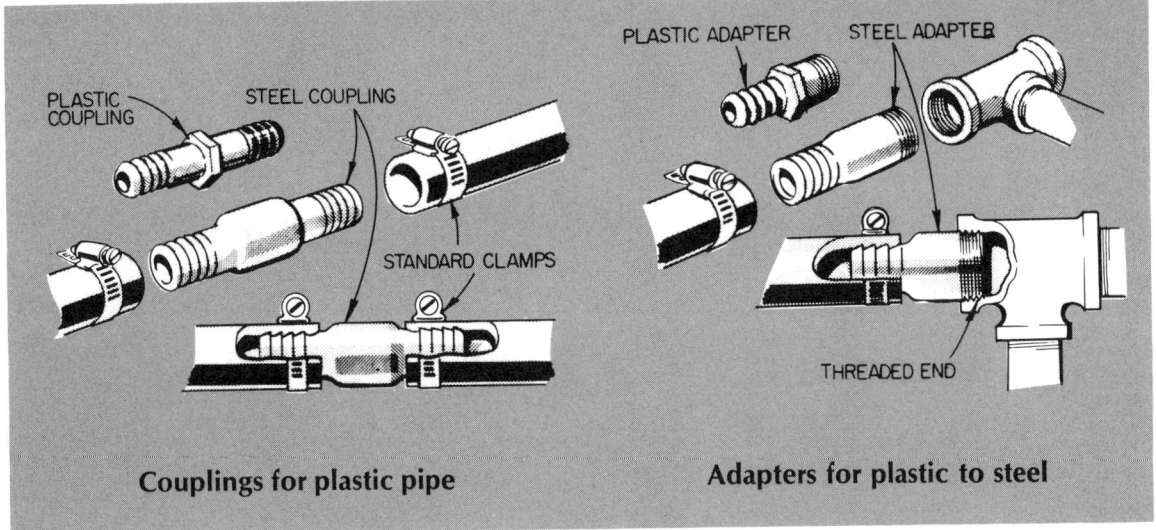

Couplings for plastic pipe

Adapters for plastic to steel

peratures over 180 degrees for only short periods.

One plastic pipemaker recommends water heater setting of 140 degrees but approves of settings as high as 180. This is hotter than you'd want water for safe use outside a dishwasher or washing machine.

Overpressures on pipes in a plastic system must be guarded against. If you turn on the water full blast, then turn it off quickly, whammo, water hammer. The fast-moving water slams against the closed valve and kicks up its heels in all directions. You've created an instantaneous pressure of perhaps 500 psi. Copper and steel pipe can take some of that. Plastic can't. Fast shutoff occurs regularly in washing machines and dishwashers with solenoid valves. Also with some of the new fast-acting faucet valves.

The solution is to see that your plastic plumbing system is fitted with 12-inch-long air chambers as close as practical to every water use. Such air chambers are standard in most plumbing. They're formed by capping lengths of pipe and extending them upward from tees at the stub-outs leading to each fixture. Often the air chambers for a solenoid-valve-controlled outlet are made 18 inches long and of one size larger pipe than the supply pipe.

Protect plastic piping with metal strips where it crosses studs so that nails don't get driven into it.

One last thing to keep in mind as you install plastic pipe is to allow for expansion and contraction of long, straight runs of pipe. A 10-foot length will expand ½ inch when heated from room temperature to 180 degrees. The pipe should be supported every 3 feet or less in hangers that permit linear movement and don't compress, cut or abrade the pipe. Use hangers designed for plastic pipe installation.

One other drawback, plastic piping cannot be used for an electrical ground. Find some other method.

Installed with good plumbing practice, CPVC plastic pipe is great. It's the best thing to hit plumbing since the flush toilet.

OTHER PLASTIC PIPES

CPVC isn't the only kind of plastic pipe you can use for a plumbing supply system. Rigid PVC and ABS (acrylo-mitrile-butadiene-styrene) can be used for cold water pipes, but not hot. These pipes come in 10-foot lengths with matching fittings. Since they cost only one-fifth as much as CPVC pipe, you might consider using one of them for cold water and CPVC for hot water. However, there's always the chance of a mix-up in fittings or pipe when running your hot water installation. The saving may not be worth that risk.

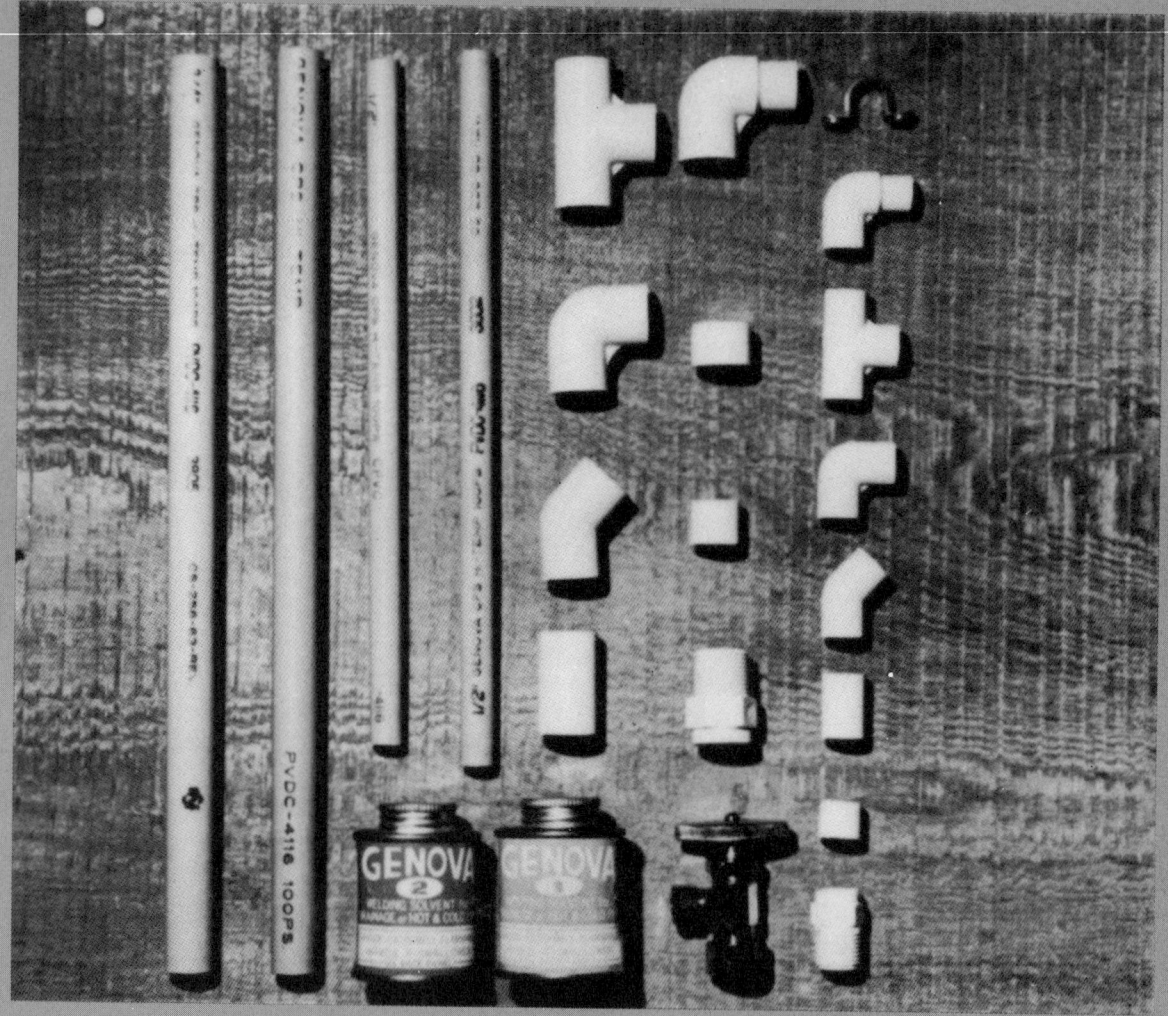

Pipe and fittings for a plastic water supply system let you build it the easy way. Included are: color-coded hot and cold pipes in ¾" and ½", tees, 90° street elbows, 45° elbows, couplings, ¾"-½" reducer, threaded adapters, joining cements for plastic pipe.

Polyethylene pipe is the flexible black pipe you may already be familiar with. Like PVC and ABS pipe, poly is to be used for cold water runs only. It's flexible, letting you negotiate gentle curves without the need for fittings. Poly pipe comes in 100-foot coils or longer and is cut to length with a sharp knife or hacksaw. There are various grades, from downright economical to more costly. Which of these to use depends on the strength needed. For water supply use 100 psi. pipe. For sprinkler systems you can use the cheaper 80 psi. pipe. Poly pipe is slipped over long, ridged plastic fittings and held in place with screw clamps. The joints can be taken apart and put together many times and remain leak-free. If a poly pipe resists pull-off after its clamp has been loosened, pour hot water over the end of the pipe to soften it.

The primary use of poly pipe is where lightweight, easy installation and flexibility are needed for a cold water run. Think of poly for a service entrance, well pipes down a well or a buried lawn sprinkling system.

JOINING PLASTIC PIPE

Plastic pipe can be installed with a few ordinary tools. You need a fine-toothed saw to cut it (9 to 14 teeth per inch) or a 24-tooth-blade hacksaw. You can cut plastic pipe with a power saw, too, if you like. If you use a vise to hold the pipe, wrap it with cloth to prevent damage to the pipe. You'll need a small knife or sandpaper to remove burrs from the insides of pipes after cutting.

Lastly, you'll need one or two nonsynthetic bristle brushes with coarse bristles for applying joint solvents.

Plastic pipe will amaze you in its ease of installation. First cut it to length and remove the burr. Clean the pipe end and inside of the fitting. Next (with Genova pipe) brush the fluxing solvent from the first can on the outside of the cleaned pipe end for a distance equal to the depth of the fitting. Brush the inside of the cleaned fitting too. Don't brush the solvents out. For best results the brush used should be about half as wide as the pipe.

Immediately follow by liberally brushing the thicker solvent from the second can on the pipe end and a light but even coat in the fitting. Best results are had by brushing in the direction of the pipe and making sure that all mating surfaces are coated with cement.

Ideally, doping of both the pipe and fitting should be done in less than a minute. Without waiting, push the pipe and fitting together with a slight twist until the pipe bottoms in the fitting. Quickly adjust the fitting direction and that's it. Some instructions call for the fitting to be held on for 15 seconds. It's not necessary with CPVC pipe. Don't disturb the joint for about three minutes after assembly. The fitting will become immovable within seconds after insertion on the pipe.

Get it properly aligned without delay. This is the only hang-up of working with plastic pipe. If you blow it, the fitting must be sawed off and a new one used.

The CPVC tubing system is designed to have an interference fit. Check the fit before doping each joint by slipping the pipe into the fitting without a solvent. Proper fit is when the tubing makes contact with the fitting walls between one-

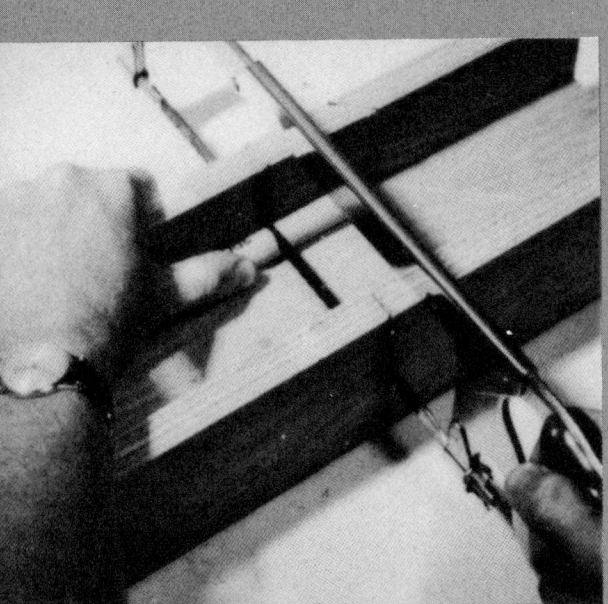

For a square cut in plastic pipe saw it in miter box with a 24-tooth blade in hacksaw. Remove burr on inside of pipe with penknife.

Coat outside of cleaned pipe and inside of plastic fitting with solvent. This Genova joining system uses 2 solvents; #1 and #2.

After coating, assemble joint with slight twist, getting pipe all the way into fitting. You must align it before joint sets.

third and two-thirds of the way in. Reject CPVC pipe and fittings without an interference fit.

Solvent cement that has jelled, discolored or noticeably thickened should not be used. Don't breathe the vapors of the solvents used to join plastic pipe. Work in a ventilated room and keep the solvent away from fires.

PRESSURE-TEST

The joints you produce in plastic pipe are stronger than the pipe itself. They're leakproof and will stand many pounds of pressure within a few minutes, but it's best to wait at least 16 hours before pressure-testing the system for leaks. A normal water pressure should be applied to the system. It should hold for about four hours in the closed system without falling off.

If a leak shows up during pressure-testing, that part of the system should be drained and the leaky joint and fitting cut out. Dry the pipe thoroughly and reinstall a new fitting, using couplings and short lengths of pipe. These joints may be assembled without rotating if you are careful to coat all the mating surfaces uniformly and completely. Allow another 16 hours before pressure-testing the repair.

Don't try solvent-welding at temperatures below 40 degrees.

An epoxy-welding technique can be used to join CPVC pipe directly to copper fittings. Genova makes a "heatless welding kit" for this purpose.

Sizes of the new plastic pipes for hot and cold water application follow those of copper pipe in order to take advantage of the labor-saving compression fittings for lavatories and toilets that are now in stock at hardware and plumbing supply outlets. Be sure to replace the brass ferrules with special plastic ferrules designed for use with plastic pipe. CPVC pipe is easily available in ½- and ¾-inch sizes.

Plastic pipe can be joined to present copper water pipe with one simple compression fitting. To connect it to an existing steel pipe system, a threaded steel pipe adapter is all you need. Never thread plastic pipe. Use threaded adapters when threads are necessary. Don't overtighten threaded joints with plastic fittings. Get them hand-tight, then give not more than 1½ turns additional tightening with a strap wrench. Using a pipe wrench or chain wrench on plastic threaded adapters is a no-no. The teeth chew heck out of the fitting. Use a recommended pipe joint compound on all threads. Teflon tape is a good one.

Don't try to paint plastic pipe. To give built-in color-coding, Genova CPVC pipe is made in two colors—green for cold water lines and red for hot water lines. Other than color, there's no difference in the two. You can switch the colors if you need to fight the establishment.

COPPER PIPE

Copper pipe is sized nominally according to its inside diameter. The outside diameter is always 1/8 inch more than the stated size. Actual inside diameter depends on the thickness of the walls. This varies by type. You have a choice of three types of copper water tube, as it's called, types *K*, *L* and *M*. Type *K* (heavy-wall, color code green) comes in both hard-temper (rigid and straight) and soft-temper (flexible). Diameters are 1/4, 3/8, 1/2, 3/4, and 1 inch.

Type *K* is for underground pipes such as a buried service line. Never bury copper pipe (or any pipe) in contact with cinders. Cinders eat 'em up.

Type *L* copper pipe (medium-wall, color code blue) also comes in both hard- and soft-temper and sizes from 1/4 inch to 1 inch. It's used for interior plumbing and heating lines with solder, flare or compression fittings.

Type *M* (light-wall, color code red) copper pipe is the least costly because of its thin walls. Type *M* comes in 3/8-inch to 1-inch hard-temper only and must be used with soldered joints. Type *M* is suitable for interior plumbing or heating applications. It is your best bet, within the limitations.

Soft-temper pipe can be used for concealed piping. Hard-temper, since it makes a better looking job and is more resistant to denting, is often used for exposed piping.

Rigid copper comes in 1-foot lengths. Soft copper comes in coils of 30 or 60 feet. Soft-temper pipe is great for remodeling and modernization jobs where it can be worked down through existing partitions and walls through small openings.

Copper pipe is easiest to cut with a hacksaw in a miter box. Use a 24-tooth blade. A tubing cutter also may be used. After cutting, remove all burrs with a round file or reamer. Sizes to 1½ inch are easiest and best cut with a tubing cutter. Don't use cutting oil. If a hacksawed cut doesn't turn out square, file it square with a flat file.

The best way to hold a pipe while sawing it is in a miter box. This also ensures square cuts. A vise tends to crush it. If you must use a vise, clamp the pipe 6

Use steel-to-plastic adapter to go from an existing steel pipeline to plastic system. From this point on, plastic pipe can run all the way.

The easy way to get from plastic water supply pipe to fixture: angle-stop is made to go with the pipe. Tighten nut, it's sealed.

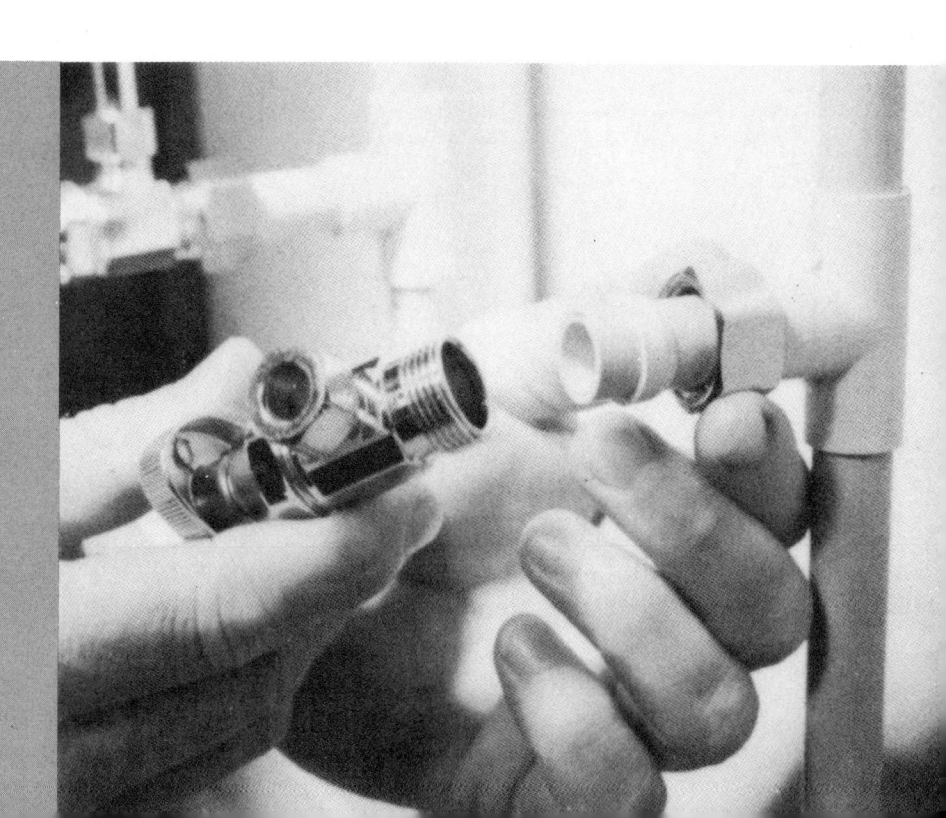

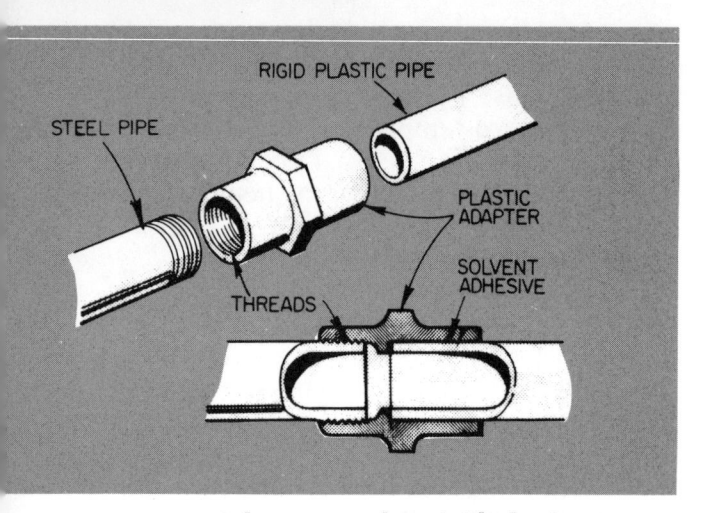

Adapter—steel to rigid plastic

inches from the end to leave the end uncrushed.

Fittings for copper water tube are of cast bronze, wrought copper and bronze, and brass. Wherever you have a choice of using a short-radius fitting or a long-radius one, choose the long radius. It passes water with less restriction.

SOLDERED JOINTS

Copper plumbing is most often done with soldered joints. These are sometimes termed *sweat joints*. The fittings for them cost the least of any.

Sweating a joint is easy. To do it, first polish the outside of the pipe and inside of the fitting with No. 00 steel wool or fine sandpaper. Get the metal bright and clean. Don't use a file. It scores the metal. The tube end must be round, not squashed. Cut off any out-of-round end and start again. Apply a thin coat of noncorrosive flux or soldering paste to the cleaned portions of the fitting and pipe. Slip the two together, removing any excess flux around the fitting. Heat the joint evenly with a propane torch or blowtorch. Move the torch back and forth to spread its heat.

Plastic pipe can be joined to flare fittings by flaring. Do this in usual way using a flaring tool, but be careful to avoid damaging edges. If they crack, cut and try again.

Test the temperature of the joint by touching it with solder as you heat. Test opposite the side being licked by the flame. When the solder will melt, remove the flame and feed solder into the joint. Capillary action will do the rest. Solder will even be drawn upward into a down-facing fitting. The joint is complete when a line of solder shows all around it. Remove any surplus solder by wiping or brushing. Let the joint cool before moving it. This shouldn't take more than a minute. Although 50/50 tin/lead solder is best, 40/60 solder may be used. Always use solid-core solder.

Sometimes to save time, all the fittings in one area can be cleaned, fluxed and assembled. Then all can be soldered in succession. Don't wait more than an hour to solder or the joints will oxidize again.

To avoid melting out a previously made solder joint when you sweat a new joint on the same fitting, wrap the completed joint with a wet rag.

Don't get a joint too hot or the flux will burn and the solder won't bond properly. An overheated joint must be taken apart, cleaned and resoldered. Likewise, any soldered joint that leaks after the water is turned on will have to be drained, taken apart, cleaned and resoldered.

If you ever have to unsolder a joint — and you might — heat it to melt the solder, then pull the pipe out of the fitting. Protect other connections in that fitting with wet rags.

When soldering a copper-to-copper valve, open it and wrap wet rags around the stem portion. This will prevent heat from damaging the valve's washer and packing.

Be careful to keep dirt and fingerprints off the prepared parts of a sweat joint. These will keep the solder from sticking to the joint.

Joints in pipes larger than 3/4 inch need to be heated on two sides for good heat distribution. Either use two torches or move the torch to heat on two sides.

Use care in working with a torch. It's fire. If a wood framing member is in the way of the flame, shield it with a piece

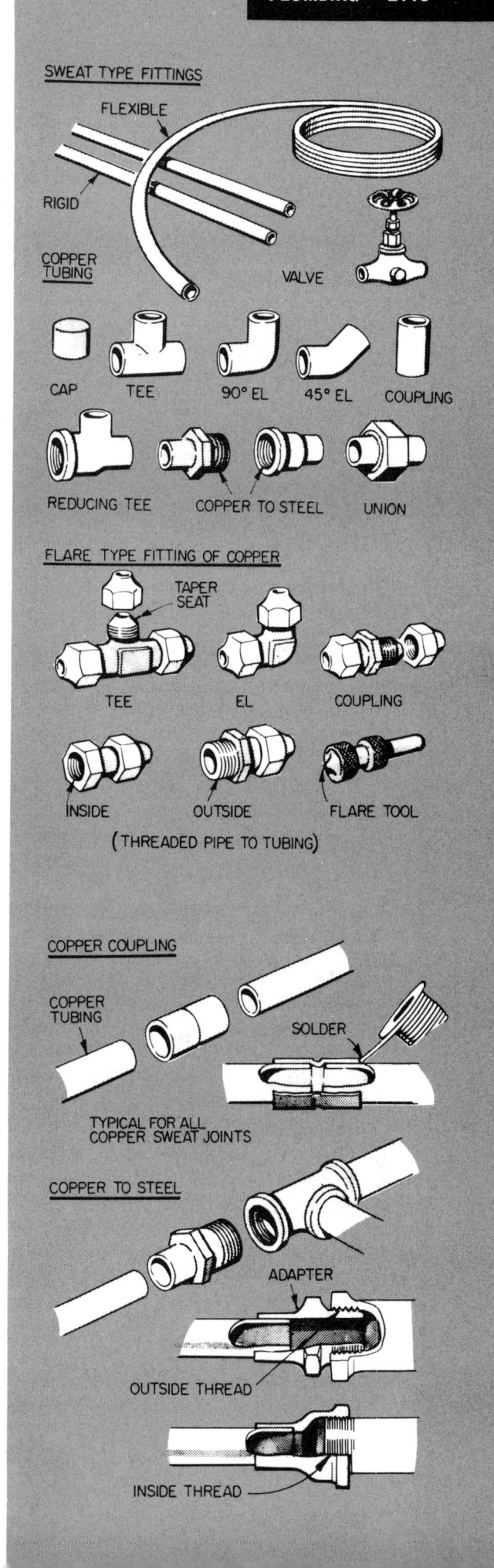

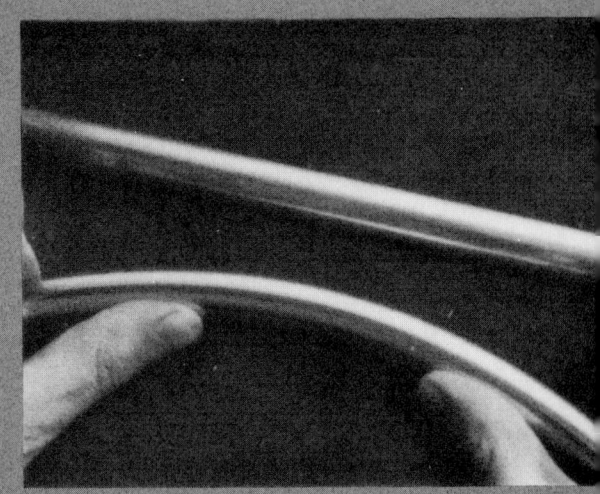

Copper pipe comes in three thicknesses, types K, L and M (from left to right above) and two tempers, one rigid and one flexible.

of metal. A cookie tray will do, if you can get it out of the kitchen unseen.

Copper pipe running through a stud wall must be protected from nails being accidentally driven into it. Put a metal strap over every stud across the pipe's notch-out.

FLARE FITTINGS

If you want an ideal working method for plumbing with soft-temper copper pipe, it's the use of flared fittings. Flaring is easy. Any line can be taken apart at any time. The cost of the fittings is the kicker. This method of joining is popular for splicing a copper house service line in the trench under wet, dirty conditions where soldering would be rough.

Flaring is done with a special tool, either the screw-down type or the simpler pound-in type. Be sure to put the flange nut over the pipe, threads facing outward, before you make the flare. It's maddening when you forget. The flange nut holds the pipe tightly to its flare fitting. Don't use flared joints in inaccessible locations where there might be enough vibration to work them loose.

With a pound-in flaring tool, you'll need a different tool for each pipe diameter. Hold the end of the tubing in one hand while you tap the tool with a hammer in the other. Keep tapping until the tubing's end has been spread enough so that the threaded side of the flange nut will just fit over it. Take care to spread evenly all around.

A screw-in flaring tool has a series of various-sized openings between a pair of steel bars. Each opening is designed to take a single size of pipe. Find the right opening for the pipe you're flaring and clamp it tightly between bars with the chamfered edge of the bars toward the end of the pipe. The pipe should be flush with the bars. Then put the flaring cone over the tube and screw it down tight on the pipe's end. That does it.

With either flaring method, be sure there are no burrs or dirt to spoil the contact.

To assemble the flared joint, start the nut onto the fitting's threads by hand. Tighten as much as you can by hand making sure the threads are started right. Complete the joint by tightening securely with a pair of open-end wrenches, one on the flange nut, the other on the fitting. Never tighten the nut alone. It puts all the torque onto the pipes supporting your fitting. This can easily ruin the con-

PLUMBING • 2117

To make a soldered joint in copper pipe you sandpaper end of pipe and inside of fitting. Apply flux sparingly and slip them together.

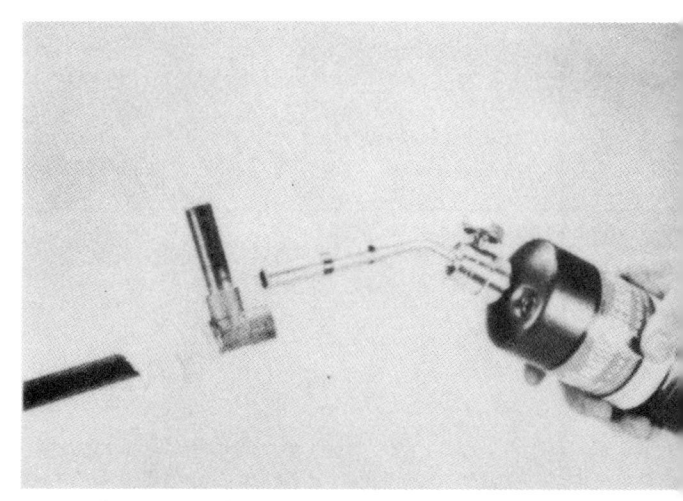

Heat fitting with propane torch. Move it around to spread heat evenly. Test temperature of the joint by touching with solder.

nection at the other side.

COMPRESSION FITTINGS

A third method of joining copper pipe is with a compression fitting. It consists of a fitting—coupling, angle, tee—plus a brass compression ring and flange nut for every pipe coming into it. The compression ring is slipped over the pipe after the flange nut. Then the nut is drawn down onto its fitting. This action squeezes the compression ring tightly between pipe and fitting, sealing the joint. No tools other than a pair of open-end wrenches are needed. Like flare fittings, compression fittings can be taken apart and reassembled whenever necessary. They're rarely used for extensive plumbing because of their cost. Solder fittings are much more economical. For an occasional small job, compression fittings are not bad.

Bending soft-temper copper pipe can be done in your hands. To bend rigid copper pipe you need a tubing bender to get a smooth job. A smooth bend is less restricting to the flow of water than an angle fitting. It also saves the cost of the fitting and making two soldered joints to go with it. Don't try to bend Type *M* pipe. The walls collapse.

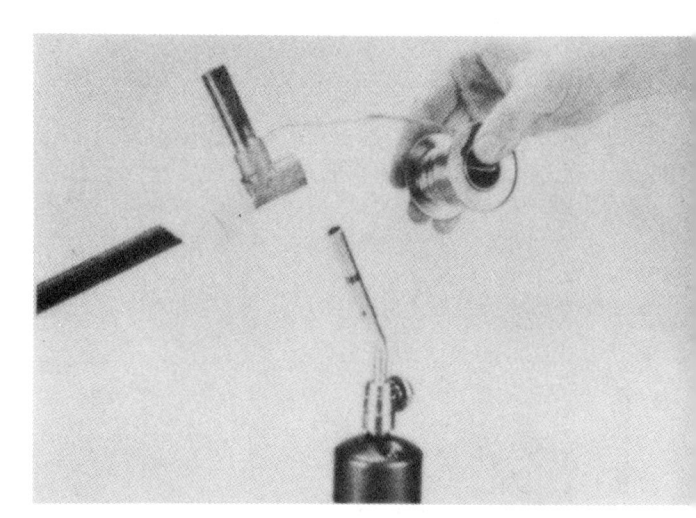

Take torch away and apply solder to heated fitting. It should flow in by capillary action, if temperature is right, and leave a fillet.

When you solder joints that are close to a flammable material, protect from heat with either a baking pan or other metal shield.

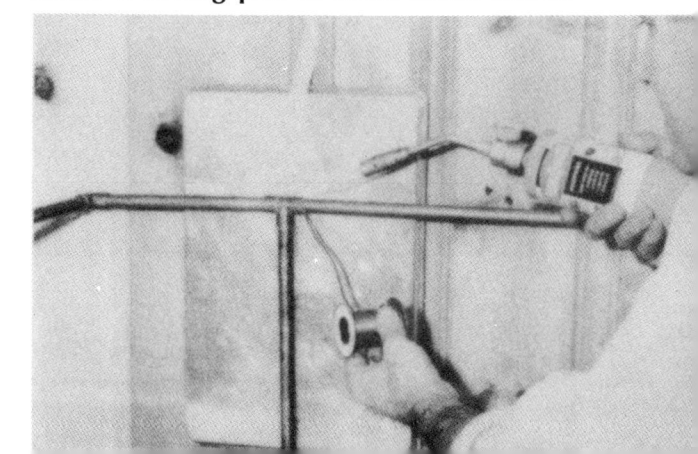

2118 • PLUMBING

FLARED ENDS COMPRESS TO TAPERED FITTING

FLARE FITTING FOR FLEXIBLE TUBING

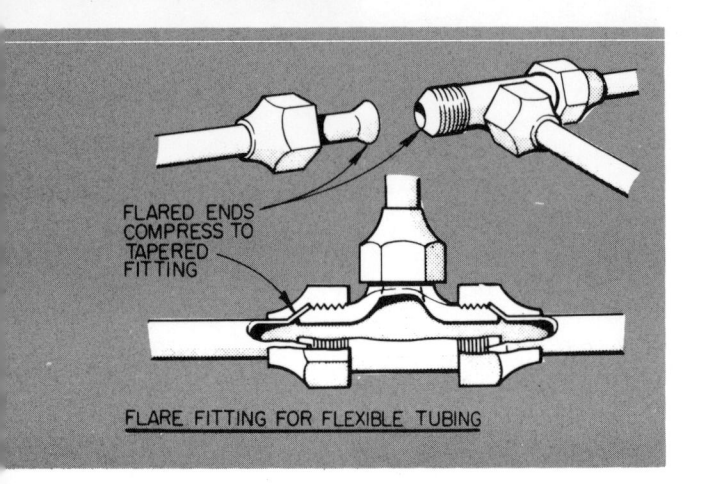

STEEL PIPE

Steel pipe comes galvanized (for plumbing) and in black iron (for gas lines). Its inside diameter is its size. For example ½-inch steel pipe measures ½ inch in inside diameter. You can buy 10-foot lengths, 21-foot lengths or lengths cut to order. If you buy cut-to-order lengths—as you should for small jobs—you may as well have them threaded too. For larger, more extensive work, you'll find it better to rent or buy a set of pipe

To flare a soft-temper copper tube with a screw-type flaring tool, clamp it in tool and tighten down on flare screw as far as possible.

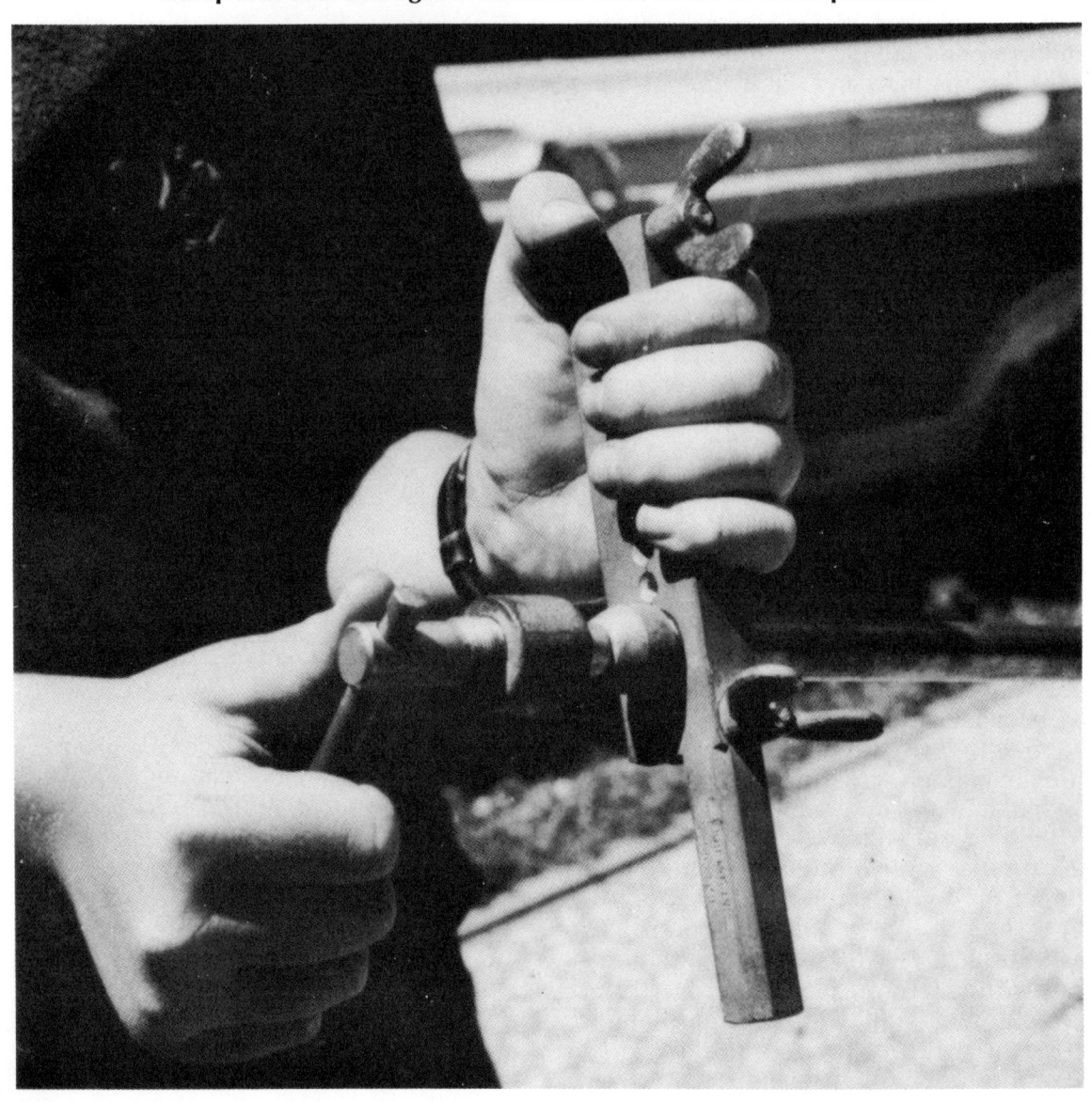

threading tools and have them on hand when you work.

Cut steel pipe with a hacksaw or pipe cutter. The cutter does the neatest job with the least effort. Lock a length of pipe to be cut in a pipe vise. This won't tend to crush it like a bench vise would. Many metal-working vises have a set of pipe jaws already in them. To use a pipe cutter, slip it over the pipe with the cutter wheel resting on the "cut" mark. Tighten the handle until the wheel bites. Apply some thread-cutting oil and rotate the cutter one turn. Then tighten again. Keep rotating, oiling and tightening until the pipe has been severed. As you get almost through, support the pipe's end to keep it from sagging or falling as it is cut through.

To cut steel pipe with a hacksaw, take long, uniform strokes, applying pressure only on the "pull" strokes. The teeth, of course, should point toward the handle of the saw. Install the blade that way if it isn't already. File off any jagged edges on the outside of the pipe.

Burrs inside the pipe must be removed, otherwise they'll restrict the flow of wa-

Smooth, kink-free bends in soft-temper copper pipe can be made using a tubing bender slipped over pipe to reinforce its walls.

The flare nut, which was inserted before making flare, will hold pipe in tight seal with any flare fitting. Fittings are costly.

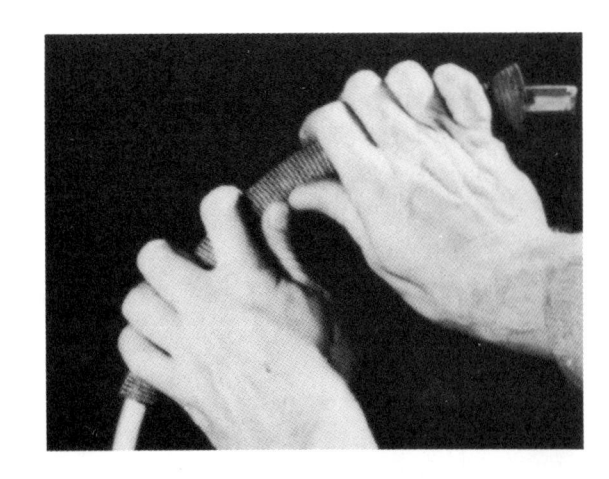

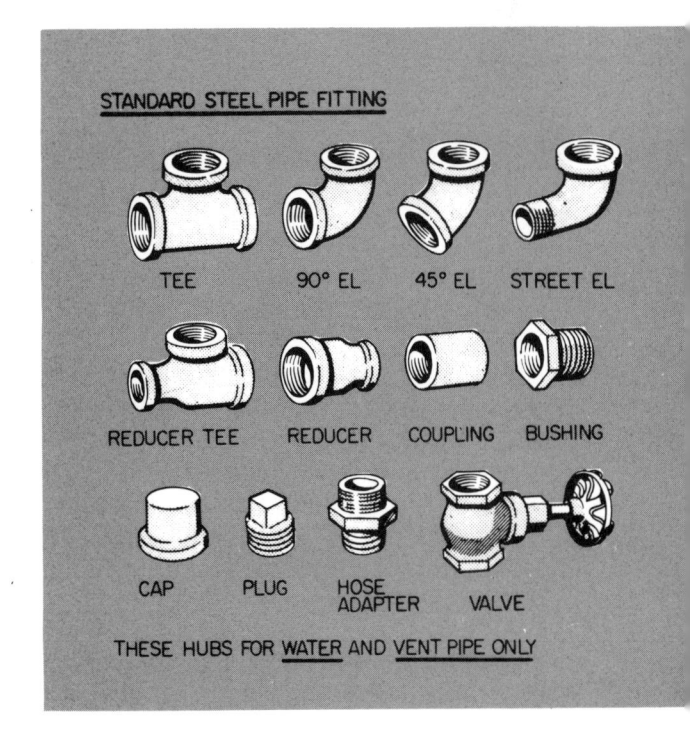

STANDARD STEEL PIPE FITTING

TEE   90° EL   45° EL   STREET EL

REDUCER TEE   REDUCER   COUPLING   BUSHING

CAP   PLUG   HOSE ADAPTER   VALVE

THESE HUBS FOR WATER AND VENT PIPE ONLY

2120 • PLUMBING

To make threaded joints in steel pipe, cut pipe to the proper length with pipe cutter. With each cutter rotation, tighten handle.

Ream out burr left on inside of cut pipe. Use pipe reamer or, lacking reamer, use a rounded file. A pipe vice and stand help.

Thread pipe with stock and die. Turn stock clockwise. Back off quarter-turn, if it is hanging up, to clear chips. Also use oil.

Apply joint compound in pipe's threads and assemble the joint. Make sure the threads start straight. Tighten with pipe wrenches.

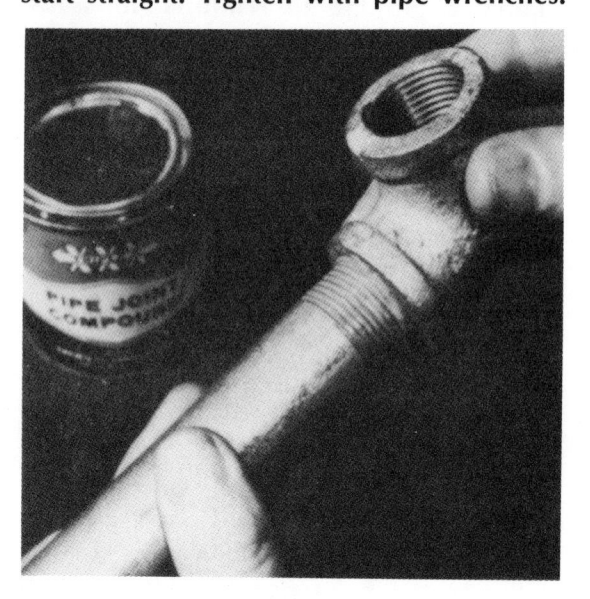

ter. Use a rounded file or a tapered pipe reamer chucked in an electric drill or bit brace.

Steel pipe is threaded with a pipe die held in a *stock* (handled die holder). The stock has a square opening on one side for insertion of the square die. On the other side is a pipe guide. The guide gets the die started true. Use the same size die and guide as the pipe to be threaded.

The printed side of the die should be placed facing away from the guide. If you put it in backward you'd have real trouble starting the die and the threads wouldn't come out tapered, as they should.

Place the stock over the end of the pipe being threaded. As the die contacts, begin rotating the stock handle clockwise. Keep pushing while getting the threads going. Apply thread-cutting oil generously to the pipe and die. Once started, you can stop pushing. The threads will take hold and pull. Rotate slowly and continuously until the pipe's end sticks out one full thread beyond the outer die face. Then back off the die by rotating counter-clockwise. If the die

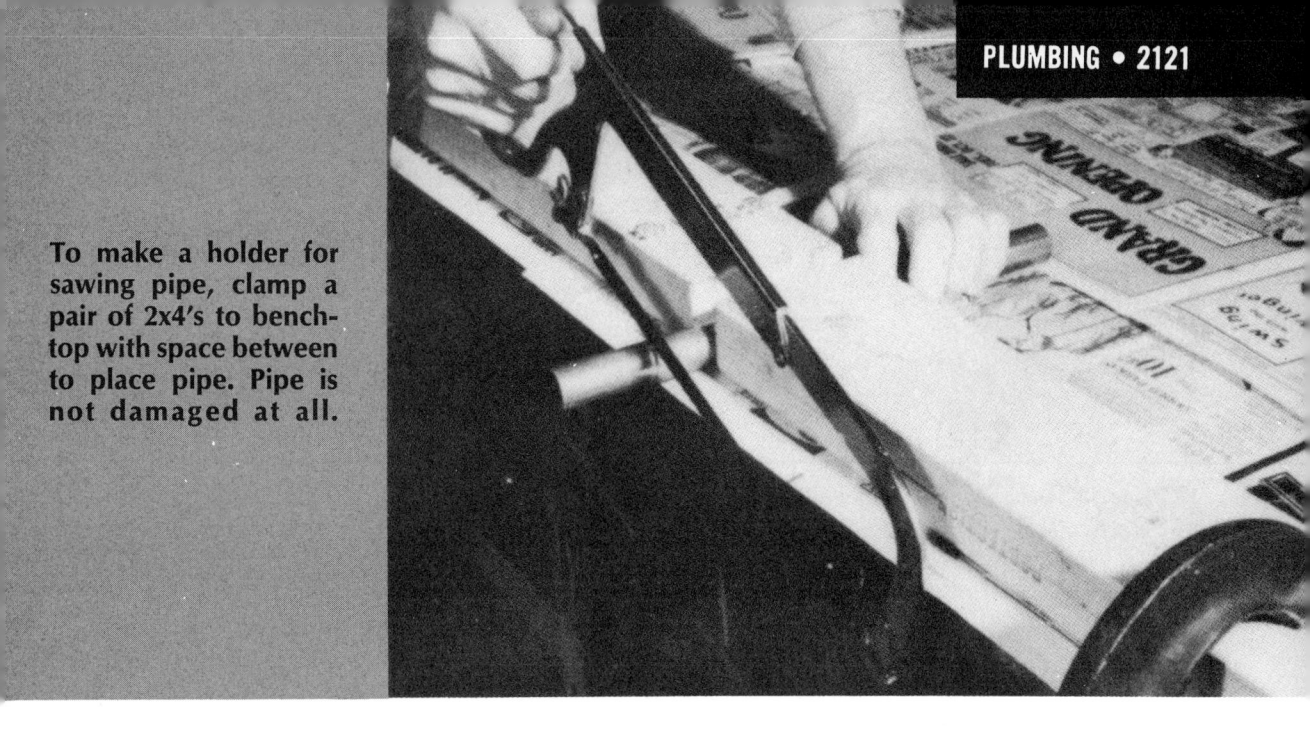

To make a holder for sawing pipe, clamp a pair of 2x4's to benchtop with space between to place pipe. Pipe is not damaged at all.

should tend to hang up while threading or backing off, unhang it by reversing the rotation for a quarter-turn. This should clear any cuttings out of the way. They're usually the hang-up. Clean up excess oil and chips with a cloth.

Before making up a steel pipe joint, remove dirt and chips from inside the pipe and around the threads. Apply pipe joint compound to the outside threads only. Never to the inside threads of the fitting. Use pipe joint compound sparingly with just enough to fill the threads evenly. No excess or barren spots. Don't get compound inside the pipe or over its end. Start the threads by hand to make sure they're not cross-threaded.

Steel pipe fittings are tightened with a pair of pipe wrenches, one on the pipe and a larger one on the fitting. A 10-inch wrench will handle pipes to 1 inch, an 18-inch wrench, to 2 inches.

A word of warning. While a threaded joint must be leakproof, you can easily overtighten the threads of ½-inch or ¾-inch pipes. With a new fitting and newly threaded pipe made as described, the joint will be tight enough when about three threads are still visible outside the fitting. Each time you remake the same joint, however, you'll have to tighten a little more to get the proper fit. Never, never turn a pipe in more than one turn after the last thread has disappeared inside the fitting. You'll likely blow the fitting if you do. After you've made up a few joints, you'll quickly get the feel of how tight a joint should be.

STAINLESS STEEL PIPE

A new kind of water supply pipe now on the market is made of stainless steel. It's called *Ti-Krome* by the manufacturer, Tubotron, Inc. The cost is about one-third that of equivalent grade copper pipe. Regular copper sweat fittings should be used until stainless steel fittings are made available. The procedure is much the same as for joining copper water tube, except that a corrosive flux is used. This must be thoroughly cleaned off before you leave the joint.

As you might expect, stainless steel pipe is highly resistant to corrosion and isn't much affected by mineral deposits from hard water. The pipe can be cut with a hacksaw or tubing cutter, soldered with your propane torch. You can bend it with a pipe bender the same as rigid copper tubing but it's tougher to bend because of its strength. Stainless steel pipe is too new to be included in many building codes, so you may have to interpret code provisions regarding its use. The pipe should be available through your local plumbing supply dealer.

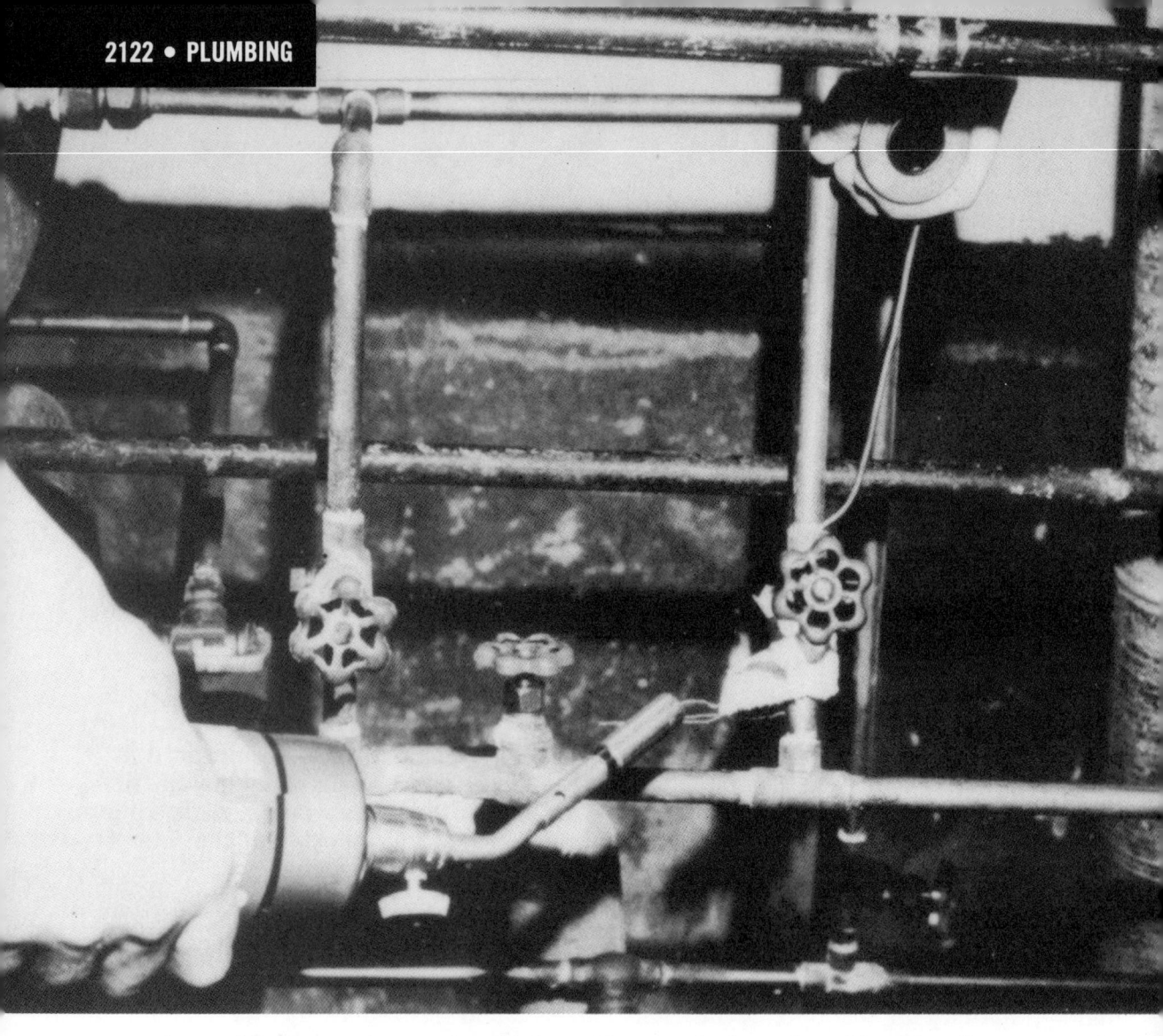

When soldering, wrap completed joint with wet cloth so the old solder does not melt.

TIPS ON RUNNING PIPES

Plan water lines to travel the most direct routes to fixtures

Modern fittings and fixtures have taken many problems out of running pipes. You don't need to be an experienced plumber to do it. Anyone who can follow a few simple directions can turn out a creditable job the very first time. It's merely a matter of measuring, cutting and assembling the pipes and fittings according to a set of sensible rules.

Pipes need carry only so much water. Beyond a certain point a larger pipe size is only wasteful. The following are fairly standard sizes for house pipes.

Service entrance — 1 inch.
Service to water heater — ¾ to 1 inch.
Hot and cold mains — ¾ inch.
Branches to sinks, showers, bathtubs, laundries and dishwashers — ½ inch.
Branches to lavatories and toilets — ⅜ inch.
Soil stacks and house drains — 3 to 4 inch.
Sewer lines — 4 inch.
Branch drains from tubs, showers, sinks, laundries, lavatories, dishwashers — 1½ inch.
Roof vents — 3 inch or more.
Many of the newer lavatory faucets

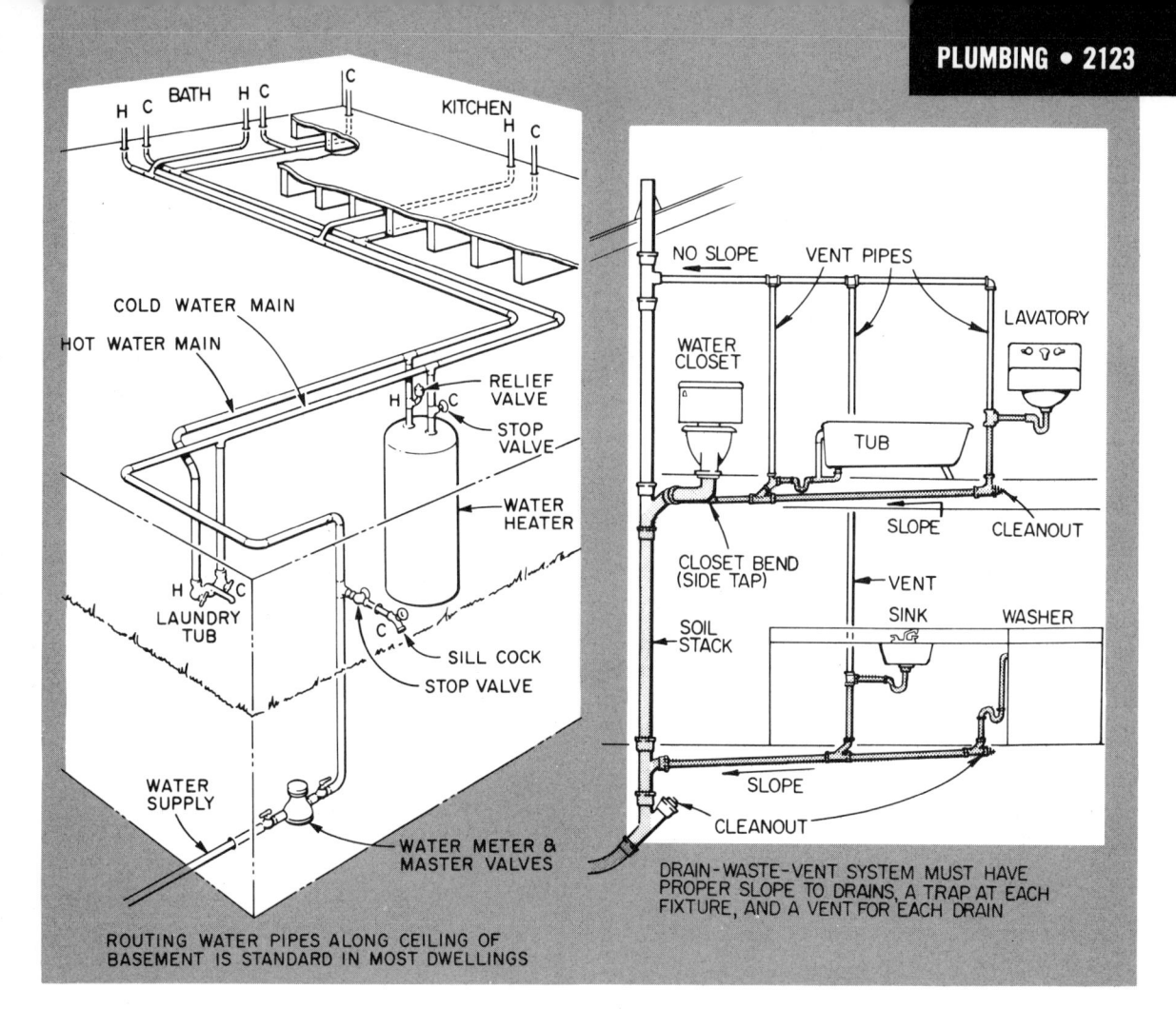

ROUTING WATER PIPES ALONG CEILING OF BASEMENT IS STANDARD IN MOST DWELLINGS

DRAIN-WASTE-VENT SYSTEM MUST HAVE PROPER SLOPE TO DRAINS, A TRAP AT EACH FIXTURE, AND A VENT FOR EACH DRAIN

come equipped with ¼-inch supply pipes from the main branch to them. If you run ⅜-inch pipes up to these, you get shot down right at the faucet. Code permitting, you can probably get along with ¼-inch branches to these lavatories.

HOW LONG A PIPE?

Measuring for pipes and cutting them would be a snap except for two things: *fitting gain* and *make-up*. Fitting gain is the amount of space taken up by the fitting a pipe goes into. Pipes in a run, or ones coming to an angle, don't butt up against each other inside the fitting. The fitting separates them somewhat. Make-up is the amount that a pipe goes into the fitting. Both fitting gain and make-up must be allowed for in measurement and cutting of pipes.

Threaded steel pipe fittings are so standardized that the gain and make-up for them can be given in a table. There's one table for standard fittings another for drainage fittings. Plastic and copper water supply fittings and most drainage-waste-vent fittings vary in design with make. Take actual measurements of the fittings you will use and then determine gain and make-up.

Measurements for steel pipe are usually taken in one of three ways: end-to-end for a single pipe or for a pipe run with fittings; end of pipe to center of fitting for angled runs; or center of fitting to center of fitting for parallel runs.

Instead of holding a steel fitting up while taking your measurement, use the

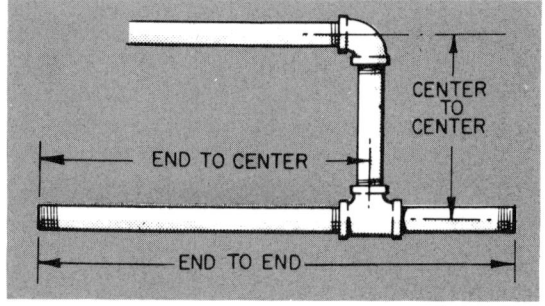

Three ways of measuring pipes.

ALLOWANCES FOR THREADED STANDARD FITTINGS

Pipe Size	Distance "X"	Fitting Dimensions (in.) A	B	C	J	K
½ in.	½ in.	1⅛	⅞	1⅝	1 5/16	1¼
¾ in.	½ in.	1 5/16	1	1⅞	1½	1 7/16
1 in.	9/16 in.	1½	1⅛	2⅛	1 11/16	1 11/16
1¼ in.	⅝ in.	1¾	1 5/16	2 7/16	1 15/16	2 1/16
1½ in.	⅝ in.	1 15/16	1 7/16	2 11/16	2⅛	2 5/16
2 in.	11/16 in.	2¼	1 11/16	3¼	2½	2 13/16

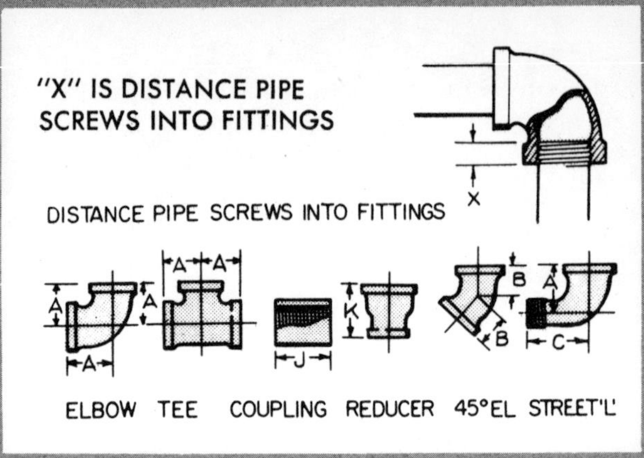
"X" IS DISTANCE PIPE SCREWS INTO FITTINGS
DISTANCE PIPE SCREWS INTO FITTINGS
X
A
B
C
J
K
ELBOW
TEE
COUPLING
REDUCER
45°EL
STREET'L'

ALLOWANCES FOR THREADED DRAINAGE FITTINGS

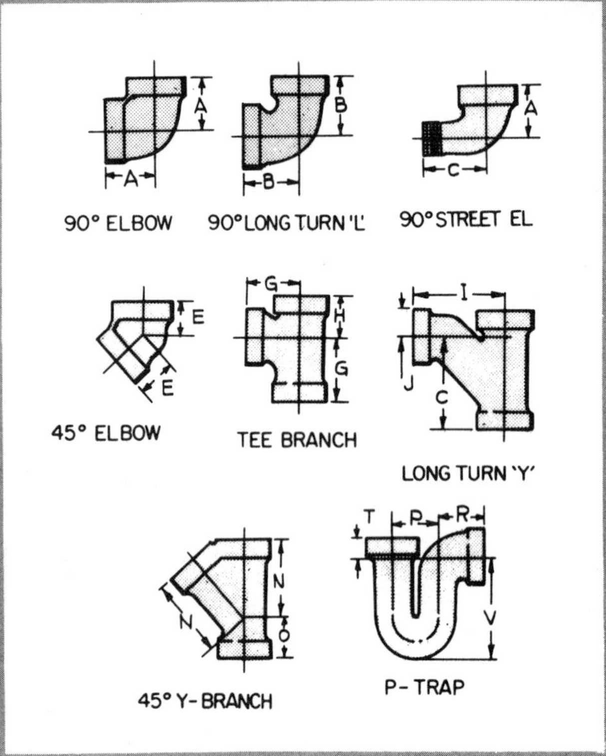
A
B
C
E
G
H
I
J
N
O
T
P
R
V
90° ELBOW
90° LONG TURN 'L'
90° STREET EL
45° ELBOW
TEE BRANCH
LONG TURN 'Y'
45° Y-BRANCH
P-TRAP

Pipe Size (in.)		1½	2
Distance "X" Pipe Screws into Fittings		⅝ (inches)	11/16 (inches)
Fitting Dimensions (inches)	A	2 3/16	2⅜
	B	2½	3 1/16
	C	2 11/16	3¼
	E	1 7/16	1¾
	G	2½	3 1/16
	H	1¾	2⅛
	I	4⅛	5 7/16
	J	1¼	1⅝
	K	4⅛	5 7/16
	N	3⅝	4 5/16
	O	1⅞	2⅛
	P	2¼	2¾
	R	2⅛	2 9/16
	T	⅞	⅞
	V	5	5 11/16

table to see how much space the fitting will occupy. Then subtract this amount from your measurement. Finally add on distance "X" and you have it.

Here's an example. A length of ½-inch pipe is to be cut running between two other pipes (see drawing). One pipe has a tee, the other is to be fitted with an elbow. Suppose you measure 29 inches center to center of the existing pipes. For both the tee and elbow the fitting gain from the table is 1⅛ inch. Make-up for ½-inch pipe is ½ inch. Subtracting the 1⅛-inch fitting gain at each end gives 26¾ inches. Adding the 1-inch make-up loss gives 27¾ inches. This is the actual length the pipe should be cut. Measure the pipe and mark it with a file or hacksaw.

FACE-TO-FACE METHOD

A simpler face-to-face method for pipe

measurement requires having the fittings in position. To find the length of a run of the pipe between two fittings, measure the face-to-face distance between those fittings. Then add twice the make-up measurement for that pipe size from the table (distance "X"). The make-up measurement is doubled because the pipe screws into fittings at both ends. Measured and cut to that total length, the pipe should fit perfectly when tightened in place.

Suppose in the previous example that both fittings were installed and you found a 26¾-inch face-to-face distance between them. Adding on twice the ½-inch make-up points to the use of a 27¾-inch length of pipe. Simple!

Even steel pipe expands as it's heated. For this reason all pipes—whether steel, copper or plastic—should be fastened to framing with pipe hangers so that some expansion can take place. Extra long runs of copper or plastic water supply pipe need an expansion loop or a special copper expansion fitting. An expansion loop is a "U" in the line. One is made with four 90-degree elbows and short lengths of pipe. Steel and rigid copper water supply pipes should be supported every 7 to 10 feet. Soft-temper copper water supply pipes need support every 16 inches. Vertical runs of pipe between the floors of a house can rest at the lower end on a header nailed between floor joists. DWV pipes need support every 4 feet (every third joist), except no-hub, which should be supported at every joist on horizontal runs.

All water supply piping should be pitched slightly backward from the fixtures to a stop-and-drain valve placed at the low point. Often this is located at the water meter. If there are other low points in the system, these should have provision for drainage too. The drain side of a stop-and-drain valve is always placed where it will not be under pressure when the valve is off. These valves permit draining the system if the house is not to be heated during below-freezing weather.

Because there is no water pressure to move the flow along in drain-waste-vent piping, all horizontal DWV runs are not

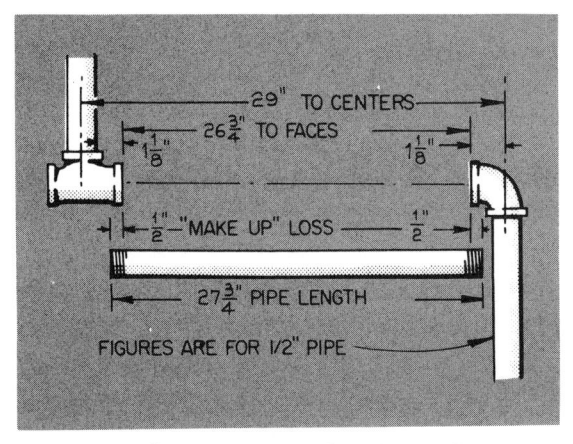

Figure fitting-gain and make-up loss.

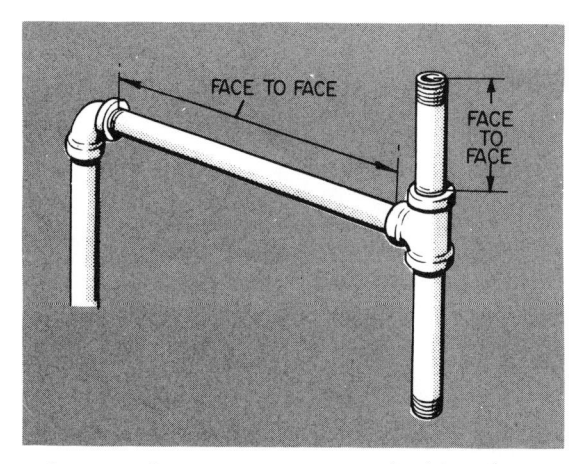

Take actual measurements and add make-up distances for pipe size, to measure pipe.

Use compact drill to bore holes for pipe runs, because other electric drills can't fit.
Stanley Tools

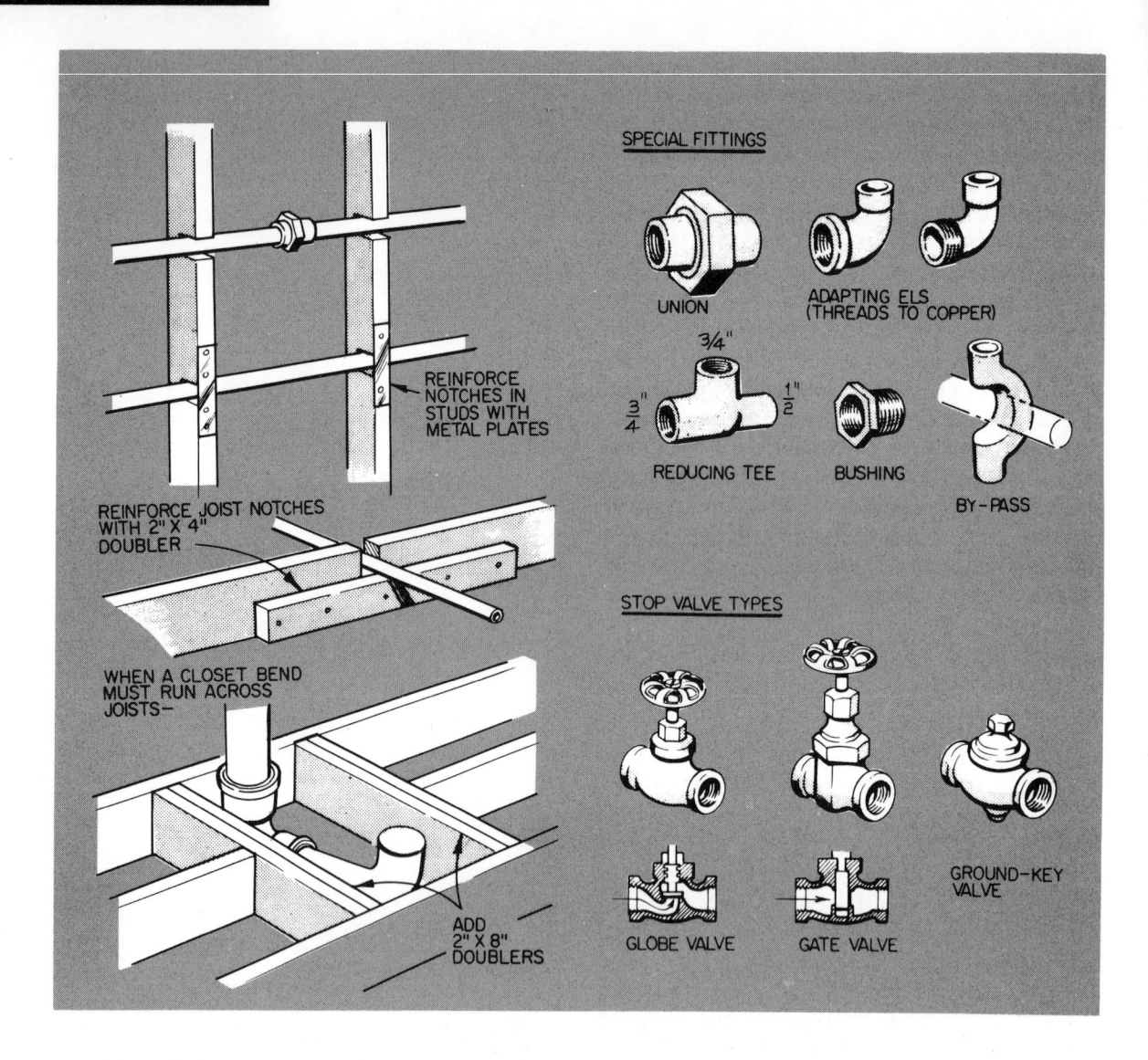

strictly horizontal. Instead they should slope ¼ to ½ inch per foot.

PIPE RUNS

With threaded steel pipe, begin each run where it originates, such as at the water heater or softener. Take it to its end. This will eliminate unions in the line. They're costly and bothersome to install. With plastic or copper pipe use any installation sequence that seems practical. You won't need unions unless you want them at appliances. Information on installing DWV piping is given in the chapter on a home addition.

Pipes in a basement or crawlspace are usually run beneath the joists and fastened at intervals with pipe hangers. If they are run up between joists, use a pair of 45-degree elbows (or ⅛-bends) to make the transition from above or below to between. Two 90-degree elbows can be used too in water supply lines, but they are more restrictive to water flow than a pair of 45's. Attic runs are generally made above the joists. Hangers are not needed there.

In new construction, pipes can be run under floors, over ceilings and inside walls. For a remodeling job you may have to fur out an existing wall, or box in a soil stack to conceal it. Pipes than run across a partition have to be notched into the studs. Since the largest of these pipes is usually 1½ inches, there's no real problem. To avoid weakening studs, don't notch them any deeper than necessary. Then after the pipe is in place, cover each notch with a strip of steel.

Pipes running across floor joists are more of a problem. Notching joists is liable to weaken them. Never notch a joist more than one quarter of its depth. Never notch near the ends and never in the center half. If you must break these rules, reinforce the dishonored joist by spiking a 2×4 or 2×6 on one or both sides at the notch. A hole can be drilled anywhere in a joist if it's roughly centered between the top and bottom edge.

The best way to run hot and cold water supply pipes is side by side. Keep them 4 to 6 inches apart to prevent the hot one from radiating its heat to the cold one. Side by side makes them easier to install.

If the space where pipes run is unheated, the pipes should be insulated to keep water in them from freezing. It may be a good idea to insulate hot water pipes anyway, to prevent heat loss. Pipes between joists can be protected by stretching blanket insulation between the joists. Pipes across joists are harder to insulate. They have to be wrapped with strips of insulation.

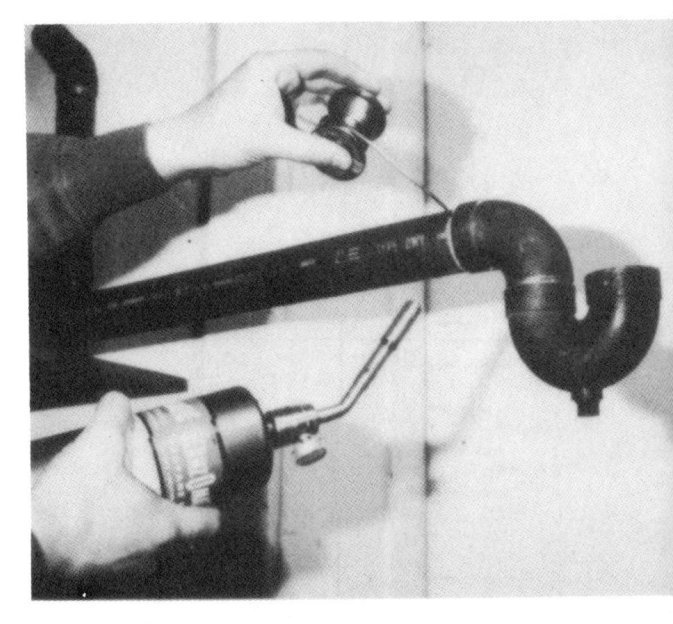

Make copper drain-waste-vent watertight joints by using big-flame tip on the torch.

If two dissimilar metals are joined together, like plastic to copper, use lots of pipe dope.

SPECIAL FITTINGS

In addition to the more or less standard pipe fittings shown in the chapter on pipes and fittings, there are special ones you should know about.

Because steel threaded pipe cannot be turned to screw into a plumbed-in fitting at both ends, a union is required at some point in the run. A union is a coupling that comes apart without disassembling the pipe run it's in. It joins two pipes of the same size and type.

To join pipes that are the same type but not the same size, use a *reducer*. There are reducing couplings, reducing elbows and reducing tees. To reduce a threaded opening in a fitting, use a reducing bushing.

When the pipes are the same size, but not the same type, an *adapter* is used. There are adapter couplings, adapter elbows and adapter tees. Seldom used are very specialized reducing-adapting fittings that combine both features.

Using special fittings, plus the standard ones, you can assemble any pipe run even though it may change size and type.

You'll have the most need for two types of valves in home plumbing—the gate valve and the globe valve. Here is the rule for which type to use: If "off" or "on" is all you want, use a gate valve. It doesn't restrict the flow of water through it. If you want to control the flow of water, use a globe valve or other flow-control valve.

A built-up leaching field for a small house. In foreground is septic tank leading to distribution box and two runs of 40 feet each. The field is made of crushed rock and will be filled 2-feet deep.

SEWAGE DISPOSAL

WHEN YOU BUILD a house, some method must be provided for the disposal of waste water and sewage. If you are a city dweller the problem is solved by tying into the city sewer line. A contractor or a city mechanic must perform the actual tying-in after all the work has been completed in the house. The lines run to the junction box at the road frontage.

In the country, however, you must install your own disposal field according to the code of the area in which you build. Many places allow *cesspools* as sewage disposals, provided they are placed not less than the approved minimum distance from the house and from existing wells. Usually this distance is 75 feet, minimum, from the well and 50 feet from the house. Cesspools are not the most desirable way of disposing of waste because of the fact that they allow

Vent stack ties into sewer pipe with a copper-to-cast iron adapter. If utilities are on opposite sides of house, it's best to have two vent stacks.

PLUMBING • 2129

The house trap and waste stack should be braced underneath to keep everything tight and true until lead has been poured and caulking is finished.

To get trenches dug for the disposal field, get a local contractor who specializes in this type of work and is equipt with power-driven machines.

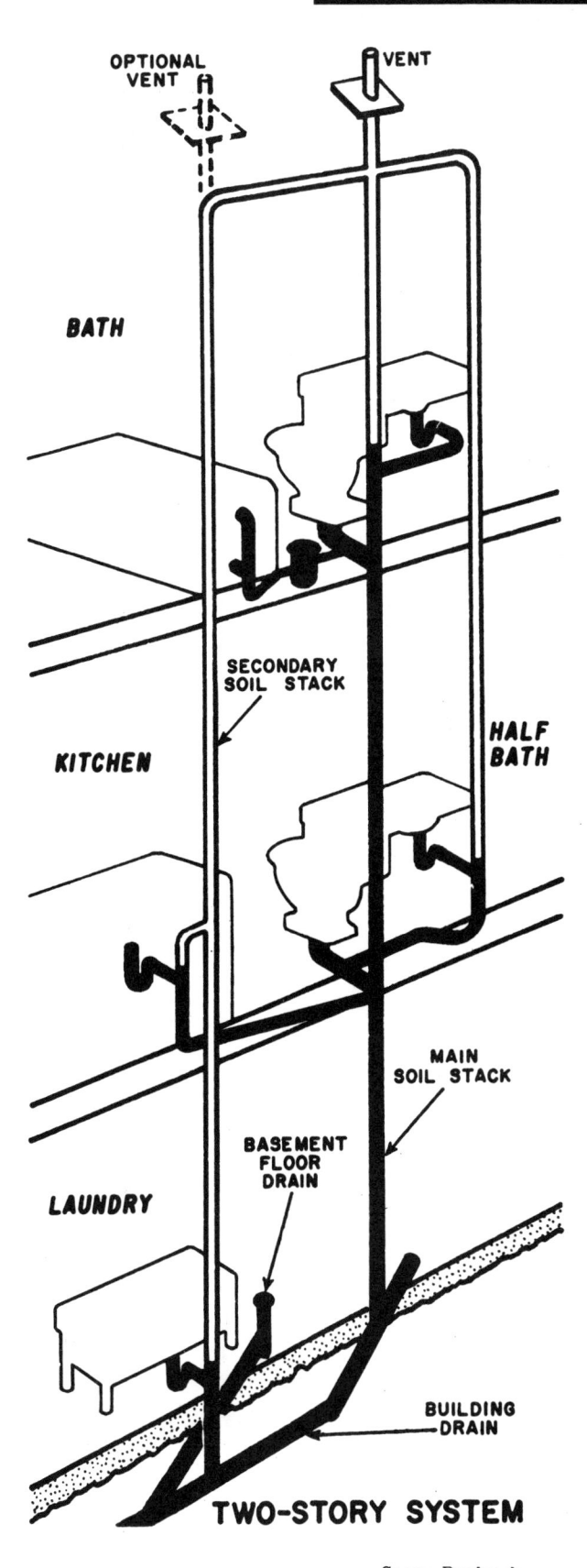

TWO-STORY SYSTEM

Sears, Roebuck

Study this layout and you will see how simple the drain-and-vent system for a two-story house can be, and the ease with which a first-floor half bath may be added to existing plumbing.

2130 • PLUMBING

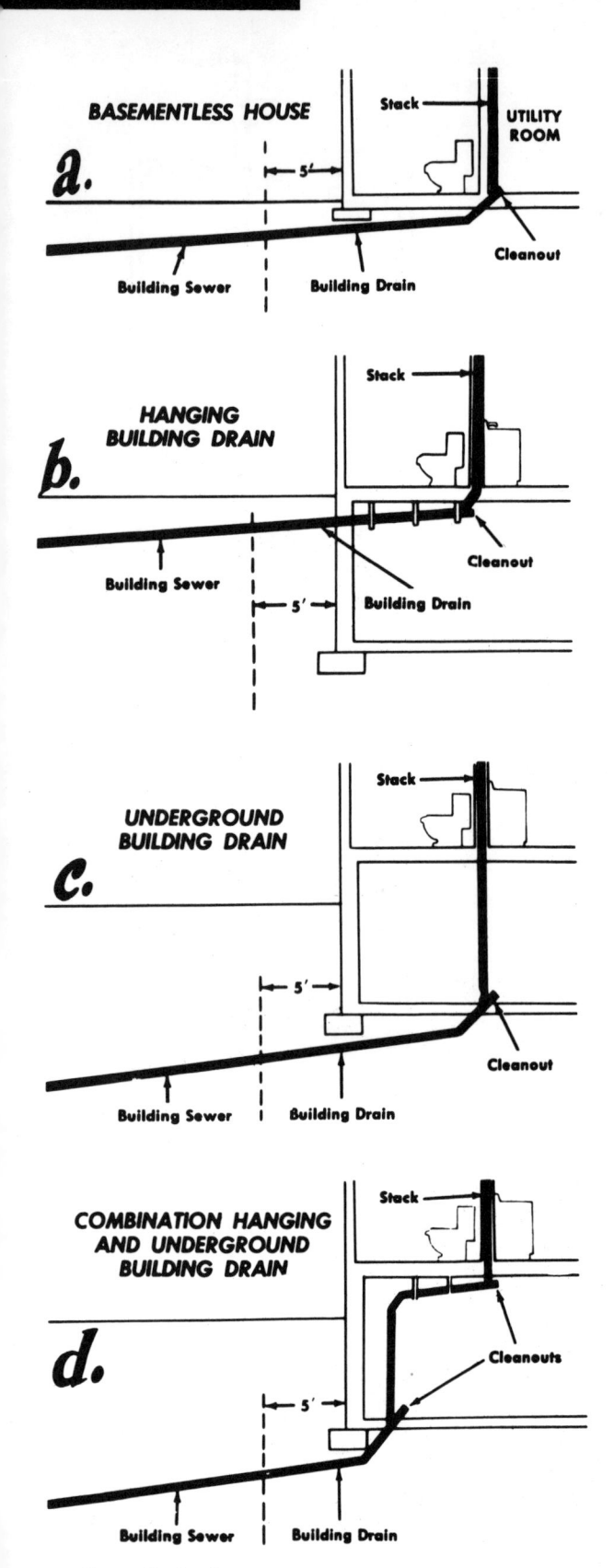

a. BASEMENTLESS HOUSE

b. HANGING BUILDING DRAIN

c. UNDERGROUND BUILDING DRAIN

d. COMBINATION HANGING AND UNDERGROUND BUILDING DRAIN

Sears, Roebuck

Here are four ways in which a drain and sewer line may be installed. And if you are adding a bathroom, you may find it simpler and better to add a second septic tank to handle its waste.

Above is a prefabricated concrete septic tank. They come in various sizes up to 2,000 gallons. Metal tanks are available from 300 gallons, up.

seepage of raw sewage into the surrounding soil, and therefore are liable to contaminate wells in the near vicinity. Where the soil is of high porosity, cesspools are generally allowed.

Septic tanks are the best method of running off sewage when building in the country. They, too, must be located at a minimum distance from the house and wells. Generally 15 feet from the house is the minimum distance permitted for the location of the tank itself, then the leaching field beyond that.

Cesspools may be purchased ready-made out of concrete, or they may be made yourself, whether out of poured concrete or out of special drainage blocks made for the sole purpose of constructing cesspools. The size of the pit is governed by the number of persons using the system, and local authorities have slightly different regulations governing this factor. Check with your authorities before building your cesspool and you will be safe.

The cement blocks are laid up without mortar on the pit until the shoulder is reached. There you start to neck-in the pit

To make cleanout holes easy to reach, put top of septic tank one foot below grade level, but check local health department on regulations.

Trenches are needed for the disposal field; hire an experienced operator to dig them. Make the trenches 18 inches deep; minimum of 6 feet apart.

Perforated fiber pipe is light in weight and easiest of all to handle when a drainage field is being installed. Joints are a simple press fit so that you will find that assembling is fast and easy.

to about two feet in diameter to accommodate a standard manhole cover. As you start to lay the blocks on the neck, mortar should be used to prevent the blocks from toppling into the pit and prevent the whole structure from caving in.

The sewer line enters the cesspool near the top, and the pit is back-filled with small cracked stone for a distance of at least 4 to 6 inches. The top of the tank should come to not more than two feet below grade if the depth of the soil allows. In places where the soil is shallow and bedrock is hit befor you have a good depth, the cesspool must be made much larger around or rectangular if need be, to gain the same cubic content.

Cesspools tend to fill more quickly than septic tanks because the solid wastes are left in the tank and are not reduced to liquid by the action of bacteria. As the sewage enters the cesspool the liquids drain off into the surrounding soil, leaving the solids which build up gradually until the pit must be cleaned out. This will be necessary to do every 3 to 5 years, depending on the amount of use the cesspool is put to.

2132 • PLUMBING

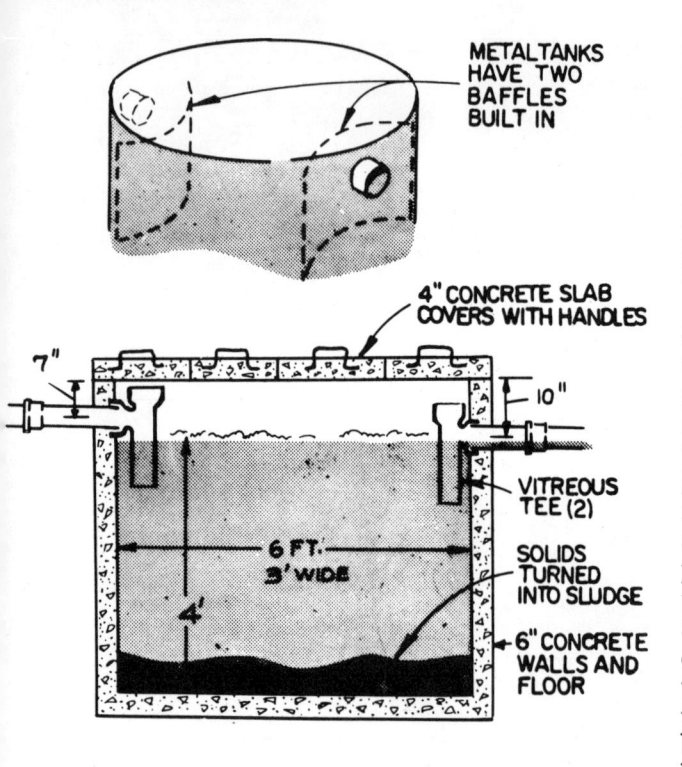

METAL TANKS HAVE TWO BAFFLES BUILT IN

SECTION THROUGH CONCRETE SEPTIC TANK (600 GAL.)
- 4" CONCRETE SLAB COVERS WITH HANDLES
- 7"
- 10"
- VITREOUS TEE (2)
- 6 FT. 3' WIDE
- 4'
- SOLIDS TURNED INTO SLUDGE
- 6" CONCRETE WALLS AND FLOOR

In rural areas there are regular companies which do nothing but pump out cesspools and septic tanks. The charge is not too high —about 25 to 35 dollars for an average tank, and the cleaning should be done regularly, because if it is not pumped clean at intervals, the tank may pack up and saturate the soil with solid waste, prohibiting the flow of liquid waste matter.

Septic tanks can also be made yourself, or can be purchased ready-made with concrete covers, delivered and lowered into your pit. The pit for either a septic tank or cesspool should be dug by a contractor with the proper equipment. This is a big job and the amount of dirt that must be moved is quite large. If you are installing a septic tank, the contractor will dig the pit for the tank, the trench from the house to the tank and the leaching field trenches all at the same time. The cost is very low considering the amount of labor it would take to perform the service. The size of the tank is determined by the number of bathrooms and other facilities in the house. Not less than a 750-gallon tank should ever be installed in a home, unless it is a small summer cabin or other campsite.

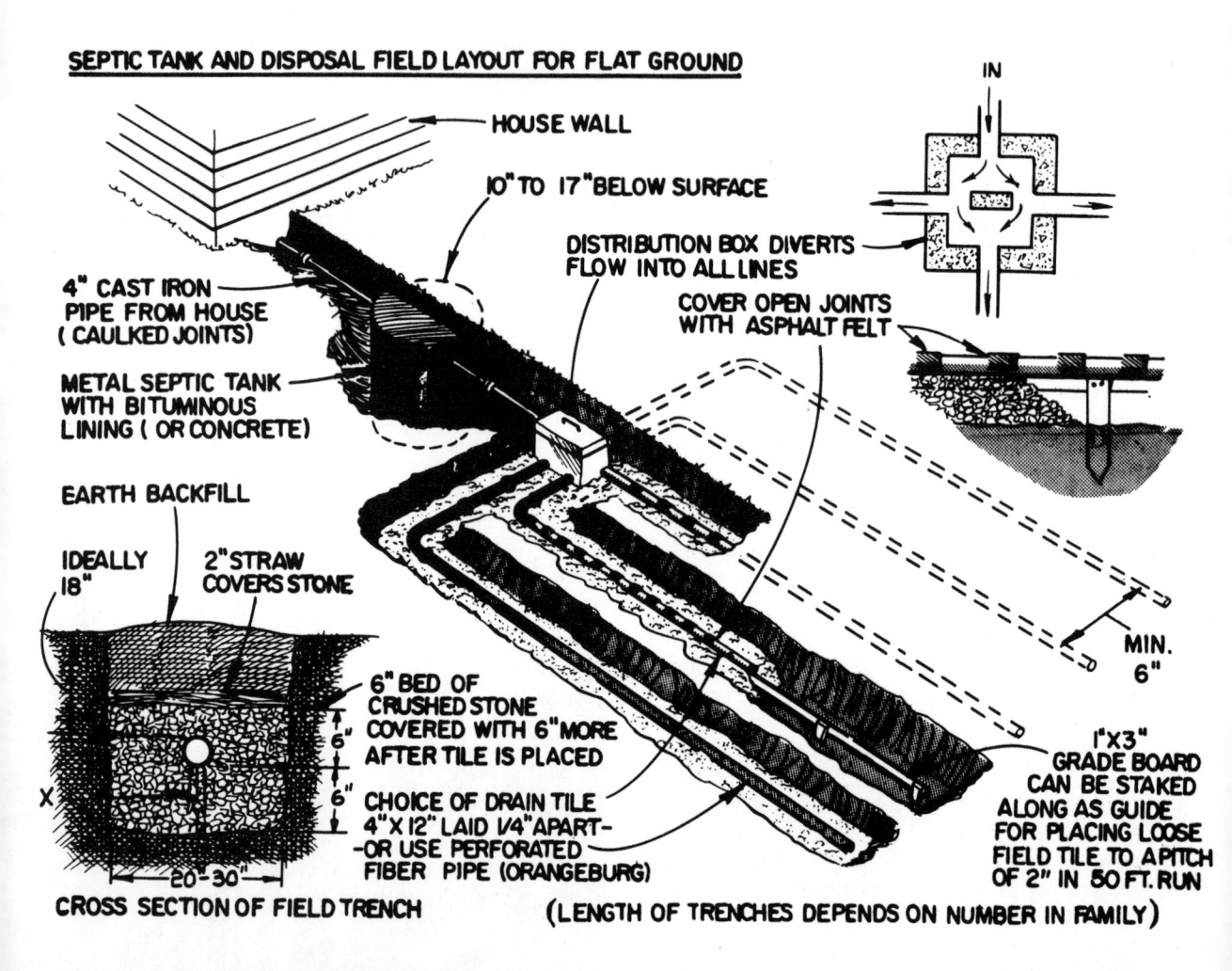

SEPTIC TANK AND DISPOSAL FIELD LAYOUT FOR FLAT GROUND

- HOUSE WALL
- 10" TO 17" BELOW SURFACE
- DISTRIBUTION BOX DIVERTS FLOW INTO ALL LINES
- 4" CAST IRON PIPE FROM HOUSE (CAULKED JOINTS)
- COVER OPEN JOINTS WITH ASPHALT FELT
- METAL SEPTIC TANK WITH BITUMINOUS LINING (OR CONCRETE)
- EARTH BACKFILL
- IDEALLY 18"
- 2" STRAW COVERS STONE
- 6" BED OF CRUSHED STONE COVERED WITH 6" MORE AFTER TILE IS PLACED
- CHOICE OF DRAIN TILE 4"x 12" LAID 1/4" APART— OR USE PERFORATED FIBER PIPE (ORANGEBURG)
- MIN. 6"
- 1"x 3" GRADE BOARD CAN BE STAKED ALONG AS GUIDE FOR PLACING LOOSE FIELD TILE TO A PITCH OF 2" IN 50 FT. RUN
- 20-30"

CROSS SECTION OF FIELD TRENCH

(LENGTH OF TRENCHES DEPENDS ON NUMBER IN FAMILY)

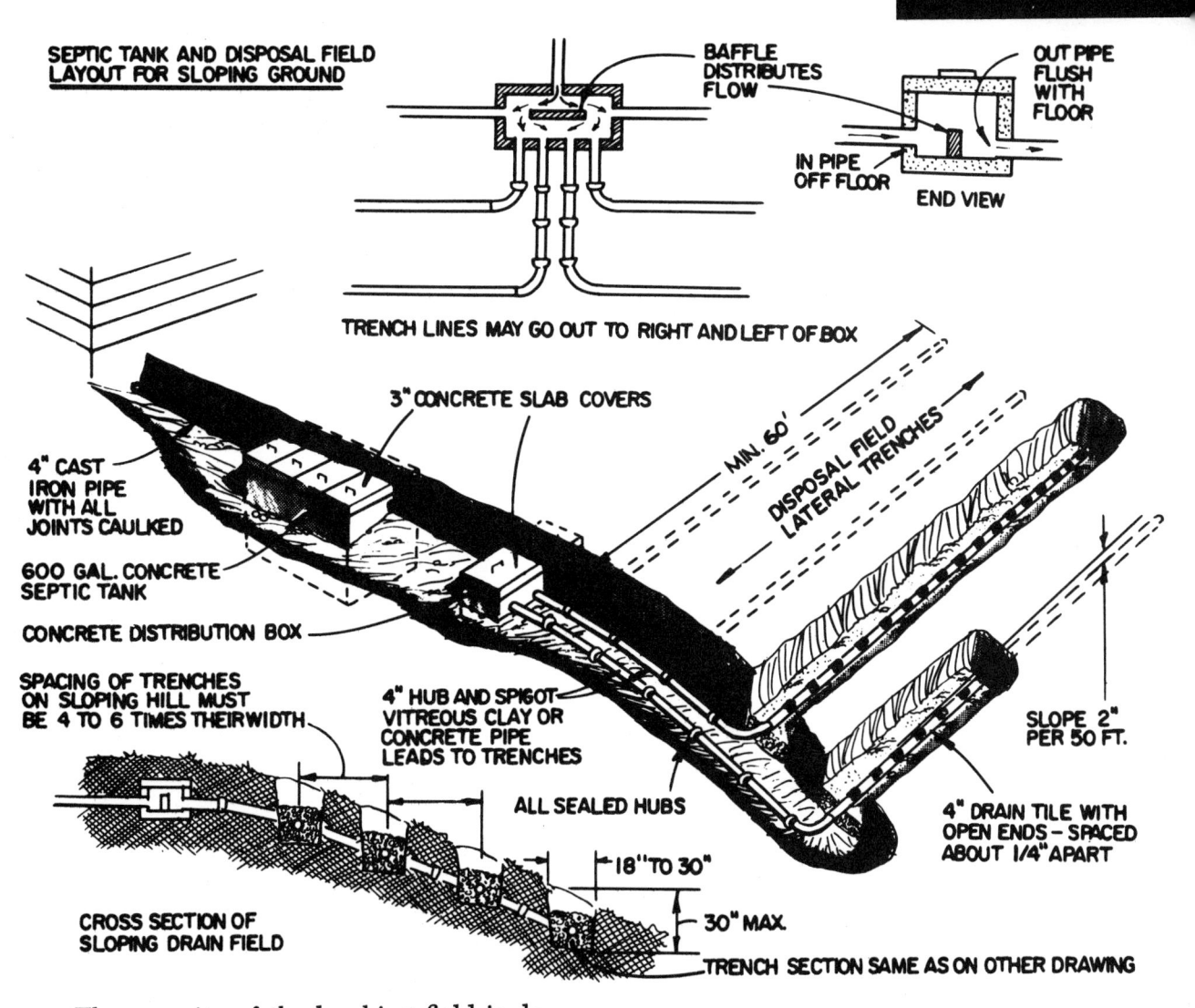

SEPTIC TANK AND DISPOSAL FIELD LAYOUT FOR SLOPING GROUND

The capacity of the leaching field is determined by the number of persons using the facilities in the home—optimum being from about 15 to near 100 feet per person, determined on the percolation properties of the soil in your area. You can make your own percolation test quite easily, to arrive at the length of leaching pipe needed. You will need a wooden yardstick such as are given away free at most yard-goods stores, or a stick about two feet long marked off in inches. Dig a hole one foot in diameter and about two feet deep at the place where you intend to locate your leaching field. Stick the yardstick securely in the hole so it will remain upright, then fill the hole half full of water, stopping the fill at one of the marks on the yardstick. Time the interval needed for the water to drop one inch. The following table will tell you the length of runs *per person* for your leaching field.

2 minutes or less	16 feet
5 minutes	24 feet
10 minutes	32 feet
30 minutes	64 feet
1 hour	88 feet

House sewer should make a watertight joint with tank inlet. Sewer, preferably made of cast iron, should be carefully caulked. The line from the tank to disposal field should be watertight, too.

2134 • PLUMBING

Tile in absorption trenches is laid on 6-inch bed of crushed stone. A 1x4-inch grade board supports tiles which slope about 1 inch in 25 feet. Felt strips keep stones from filling open joints.

Crushed stones are placed around and over tile, covering the tile to a depth of 2 inches. A layer of salt hay keeps backfill dirt from filtering into the stones, also it acts as a medium of insulation.

Seventy concrete blocks are needed for a 5x5' leaching pit. Two or more may be used in series, or both may be fed from distribution box. Top tapers inward, is covered by cast concrete lid.

A leaching pit may be 3 to 6 feet or more in diameter, and may be built with blocks laid on sides. Cast iron, vitreous, or nonperforated Orangeburg pipe may be used for connections.

If the percolation time is greater than an hour, the soil is not suitable for a leaching field, and you will have to manufacture one instead of utilizing the native soil. This consists of having cracked stone hauled in and spread to a depth of at least two feet over the entire area of the leaching field. The leaching pipe-runs are laid on the surface of the stone, and more stone is spread to a depth of not less than one foot over the top of the pipes. Topsoil or other fill soil is then spread on top of the crushed stone about a foot deep, on top of which you may seed grass or other erosion control foliage such as vetch or clover. When a manufactured field is required, the length of the leaching runs should be as for one hour percolation, i.e., 88 feet per person.

When the septic tank is in place, the soil drain is attached to it from the house, using either solid Orangeburg fiber pipe, or clay tile in two foot lengths with the joints cemented together. The Orangeburg is much easier to use and is excellent for the purpose. The run from the tank to the leaching field is intercepted by a distribution box. This is a box made of concrete—or made yourself out of concrete—inside of which is a baffle against which the rush of waste is caught to disperse the flow inside the box. The waste is then diverted into all of the leaching runs instead of the one directly in front of the entry hole.

A distribution box is necessary because otherwise the sewage would shoot out of the septic tank and run into that leaching pipe which was directly in line or nearest in line with the overflow outlet. This would soon tend to saturate the field at that run and slowly fill the run, backing up into the septic tank. Thus, you would lose the effect of the desired run per person in the leaching field.

Orangeburg pipe comes perforated, for leaching runs, and is put together by slip tapered joints which tend to seal themselves after awhile and which are rustproof. The pipe is sold in 8-foot and 10-foot lengths. Four-inch diameter is used for sewer lines. They are laid in the trenches with a slope or pitch of not less than two inches per 50 feet of run. The leaching field must end not less than ten feet from your property line, and not less than 75 feet from the nearest well. The septic tank itself may be located not less than 50 feet from the nearest well. The trenches for the leaching runs should be dug about two feet deep and about six inches of crushed stone or traprock spread in the bottom before the pipes are laid. The pipes are covered with another six inches

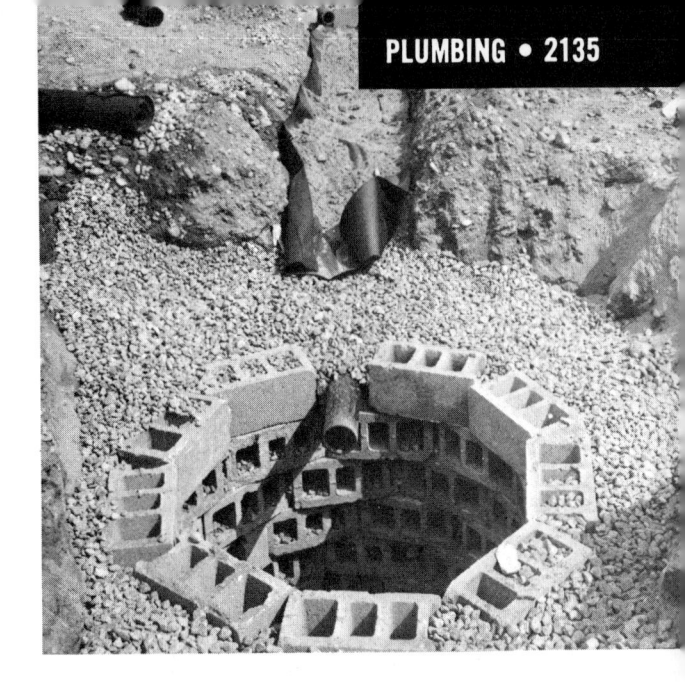

Crushed stone of 1½- to 2½-inch size is filled around leaching pit in a band having a minimum thickness of 6 inches. Top of pit is usually about 12 inches below grade, and has an access cover.

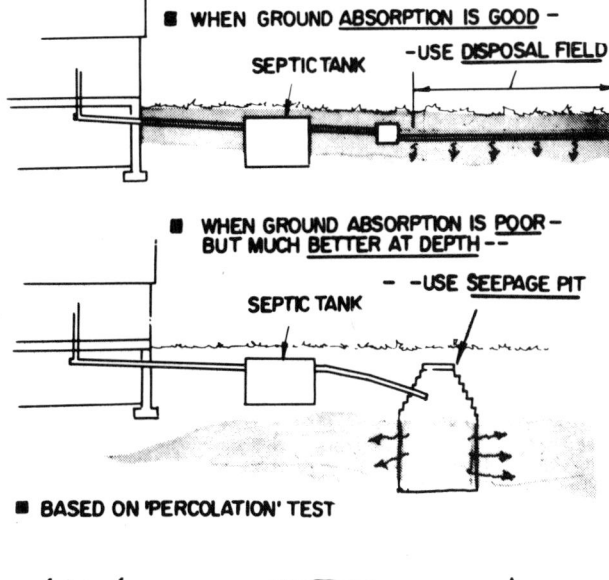

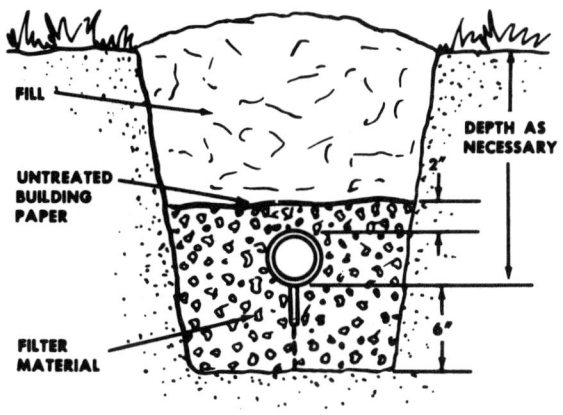

Below is section of drainage or leaching trench. It is 18 inches wide or more, and 18 inches deep. Crushed stone surrounds drain tile or the pipe.

2136 • PLUMBING

of stone, then a layer of hay or straw a couple inches thick. On top of the straw the dirt is backfilled and slightly mounded to allow settling to the original grade.

If your land is on a steep grade, it is better to put the leaching runs in lateral trenches branching out of the distribution box. Several runs can be laid, equally divided on both sides of the distribution box. Solid pipe should be used until the elbow to the lateral is reached, then the perforated pipe installed. The lateral trenches should not be spaced much closer than ten feet. Naturally, the crushed rock need not

Dry well gets a cast concrete cover just as a leaching pit does. Well can be used to disperse water from gutters, foundation and the basement drains, as well as from clothes and dishwashers.

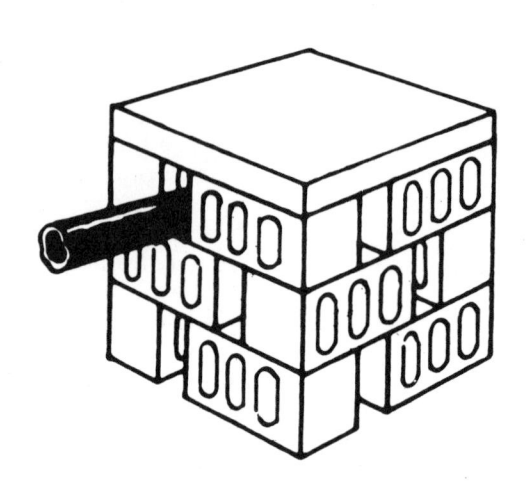

Concrete blocks are laid on side to make a good, dry well. A 3x3x3-foot hole is needed for well 1½ blocks square, 3 courses of blocks high, no mortar.

LAYOUT OF SEPTIC TANK AND DISTRIBUTION BOX WHEN DISCHARGED INTO SEEPAGE PIT(S)

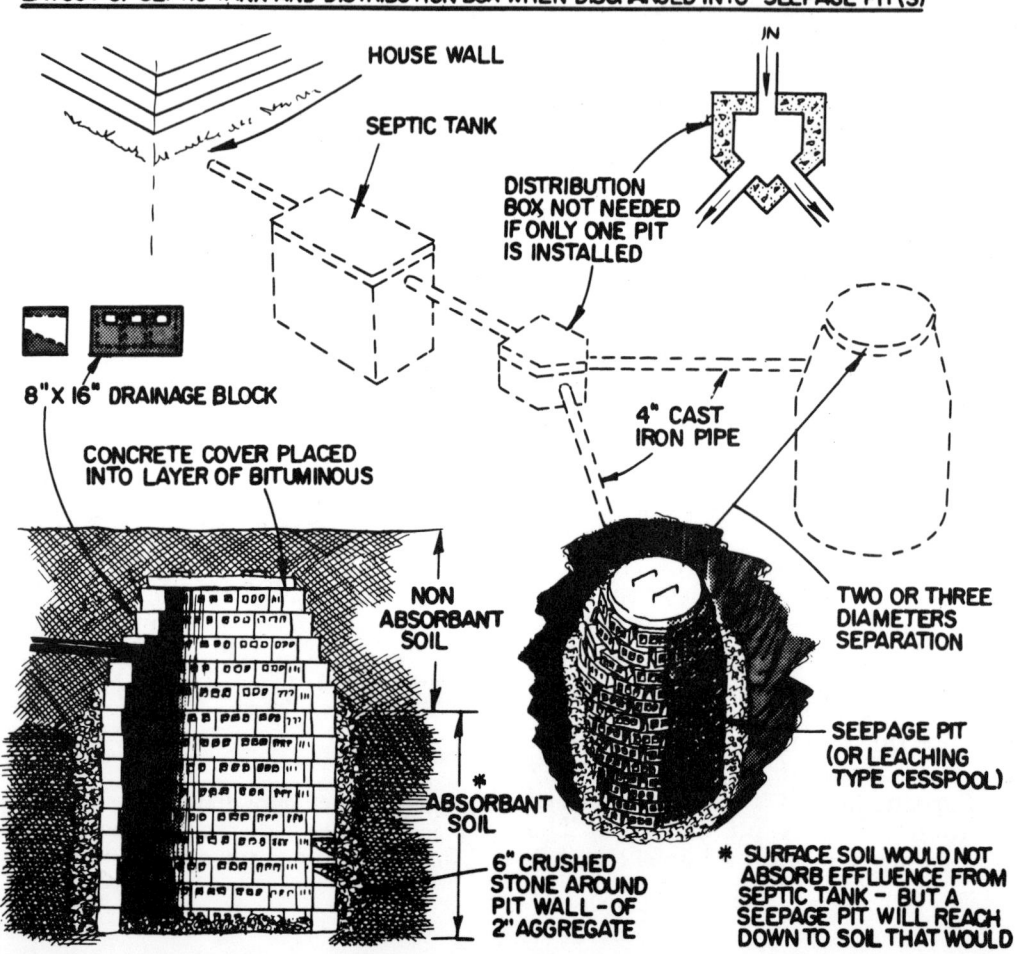

- HOUSE WALL
- SEPTIC TANK
- DISTRIBUTION BOX NOT NEEDED IF ONLY ONE PIT IS INSTALLED
- 8"x 16" DRAINAGE BLOCK
- CONCRETE COVER PLACED INTO LAYER OF BITUMINOUS
- 4" CAST IRON PIPE
- NON ABSORBANT SOIL
- ABSORBANT SOIL
- 6" CRUSHED STONE AROUND PIT WALL - OF 2" AGGREGATE
- TWO OR THREE DIAMETERS SEPARATION
- SEEPAGE PIT (OR LEACHING TYPE CESSPOOL)
- *SURFACE SOIL WOULD NOT ABSORB EFFLUENT FROM SEPTIC TANK - BUT A SEEPAGE PIT WILL REACH DOWN TO SOIL THAT WOULD

be put in that part of the trenches leading to the laterals, but the same bedding of crushed rock as on ordinary ground is required around the perforated part of the leaching runs.

Septic tanks are available in steel as well as concrete, and top models, having a double chamber, are sold by most plumbing supply houses and by the large mail-order stores such as Montgomery Ward and Sears Roebuck. The double compartment allows a considerably longer time for the solid waste to be broken down into liquid by the bacterial action, resulting in longer use before cleaning is necessary. Every tank must be periodically cleaned.

After installing your cesspool or septic tank, and leaching field, you should make a map of your property and accurately sketch in the location of the tank and the leaching field. If you make lawns or plantings over the site, or even leave a plain dirt cover, you might have difficulty remembering the exact location after a period of years has elapsed, should the tank need cleaning. "I think it's somewhere around here" can play hob with your beautiful lawn or your wife's favorite bed of petunias, when digging-up time comes around. •

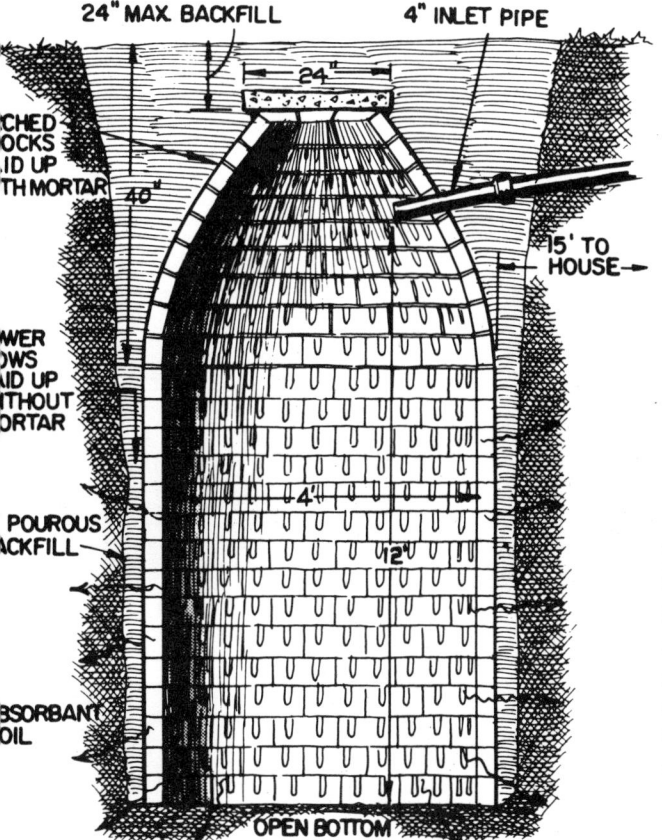

STANDARD CESSPOOL CONSTRUCTION

SOIL PERCOLATION TEST

TIME REQUIRED FOR WATER TO FALL 1 IN.	FEET OF PIPE PER PERSON
1 Minute	12
2 Minutes	15
5 Minutes	20
10 Minutes	30
30 Minutes	60
60 Minutes	80
Over 60 Minutes	Unsuitable

Example: It is found that it takes 30 minutes for the water in the percolation test to fall 1 inch. Find the feet of drainage pipe needed if five persons will be served by the system.

Solution: Refer to Table B. When, in column 1, it requires 30 minutes for the water to fall 1 inch, column 2 shows that 60 ft. of drainage pipe will be required for each person; therefore, five persons will require 5 x 60 feet or 300 feet of drainage pipe.

Typical layouts for a flat drainage field, and one with laterals on a slope. A brick or block in distribution box will help deflect tank liquid evenly. Box may also be used with seepage pits.

Sears, Roebuck

SERVICE and REPAIR

IN HOUSES that have been lived in for several years the plumbing often becomes in need of servicing. Pipes will deliver too small a volume of water, fixtures will gurgle while draining, or, waste water will back up in one fixture from another. If your house is a two-story home and water from the upper floor fixtures backs up into those on the lower floor, the trouble is probably a stopped-up vent stack. The first examination to make is from the roof.

Wasps and bees often build their nests in vent pipes, clogging the pipe to the extent where a back-up occurs. A pole can be used to knock the nest down the stack to the point where it will flush through the sewer system as waste matter. If the nest is occupied, first spray it thoroughly to kill or drive away all the wasps or bees. You might otherwise have a busy time on your hands dodging the angry insects when you start to destroy their home.

Another common cause of vent clogging is high-sudsing detergents in your washing machine. These suds do not flow out the drains at the same rate as water, and the

Pipe leaks are mended quickly, simply, with Plastic Steel spread on bandage, wrapped around leak.

water can actually force them up the vent stack where they will run out onto the roof. Each time a foam of suds is pumped up the stack some of the detergent remains on the walls of the stack when it dries. Gradually it builds up until the pipe is so restricted as to cause a blockage in the fixtures which the stack services.

A roto-rooter type of snake sent through from the roof will clear such stoppages and ream the vent stack clear of scale and built-up soap and grease. If it is unhandy to send the snake through from the top, then it should be sent in from a cleanout plug located at the bottom of the stack. The snake should be driven through until it comes out at the top, then reversed and sent through the sewer line until it enters the main or the septic tank or cesspool.

If the stoppage is really bad and the matter caked hard inside the vent, set a garden hose at the top of the vent and run a trickle of water. The water will serve to lubricate the cutting knives while the rooter is being operated. This will ease the load on the snake. Only in extreme cases of neglect will a section of the stack have to be replaced.

It is always better to use detergents in your washing machine that do not make large amounts of suds. The suds are not an indication of washing power in detergents anyway, and they are only death to drainage systems and septic tank operation, retarding or entirely stopping the bacterial action that is absolutely necessary if your septic tank is going to dispose of the waste properly.

Sometimes a kitchen sink will back up while all the other fixtures operate properly. This is generally an indication that the stoppage is locally confined to the sink trap or within a short distance of the trap—

A saddle clamp, assembled and disassembled, is used as a temporary repair for a leaking pipe.

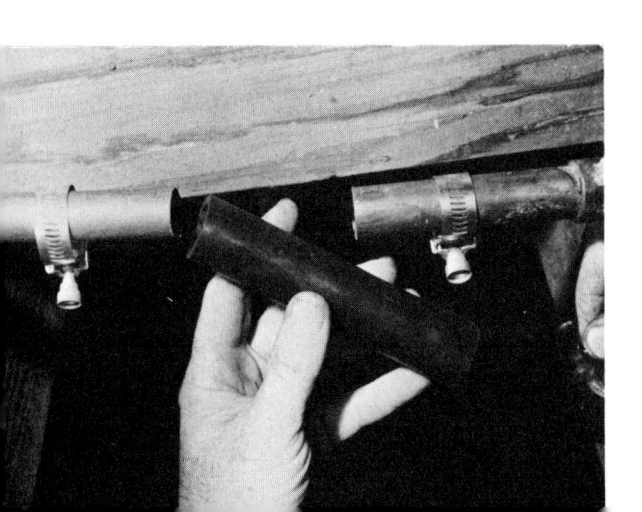

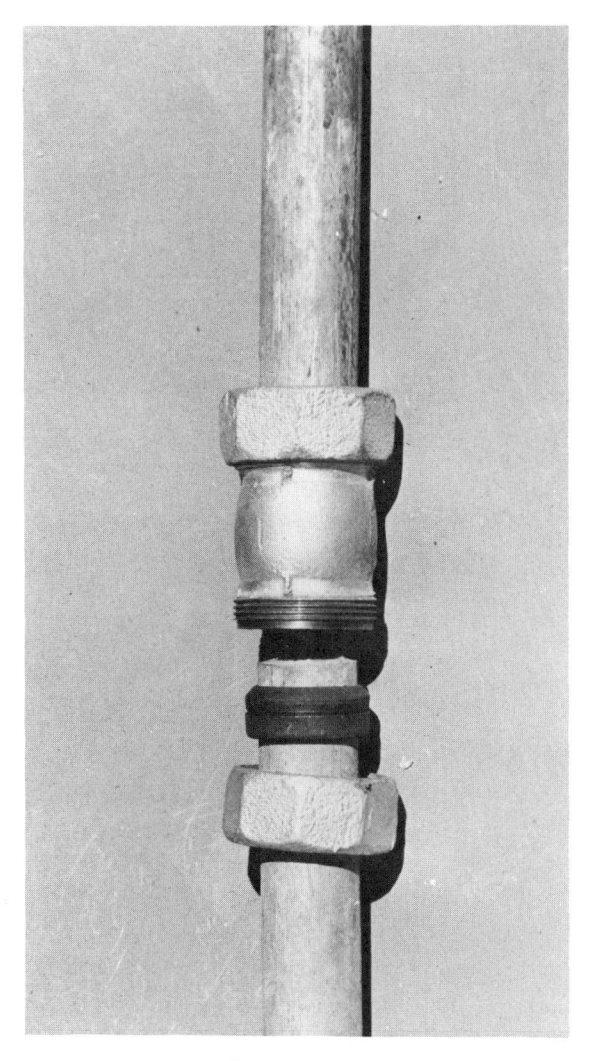

Quick repair of a damaged pipe is made by sawing out section, replacing with hose and clamps.

A Drescher fitting, partly assembled, is used to join two steel pipes without threads, or to connect a pipe to a tank with a plain fixed nipple.

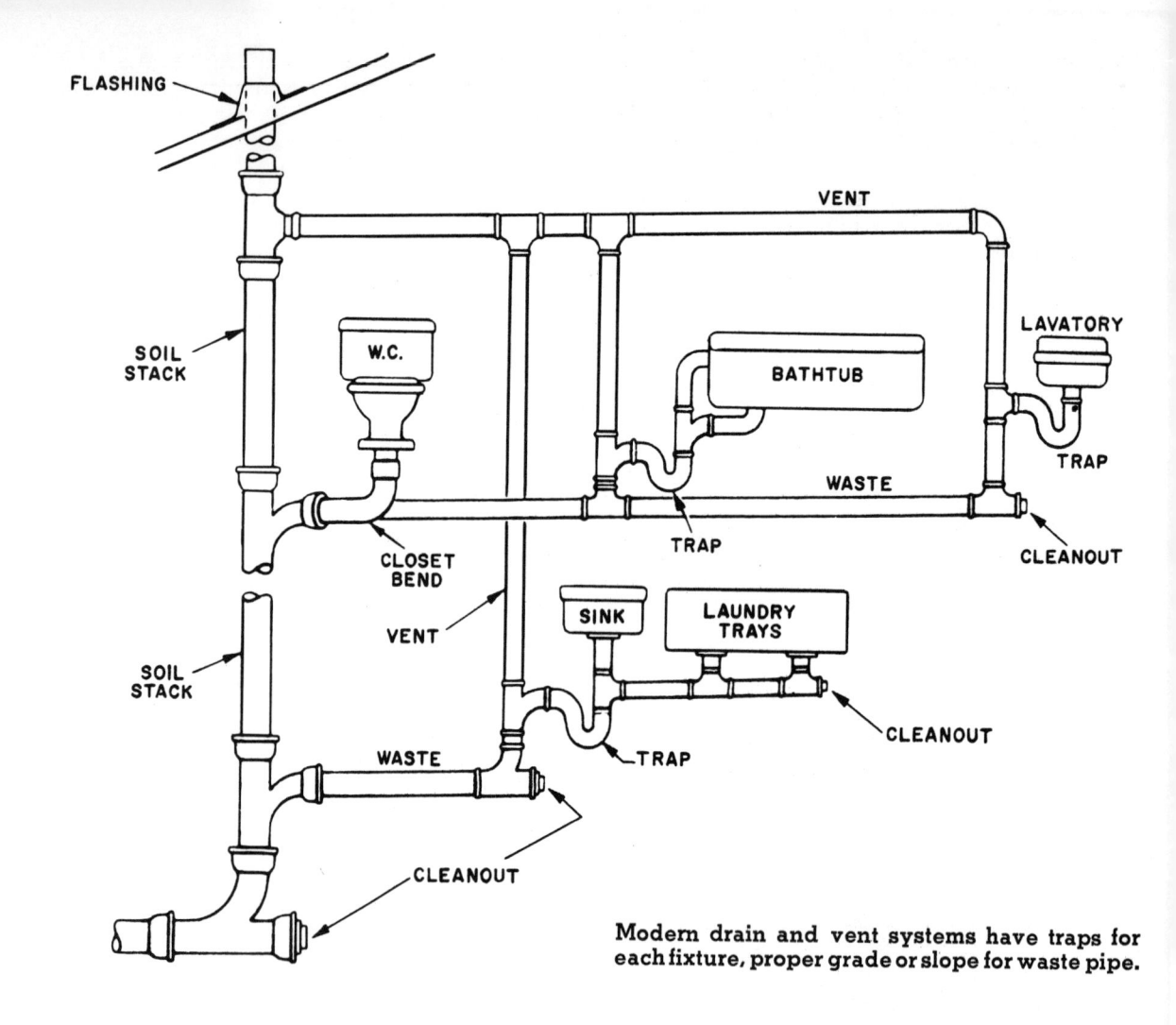

2140 • PLUMBING

Modern drain and vent systems have traps for each fixture, proper grade or slope for waste pipe.

When all house drainage is blocked, the place to go to work is at cleanout plug where house drain exists through foundation. If exterior line is clear, then check cleanouts on interior drains. where it enters the vent stack, for instance. Sink traps can become clogged in new systems if grease is indiscriminately poured down the drain; food scraps flushed out when the dishes or pans are being rinsed.

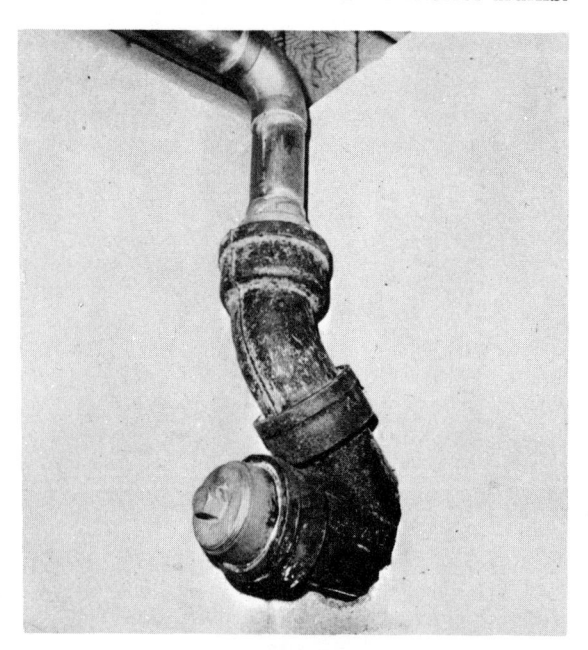

Many people think they can pour grease right down the drain while they run hot water, on the supposition that the hot water will keep the grease liquid and flush it away at the same time. Not so. The grease will stick to the walls of the drain and remain in the trap, building up to the point of stoppage in a comparatively short time. What the grease also does is attract small particles which stick in it and help to form an obstruction in the drain.

That demitasse spoon you have been missing for so long, the popsickle sticks the kids tossed in the sink, the little plastic spears from the olives, consumed during your last entertaining session, all are wonderful devices for stopping up sink drains. They rest comfortably in the trap, gayly collecting other debris until the trap is solidly filled with assorted junk. Fortunately the sink drain is easily opened for

PLUMBING • 2141

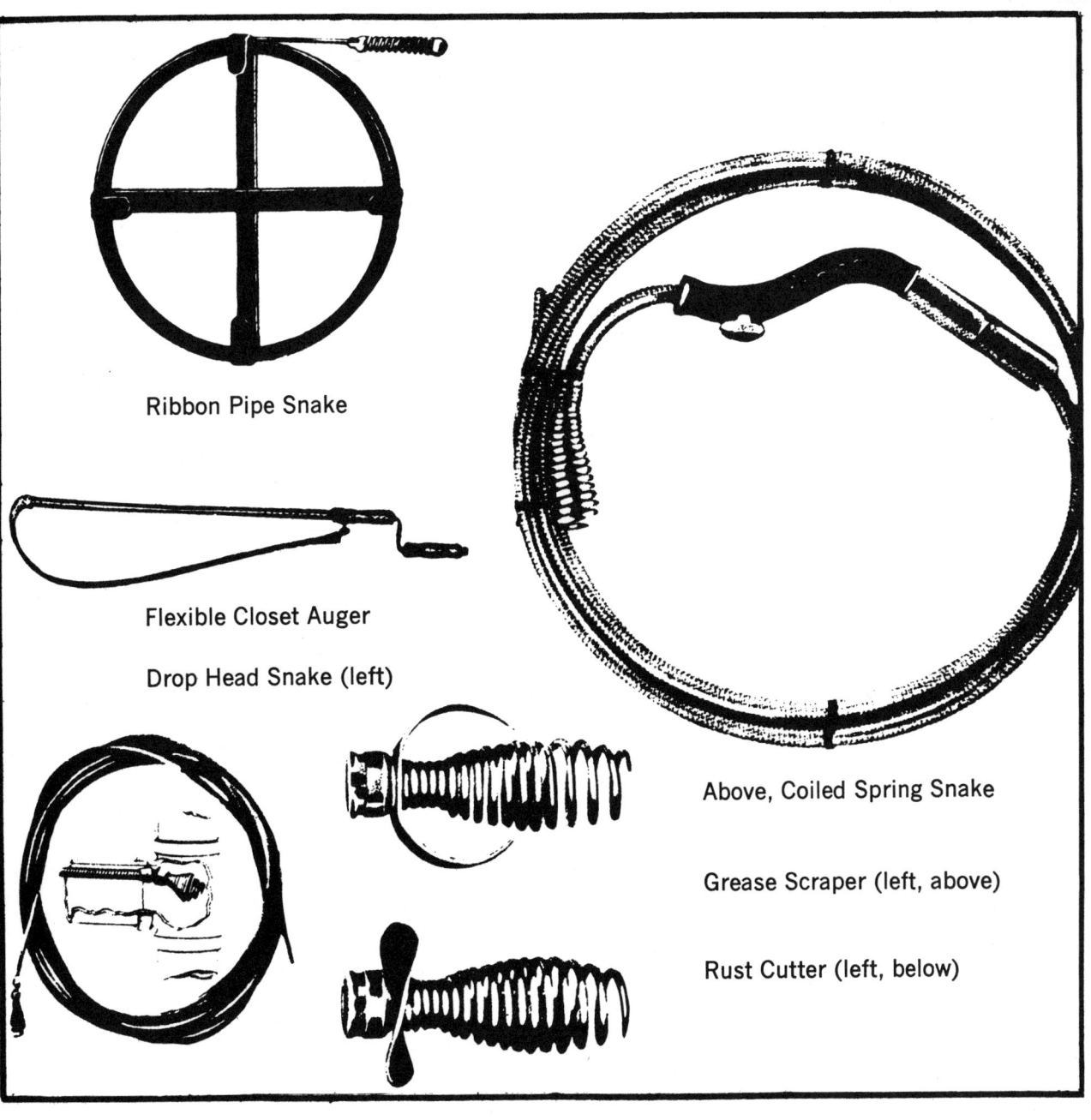

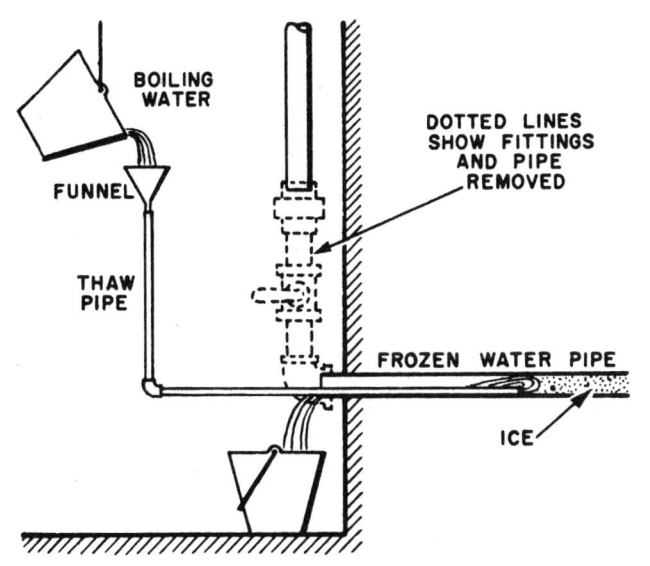

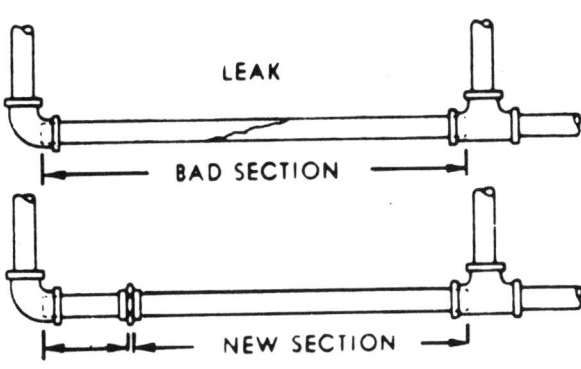

Ribbon Pipe Snake

Flexible Closet Auger

Drop Head Snake (left)

Above, Coiled Spring Snake

Grease Scraper (left, above)

Rust Cutter (left, below)

A leak in the pipe is best repaired by replacing the entire section with proper fittings, as shown.

Easy way to thaw out frozen pipes is to remove fittings, pour boiling water through thaw pipe.

2142 • PLUMBING

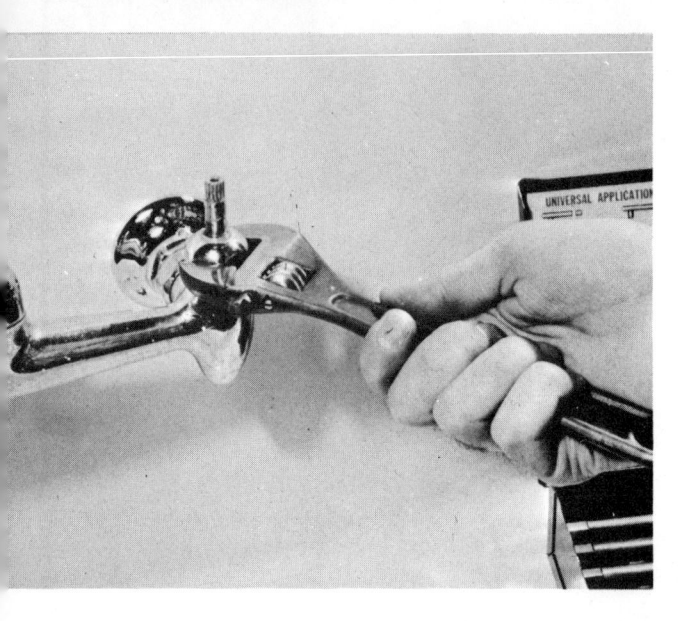

To get at faucet washer, remove handle, then unscrew cap nut or bonnet, as shown. Stem or spindle will then unscrew from the faucet body.

On some models, stem will unscrew right along with cap nut. Others may have a second packing which will have to be removed with wrench.

Faucet washer is removed by unscrewing a brass screw at bottom. Pry out old washer and replace with new one. Beveled side should face bottom.

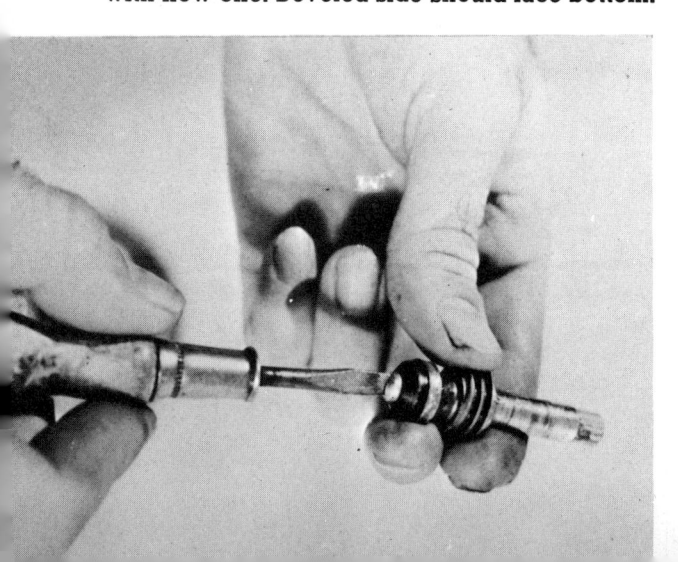

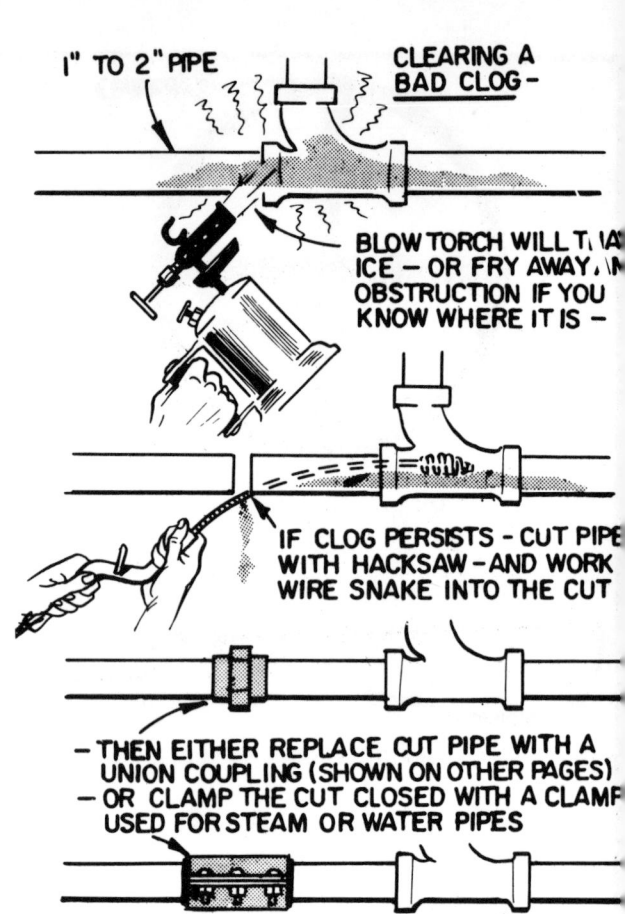

CLEARING A BAD CLOG —

1" TO 2" PIPE

BLOW TORCH WILL THAW ICE — OR FRY AWAY AN OBSTRUCTION IF YOU KNOW WHERE IT IS —

IF CLOG PERSISTS - CUT PIPE WITH HACKSAW - AND WORK WIRE SNAKE INTO THE CUT

— THEN EITHER REPLACE CUT PIPE WITH A UNION COUPLING (SHOWN ON OTHER PAGES)
— OR CLAMP THE CUT CLOSED WITH A CLAMP USED FOR STEAM OR WATER PIPES

cleaning, and most often all that is needed to clear up the stoppage is to unscrew the cleanout plug and dump the waste matter into a collecting pan. Feel up in the trap both ways with a finger to make sure nothing else is lodged inside, then screw back the plug and fill the sink with good hot water. Pull the stopper and the water should rush down, completing the cleaning action for you. If the water runs out slowly, you still have a partial stoppage farther on in the line from the trap. The treatment is to run a snake through the drain until it breaks clear in the vent stack.

An occasional shot of any of the prepared drain cleaners is good insurance against stoppage. If you have installed ABS-DWV pipe in your drainage lines, make sure that the cleaner is not one of the ones using sulphuric acid. It will damage the plastic pipe. Drano, Sani-Flush and similar products have no affect on the ABS pipe. Stoppages occuring in the bathroom wash basins are generally caused by one thing only—the gradual accumulation of hair in the pop-up part of the drain. If, when you install your fixtures, you use one of the better-quality pop-ups, the plug stopper will easily lift right out of the drain for cleaning. If, then, you schedule a regular routine of lifting out the plug and clean-

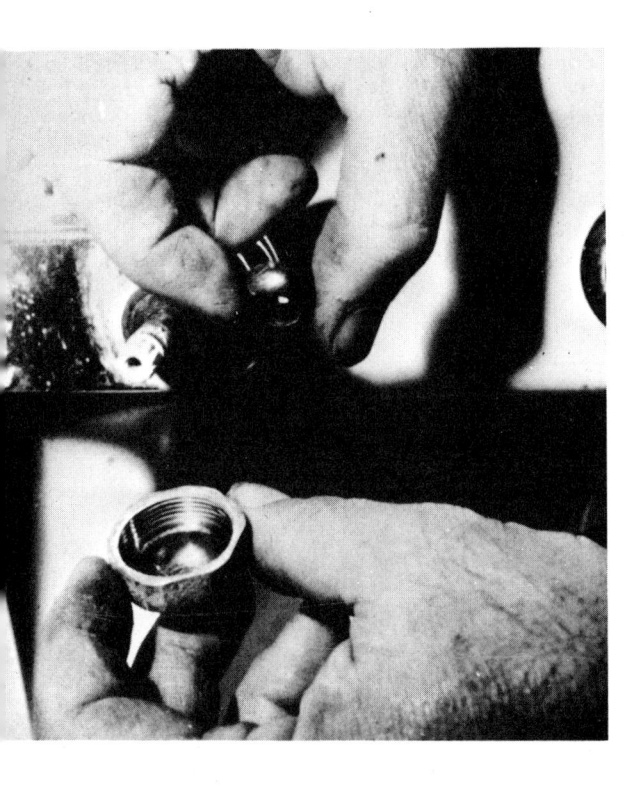

PLUMBING • 2143

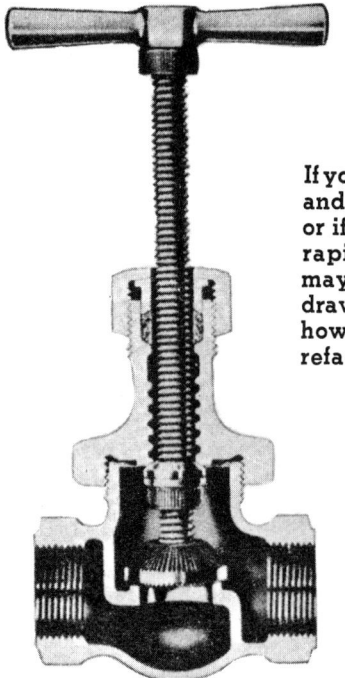

If you put in a new washer, and the faucet still leaks, or if the washer wears out rapidly, the faucet seat may need refacing. The drawing at the left shows how a very inexpensive refacing tool fits in easily.

O'Malley Valve Co.

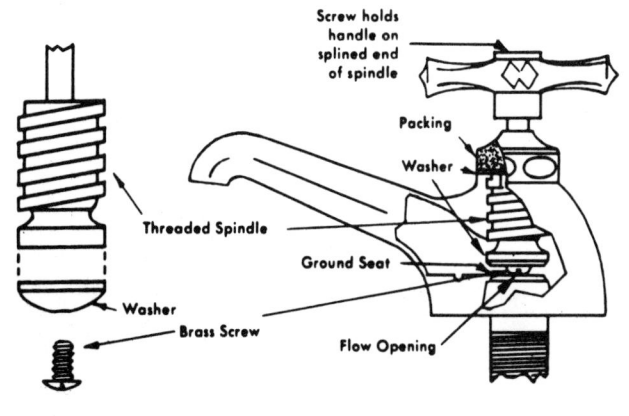

Gumdrop-shaped packing washers are graphited, come in different sizes and types. To get a replacement for one, take worn washer or faucet assembly along with you when you go to store.

Above is a diagram of a typical faucet with all the parts. Note the positions of each unit of the faucet and the order in which they are put on the unit. Also see how packing is above washer.

ing it, say once a month, or each time you clean the bathroom, you will never have a stoppage in the lavatory. Girls' hair, especially, is the big offender, because it is long and fine; sticks easily to the plug.

Sometimes the slug of matted hair is so dense that the plug is locked into the drain and cannot be removed at all. Patient rotation of the plug, sawing it back, forth, up and down for as much as an hour are sometimes necessary before it can be removed. Sometimes the plug has to be cut apart and taken out in sections—a new plug then being purchased for the drain. If you have several females in your family, this should be taken into consideration and the pop-ups cleaned regularly, without fail. It will save a lot of future grief.

Toilet stoppages are from several causes. The thing that makes the quickest stoppage is the use of too much toilet paper. Generally teen-age youngsters are the biggest offenders and the hardest to break of the habit. Traps in toilet fixtures are not always as smooth and direct as they should be. If you were unfortunate enough to get a rough one, nearly every time a king-sized wad of paper is sent down it will hang up on some small obstruction. The next flushing goes all over the bathroom floor.

One shot with a force-ball type of plun-

Plug type drain is removed for cleaning by a quarter turn and lifting out. Older plunger type requires loosening net under bowl at back. Pull out rod attached to plunger and lift the stopper.

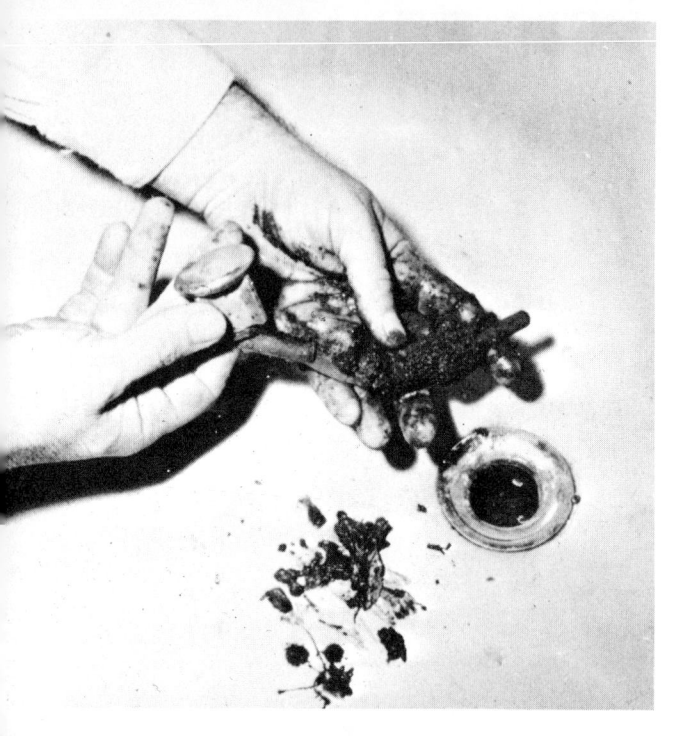

Some pop-up bathroom drains can be removed by getting a hold around their rim and lifting up while jiggling the drain control handle. Matted hair is often the number one cause of clogging.

Below, a good trap has plug at bottom. It saves the labor required to take apart a clogged trap.

Left, never use a toothed tool on chrome fitting. Smooth-jaw Channellock pliers are best for them.

ger is usually all that is necessary to clear the stoppage, unless several flushings have gone through, partly obstructing the drain each time. In this case you may have to resort to the use of a toilet auger, which is a short snake in a pipe sheath with a crank on the upper end and a spring-type of hook on the other. You start the snake through, then crank away until it tightens up. Then heave back, pulling out the obstruction which has been caught on the hook.

In cases where a foreign body has fallen into the toilet and been flushed part way down, or in extreme cases of stoppage, the toilet may even have to be removed from the floor, turned upside down, and the stoppage pulled out from the bottom, or pushed back up through the trap until it can be reached and lifted out of the bowl. When this drastic measure has become necessary, don't forget to replace the wax seal on the floor flange before reseating the bowl. The old seal should be scraped away and cleaned off the toilet, as well as the flange, before using the fresh wax. A large rag or sheet of newspaper should be stuffed down the lead bend before scraping the wax away to keep pieces of the insoluable wax from going down the drain. Do

PLUMBING • 2145

To get at a washer in a recessed tub or shower faucet requires a socket wrench of correct size.

First step in disassembling faucet of this type is to remove handle and the decorative housing.

Then slide socket wrench over the stem until it fits over packing nut on the inside, and unscrew.

Simplest cure for a toilet that won't flush is a good working over with large rubber force cup.

not force the rag or paper so far down the drain that you cannot reach down to pull it out when you are ready to reinstall your fixture.

When, in a hurry, a rough edge or projection may be left on the lead pipe where it was soldered to the floor flange. This projection can catch on paper going down the drain and hang it up, causing a build-up and eventual stoppage. The only remedy is to unseat the bowl, file the edges of the lead bend smooth, and then replace the wax seal and reseat the fixture.

Failure of the system due to pipe rusting or splitting is harder to correct. Splitting is generally caused by a pipe freezing in the winter time, then opening at its weakest spot when the ice expands within it. Sometimes the split pipe can be repaired without having to cut it out of the line and replacing it. There are several cements on the market which might do the job. Epoxy cement will stick fast to metal and will form a waterproof seal if applied according to the mixing directions on the tubes. It should be held in place with some kind of pressure band. Either a clamp around the pipe at the split, embedded in the epoxy and tightened in place before the cement has set, or the epoxy can be spread on a

2146 • PLUMBING

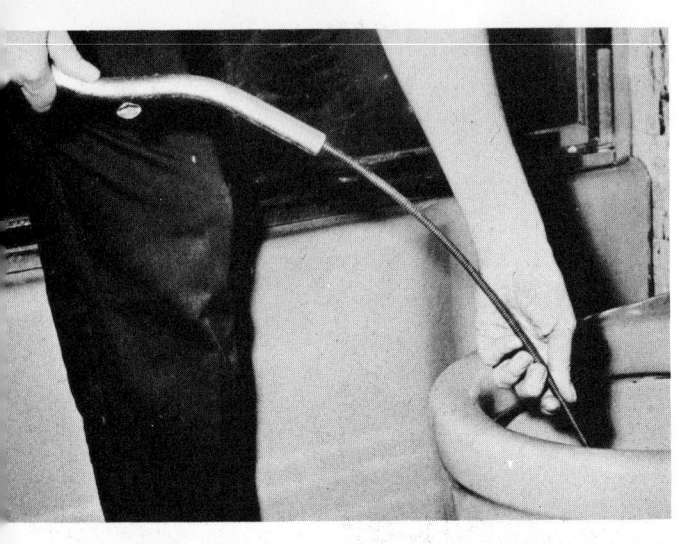

Most toilet bowl stoppages are right at the top bend of the trap and can be cleaned with an ordinary auger. In using auger, exercise extreme care not to scratch bowl or to let tool strike it.

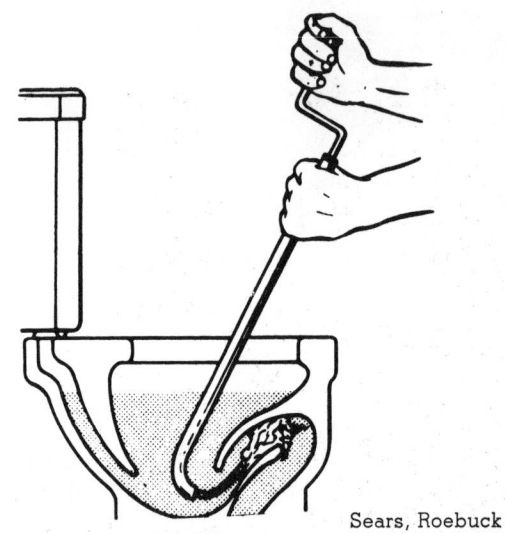

You can get a special auger, designed for toilet traps for a small sum. Type shown has a wooden handle, rubber guard, and is 5½ feet long, ample for reaching all the way through the toilet trap.

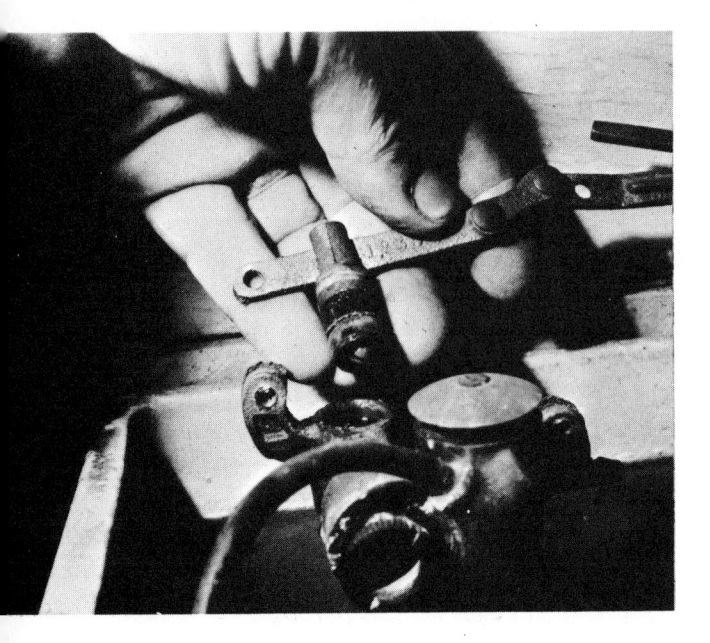

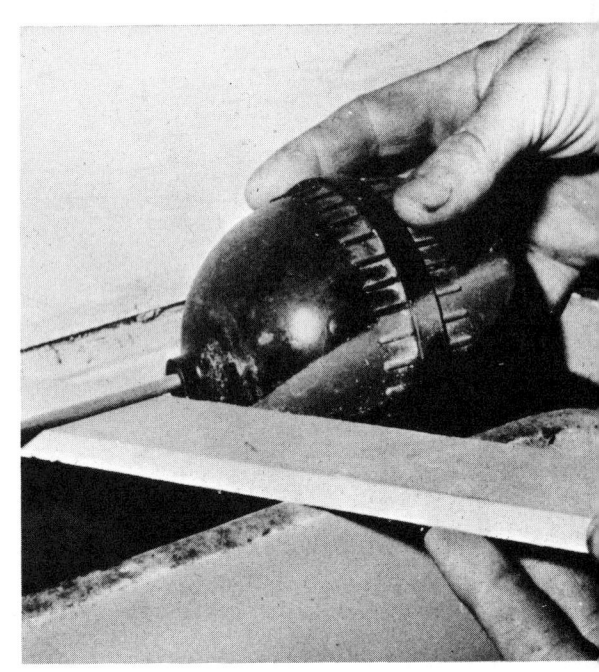

Sears, Roebuck

To prevent the toilet tank from refilling as you work on it, prop float up with a stick, as shown.

If toilet dribbles, a ball cock washer may need replacing. Faucet seat may be a porcelain unit.

Left, toilet may have a device like this to control refill flow. Increase flow to reduce noise.

INSTALLATION OF TANK ON BATHROOM WATER CLOSET

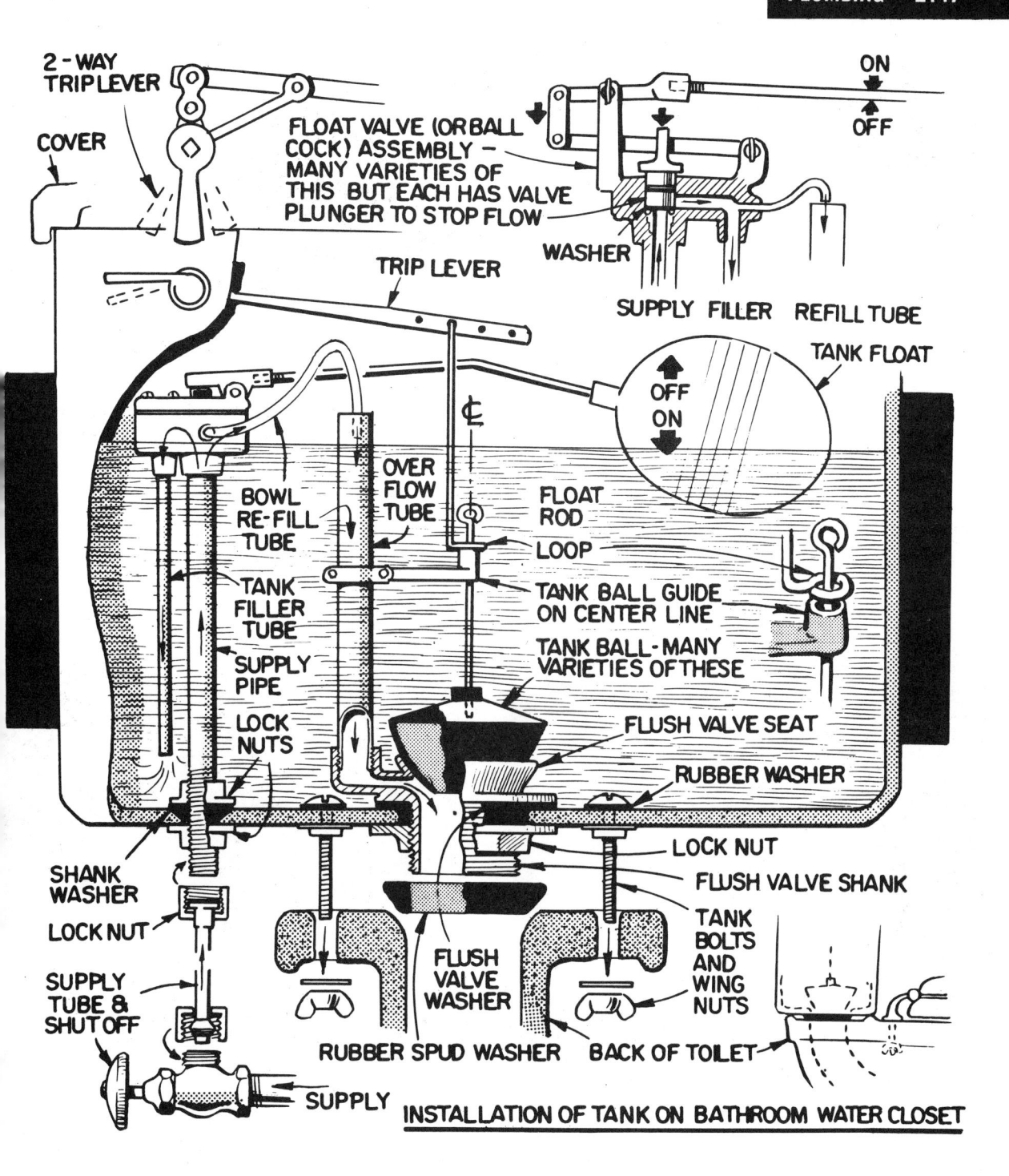

strip of canvas and the band tightly wrapped around the pipe and clamped in place.

The pressure must be relieved in the pipe when making such a repair, and the pipe emptied and left out of service for 24 hours while the epoxy cures and hardens. Plastic steel may be used the same way, spread on a band and wrapped around the leaking area. In the case of plastic steel, the pipe may only be taken out of service for a couple of hours, since the plastic steel hardens rapidly after mixing. A strip of old innertube covering the split and in turn covered and held in place with pipe clamps may do the trick. Commercial repair clamps are available which operate in much the same way and which perform repairs which will last the life of the pipe.

When all else fails, you may have to cut out the section and replace it. The replacement may be fastened into the line with a coupling on one end and a ground-joint union on the other. A fitting is made with which a new length of pipe can be inserted in a line without having to thread the ends of the insert, or the pipe which is being repaired. This fitting has two rubber bush-

2148 • PLUMBING

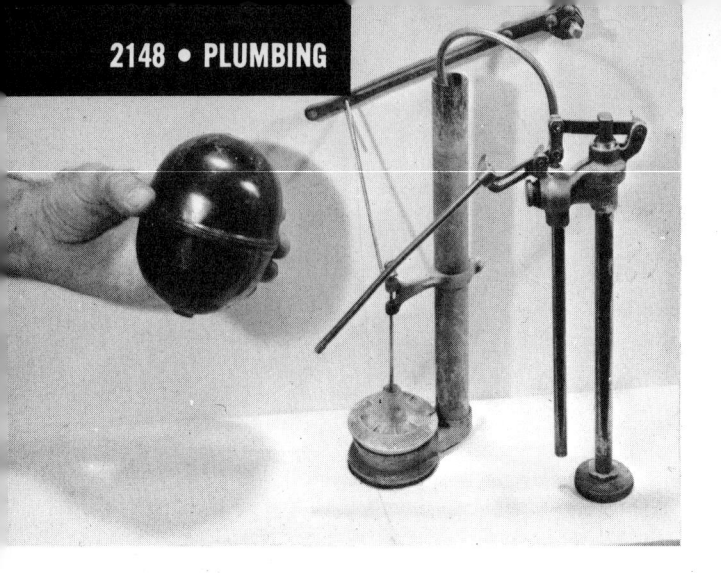

A leaky float ball will not rise high enough to shut inlet valve completely. To check, unscrew ball from the arm and shake for sound of water.

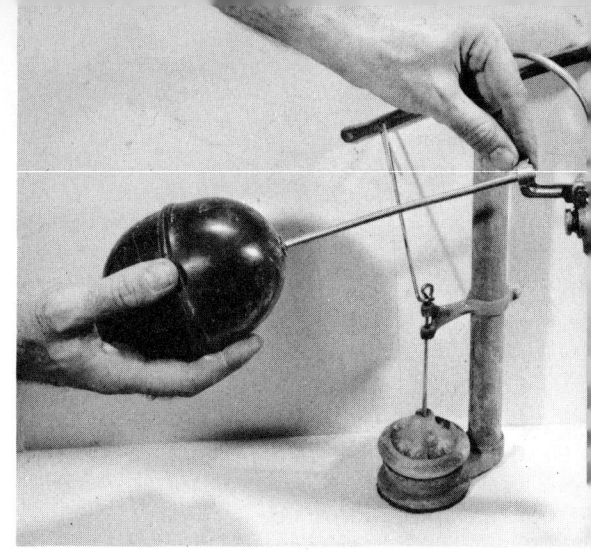

Height of float ball can be adjusted to regulate height water will rise inside tank. Some models have adjustment screw. Otherwise, bend arm.

To replace washer on the inlet valve inside of the tank, first remove turnscrew which holds the horizontal level in place across top of plunger.

Lifting up on this lever will then enable you to lift out plunger. On some models, though, you may have to disconnect the float ball arm, first.

ings and a tightening nut on each end, and is called a *Drescher fitting*. One end of the fitting is slid over the ends of the existing pipe, then the inserted piece held in position while the fittings are slid halfway to lap both the insert and the existing run. The two expanding nuts are tightened in place and the repair is made. The fitting serves as a sort of expansion joint, too.

If the expansion fitting is not to be used, then the split part of the pipe must be removed. The remaining ends of the run will have to be unscrewed from their fittings and threaded on their cut ends. The flange half of a ground joint union is threaded onto one of the newly threaded ends and that section replaced in its fitting. Take care to screw it in tightly and to put pipe joint compound on the threads before installing it. The second section is compounded and rethreaded into its fitting. The coupling end of the ground joint union is now installed on the replacement section and an ordinary coupling on the other end. Now screw the replacement section onto the existing pipe at the coupling end. You may have to have a helper hold the existing pipe out of line until you get the new piece started, then you can screw it in place until the ground joint union clears

The inlet valve washer fits on the bottom of the plunger. In some models, the washer is held with a brass screw. In others, washers are press fit.

Flow of water into tank can be regulated by turning adjustment valve at side of ball cock mechanism. Slow water flow makes quieter tank.

Antihammer chambers for water pipes are usually concealed inside the walls, but you can buy commercial devices, to serve the purpose, which can be installed outside walls, like one shown above.

its mating part and can be assembled. Run the union up tightly and the repair is complete.

In old houses the piping may become clogged up with accumulated rust, mineral deposits from the water, and scale. When this happens, generally the only thing that can be done is to replace the plumbing throughout the house. Sections of pipe may be removed and a rod worked through them to clear the obstructions, but you will find the job tedious and difficult. The results are not good anyway, since all the galvanizing is gone from the inside of the pipe, and the pipe has been weakened by the rusting and scaling. It is far better to replace the plumbing, and, whenever possible, replace it with copper rather than galvanized iron. If only certain sections of the pipe are restricted with the scaling and rust, these sections can be replaced with copper-to-galvanized adapters. •

A cable-rigged machine in action. Operator usually keeps his hand on cable to gauge the "feel" of the drilling at bottom of the bore and to guide cable as it keeps turning with each impact of the bit.

WELLS

IF YOU ARE GOING TO BUILD a home in the rural district the chances are that you will have to use a well as your water supply. There are several different kinds of wells, including dug wells, drilled, and artesian. Of course, there is the possibility of taking your water supply from a lake, pond or river. This is something of a hazard, however, because of the likelihood of contamination from one cause or another.

A dug well is not too good either, for the same reason. Too often, the dug well only collects surface water and run-off rather than water tapped from the water table.

Dug wells are useful where the water table is very close to the surface of the ground—that is, fifty to sixty feet, or less, and when the ground is workable with a pick and shovel. If rock is present in any great quantity, digging a well becomes a tedious proposition, and if the rock is in the form of a stratum, a dug well is impossible unless you use dynamite.

A properly constructed dug well is more than two feet in diameter. The bore is lined with concrete blocks or rock, set without mortar for the lower half. The upper walls are lined with poured concrete, concrete

The bit on this cable-rigged well driller is raised and lowered by a walking beam which raises the one ton bit, then drops it into the bore. The impact crushes the material being drilled and tailings are washed out by water.

Looking down casing of a well being dug with a cable-rigged machine. Casing has been driven 22 feet, and the top 8 feet cemented in place.

blocks or bricks set in mortar. The top should be provided with a tightly-fitted cover to prevent small animals from falling in and drowning, thus contaminating the supply. Force pumps should be used in dug wells since deep-well pumps are not required and pitcher pumps require priming with every use. The cylinder of the force pump should be submerged in the well. A dug well has two advantages—it is cheap to construct and it provides a large reservoir of water for immediate use. However, the reservoir can be quickly used up if you are drawing any considerable

2152 • PLUMBING

"Feeling" the bite on a cable-rigged driller. The tall shaft in foreground is the bailer, holding 10 gallons, used to bale out the tailings and to gauge the flow in the well.

amount for watering lawns, trees, etc., and, unless the recovery rate is fast, you may have to wait for it to refill each time you use it.

Drilled wells are made in several different ways. *Cable-rig*, also called *Spudders* and *Shock-Machines; Rotary Drills; Stove-Pipe Drilling; Hydraulic Jet* and *Core Drilling* are some of the methods used in different locations and in different types of ground. Where the substrata are composed of sand, loose dirt, gravel or other unconsolidated material, the stove-pipe or the jet methods are practical.

Stove-pipe drilling has been used extensively in the Far West. This method employs a hydraulic ram to push short lengths of steel tubing into the ground. The tubing is double—that is, two sizes are used, one which slip-fits inside the other. The joints are staggered, and as the pairs of pipes are shoved into the ground, they are keyed together with a punch or deforming tool. After the pipes have been run as deeply as necessary a special saw is lowered into the well and slots are cut through the walls of both pipes so the water can enter the bore. The casing is capped and the pump installed the same way as in other types of drilled wells. Naturally, this method is not possible when rock strata are encountered.

If your well is in sandy soil, a casing must be installed clear to the bottom of the bore. This can be quite expensive since the going price for six-inch casing is around six dollars a foot. The casing can cost more than the well. Yet, unless you have it installed, your well may become useless within a very short time and you will have lost the entire cost of the whole installation. The casing keeps the walls from collapsing in the bore, and holds back sifting sand and silt. If you are fortunate enough to be in a rock area where the bore is through shale or other compacted material, you can get away with a very short casing —just to keep the topsoil from entering the shaft. When casing is put to the bottom of a sandy well, the bottom section has a screen to let the water in, and to keep the dirt and sand out.

Every well, regardless of its depth and the type of pump used, should have an equalizing storage tank installed between the pump and the supply feed to the plumb-

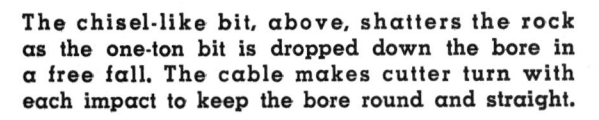

The chisel-like bit, above, shatters the rock as the one-ton bit is dropped down the bore in a free fall. The cable makes cutter turn with each impact to keep the bore round and straight.

The cutter bit for a rotary drilling rig is at top right. Center horn on lower right gear is the "breaker" which starts the hole in the rock. As the bit rotates, water washes out the debris.

The hydraulic motor is at top of the drilling tower. A planetary gear system drives drilling shaft through which water is pumped as bore is drilled. This is on rotary drilling rig, only.

ing in the house. This tank allows you to maintain even flow in the pipes, provides a settlement chamber for silt brought up from the well over a period of time and provides an air cushion against the pressure in the line so the pump is not overloaded when it starts.

Pressures in well systems can pretty much be what you want them to be. However, not less than thirty PSI on and forty PSI off should be used, or you will have such a feeble trickle at the faucet that it will take you all afternoon to fill the bathtub. A forty/sixty-pound differential is much more realistic, and, even if the pump does have to run a bit longer to hold this pressure, the convenience of "city water pressure" is worth the fractionally-extra electric bill.

In choosing the storage tank you should take into consideration whether you are a large water consumer or if only small amounts will be drawn. If you use a lot of water you should have a fairly large storage tank. If, on the other hand you do not need a large supply, a tank of about fifty gallon capacity, or even as low as thirty-two gallons will suffice, since if a larger tank were installed the water would lie dead within it for long periods of time. This would have the effect of supplying stale water every time you opened a tap. For normal good use of water, the most useful size is the eighty-two-gallon tank, and these are obtainable glass lined against corrosion and rusting. They will last for years.

Your storage tank should have an inlet fairly high up on the side; an outlet a little above the bottom, and a drain outlet right at the bottom. An additional convenience is a quarter-inch-pipe-thread outlet near the top for a pressure gauge, and another down just a bit for an air pressure control. The eighty-two-gallon tanks are supplied with these outlets all in place. All you have to do is plumb them into the system. The storage tank should not be installed outdoors where it would freeze in the winter. It can be put in the well house if that can be insulated, or if the tank is electrically heated by wires wrapped around the tank. The lines leading to and from the tank, as well as the pump, will have to be heated the same way.

Jet Drilling is used where unconsolidated

2154 • PLUMBING

The rotary rig at the start of a new section of shafting. Note the truck jacked up off its wheels. The heavy, 10-ton weight of the rig is used as a dead weight on the shaft to assist in the drilling.

The rig is almost at the bottom of its bore and the hydraulic motor is in its lowest position. The motor will be reversed to unscrew it from the shaft, then raised for a new section to be put in place.

material is encountered, such as clay, sand and gravel. It can be used only when the driller has access to water he can put under pressure in his machine. The drill bit is hollow and the water is forced through it under high pressure, washing the material out of the way as the tool is lowered into the ground. The tailings and debris are washed up out of the bore as it is dug and the casing is inserted into the well as the digging progresses. Jet drilling is not generally done in rural, domestic, well digging.

Rotary Drilling is commonly done by independent well drillers and is useful under certain conditions. A rotary drill uses a derrick much lower than a cable-rig machine, and the bit is rotated as it bores. The loosened material is washed up the bore by water which is pumped down through the bit as it is drilling. A casing is sunk from ten feet deep to thirty or more feet down the bore depending upon

At left, the hydraulic motor of the rig is being tipped back preparatory to insertion of the new shaft section. Below, drilling boom has been completely raised. The driller's helper is pushing shaft derrick away before the drilling is resumed.

the structure of the substrata. Rotary drilling finds usefulness when the well has to be dug through rock right next to the existing foundation of a building. The foundations are not as apt to be loosened as with the crushing impact of a shock machine.

When a rotary rig is set up at the point of drilling, the truck carrying the derrick is manuevered into position and then raised on three hydraulic rams, lifting the entire truck off its wheels. Since the truck and derrick combination weighs from 20 tons upward, this provides an excellent back-up weight for the drill bit. The bit is driven by a hydraulic motor through a planetary-gear drive which is mounted at the end of a hydraulically operated boom. The boom may be raised to accommodate the drill sections which are made of steel tubing ten feet long and which weigh about 200 pounds each. A length of drill tubing is screwed onto the motor drive and the drill bit is screwed onto the lower end. The entire motor and drill is then tilted into a vertical position and the drilling is started.

Water is fed down through the length of the drill tube and out the bit, washing away all the ground stone, dirt and dust. An eight-inch-diameter bore is first made for a comparatively short distance—usually about thirty feet, and a casing is fed into the bore. The casing has a six-inch inner diameter, and after it is in place the drill is raised and another bit substituted that will drill a six-inch bore for the well proper.

In ordinary rock, shale and consolidated material, a rotary drill will cut through two feet a minute, washing out all the debris as it cuts. As each length of drill lowers into the ground, the machine is stopped and a new section screwed onto the first. Length by length the drill cuts the bore until water is finally reached. When this happens the water starts to gush up

2156 • PLUMBING

out of the bore around the drill tube. When the gush seems to be a good enough flow, the drill is stopped and the water which is forced down the shaft to wash out the debris is cut off.

Compressed air is then shot down the inside of the drill tube which blows the water up out of the well as it accumulates. A dam of tailings is heaped around the well casing and a pipe buried under the dam, leading out about five or six feet. The water from the well fills the reservoir created by the dam and flows through the pipe where it is caught in some sort of measure, generally a five-gallon can. The filling rate of the can is timed and the flow of the well calculated thus.

An advantage of rotary drilling is that the well shaft is clean of debris when the well is completed, and the clearing is a slight matter. Speed is another great advantage. A well 100 feet deep can easily be dug in one day as opposed to several days with a cable rig.

In drilling with a *Cable-Rig* the derrick is set up over the location of the well bore. This derrick is generally mounted on a heavy truck which has extendible stabilizers mounted so they can be pulled out and braced at each side to provide greater stability to the derrick under the impact of the tools. The drill bit is suspended on a cable attached to a walking beam which

"Blowing off" a rotary dug well. Compressed air is blown down the bore to expel the mucky water and clean out most of the debris down the bore.

At left, the dam, around the well, built out of tailings from the drilling, is banked around a flow pipe to measure recovery rate of the well.

At right, the driller is timing flow of the well by catching water in a measured container. Air forced down drill shaft blows water out of well.

alternately raises and frees the cable, allowing the bit to rise into the air and then fall freely, thus pounding a hole through the earth bit by bit. As the drilling progresses additional cable is fed to the line by reeling a bit off the storage winch or temper screw.

When the well is started, and for the first hundred feet or so in the case of very deep wells, the walking beam is not used, but the bit is raised and lowered with the cable to the top of the derrick and let fall into the bore. The elasticity of the cable bounces the bit so it does not lock tightly at the bottom of the stroke. After several feet of hole has been drilled, the tool is removed from the line and a bailer tool substituted.

The bailer is a long tube nearly the size of the bore of the well. In the bottom end is a flap valve which opens freely as the bailer is dropped and closes tightly under the load of debris and water picked up. A good well driller who can use the bailer with speed, and accurate intervals of operation, can very nearly gauge the recovery flow of the well by the amount of water he can bring up in the bailer. An average bailer holds ten gallons and if the driller can make three trips a minute, for instance, without lowering the head, the well would have a recovery rate of not less than 30 gallons a minute.

An alternate method of gauging the flow in a cable-rig-drilled well is in general use in the Northeastern part of the country. In this method, the well, after water has been struck, is bailed out with the bailer on the drilling machine as fast as it can be operated, until the well is emptied to the bottom. The bailer is then lowered until the bottom end just touches the water in the bottom of the well, and a grease mark put on the cable right at the top of the casing. The bailer is then raised and held suspended for a time period—usually one minute. Again the bailer is lowered until it just touches the water and the distance between the top of the casing and the grease mark is now measured. The average capacity of a six-inch well bore is one and one-half gallons per foot. If the grease mark is, for example, six feet from the top of the casing, and the timed interval is one minute, the recovery rate would be nine gallons per minute.

After drilling, the well must be cleared. This is best accomplished by installing the pump and pipe and pumping the well out with direct discharge until the water runs perfectly clear. Then allow the well to stand for a day or two and pump it out a second time. If the water starts clear on the second pumping, you do not have to continue discharging. You can go ahead and couple the storage tank and tie into the house line. •

2158 • POOL

Build this
IN-GROUND LINER POOL

You'll save thousands of dollars by installing this 16' x 32' vinyl liner pool. It's easy with this popular kit.

The backyard swimming pool—complete with crystal clear water, automatic filtration, adjoining patio, sun deck, slide, etc.—is no longer limited to the wealthy; new materials, new filtering systems and engineering breakthroughs have made it possible for the average family to have their private pool; in-ground or above-grade.

Of course, substantially more above-grade pools exist than the in-ground type because a combination of low cost, lack of space or building code restrictions. But as the above-grade pool increases in size and refinement, so does the price—to a point where some above-grade pools (complete with decking) actually cost more than an in-ground unit!

There are many advantages to an in-ground pool—the prime one being that it fits in better with the overall landscaping of the home and takes on the appearance of being part of the house and is considered a permanent asset. Unlike most above-grade pools, in-ground pools automatically increase the resale value of a home, a very important consideration for any home improvement. For instance, a typical 16' x 32' pool complete with patio and landscaping can add anywhere from 5 to 10 thousand dollars to the value of the home!

You should not be surprised to learn that the majority of the in-ground pools have a vinyl liner, which in many ways is superior to the old-fashioned poured concrete or the sprayed gunite pools. Liner pools are more economical; they do not require regular painting as many old concrete pools usually do—at $40 to $100 per season just for paint. While a vinyl liner is tough, if by chance it is pierced, a simple patch (made underwater) seals the puncture! Most liners are usually guaranteed for ten years and, if a replacement is required, you merely drain the pool and "drop" in a new one!

The pool market is so huge there are many manufacturers of vinyl liner pools with dealers who will either install a complete pool or sell you a kit so you can do-it-yourself and, if necessary, help you

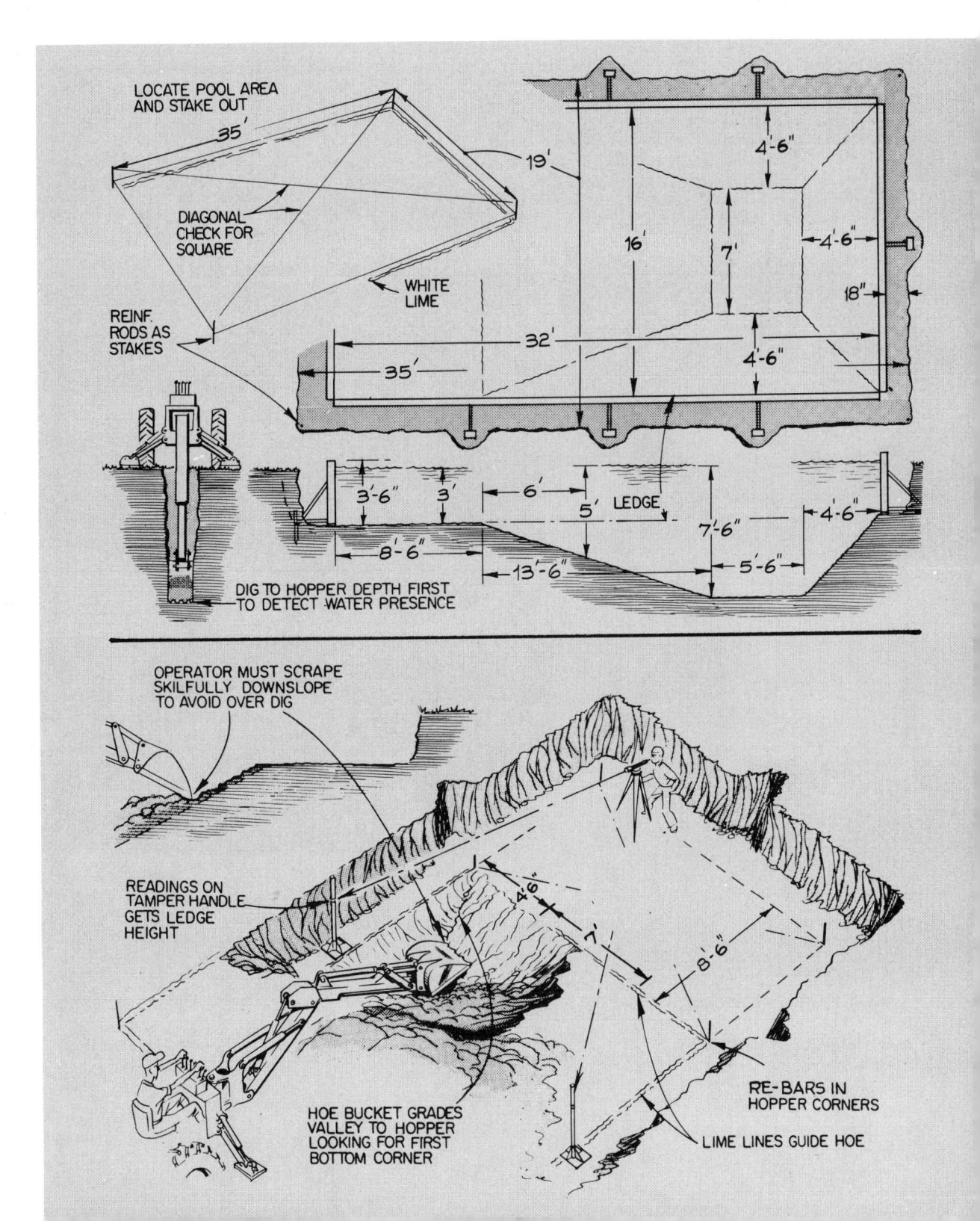

2160 • POOL

with some of the more difficult stages such as excavating or "dropping" the liner. The pool construction described on these pages is a Buster Crabbe pool by Cascade Industries, Inc. For additional information as to the sources of the materials contact Mr. Robert West, Chief Engineer, Cascade Industries, Inc., Talmadge Road, Edison, New Jersey 08817. Cascade is one of the pioneers and pace setters in the industry with a nationwide network of dealers.

This pool has many unusual features. First, the walls are built in panels from aluminum extrusions and 5/8" thick exterior grade plywood that has been chemically pressure treated to prevent decay. This treatment, called "Wolmanizing" is such an effective way to preserve wood no one has yet been able to calculate the life expectancy! 40 to 60 years would seem minimum!

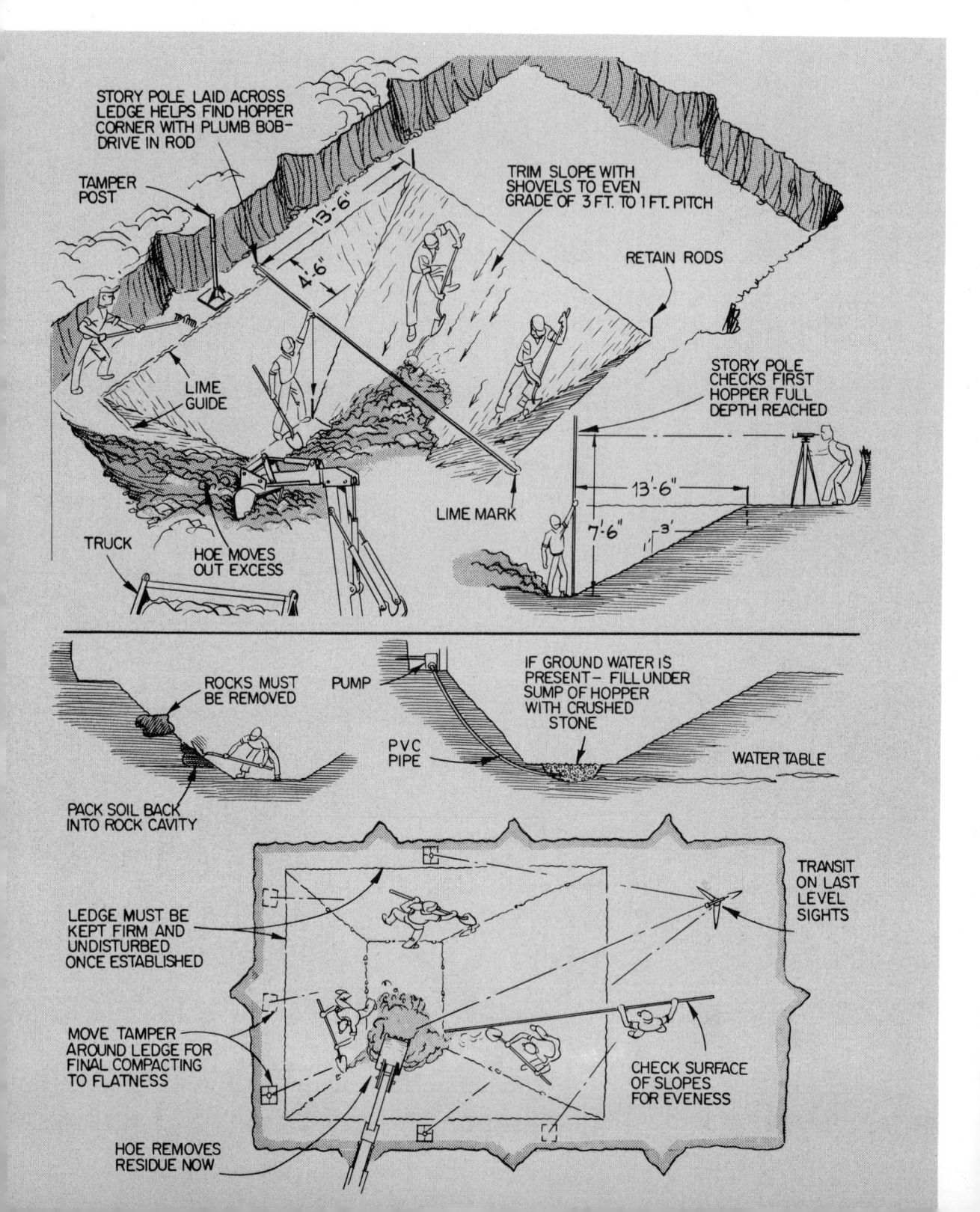

Years ago all pools had a concrete coping, but with this vinyl liner pool the coping consists of short lengths of a painted aluminum extrusion that snap in place! If you ever want to replace the liner or make a major repair merely unsnap the coping and remove the liner! One other great feature of this Buster Crabbe pool is the filter system that features the exclusive "Aqua/Genie" Feeder Skimmer. This is an unusual device that keeps the pool water clearer than any comparable device now on the market AND also automatically chlorinates the water! Simply insert the special chlorine cartridges in the skimmer tray and your pool water will be chlorinated day in and day out as the filter system works! Here is how you can build your own pool.

Excavating is the first physical step and it is best to hire an excavator who has had some experience with pools; he will have the trucks to remove the excess dirt, and the help and tools needed to make certain the ledge on which the wall panels will rest are absolutely level. Of course, most skilled backhoe operators can do the job by following the drawings and checking at regular intervals to make certain the slope for the hopper is at the correct angle and that a 2" allowance is made for the sand or vermiculite bottom that must be shaped before the liner is installed. But an experienced pool excavator can do the job faster.

All experienced contractors are aware of the procedure involved in digging to an exact depth. Most have a transit or builder's level but may not have a long enough transit rod, or "story pole." Therefore, make sure you have a straight 2 x 4 on hand. One reminder: before the ground is broken, set your transit in a spot that will not be immeditaely affected by the backhoe and sight two bench marks either on an adjacent patio or even on the side of the house. All future depth measurements will be in relation to this mark.

Excavating your pool is an extremely critical operation that requires constant supervision and careful planning before the first bucket of earth is removed.

A high water table and rock are at times unknown factors that can affect pool construction. If your land is such that you have a general idea (from previous neighborhood excavations) that the area has a low water table and little stone, you can logically assume you will experience no difficulty excavating. However, to make certain of your ground condition, rent an auger and take a sampling in the projected hopper area, going down to the full depth

POOL • 2161

Digging hopper requires finesse. Outline is marked with lime, slope checked. Note wall cut in for braces.

If you have ground water, overdig the hopper and fill with gravel. Run a sump line to permit pumping out.

Line to sump is buried in the corner of the hopper. After pool is full cap off line. Mark for future use.

2162 • POOL

Building wall panels is a two-man job; takes less than ten minutes a panel because all parts are cut to size.

Two men can handle each panel and set them in place. Ledge must be absolutely level so pressure is the same.

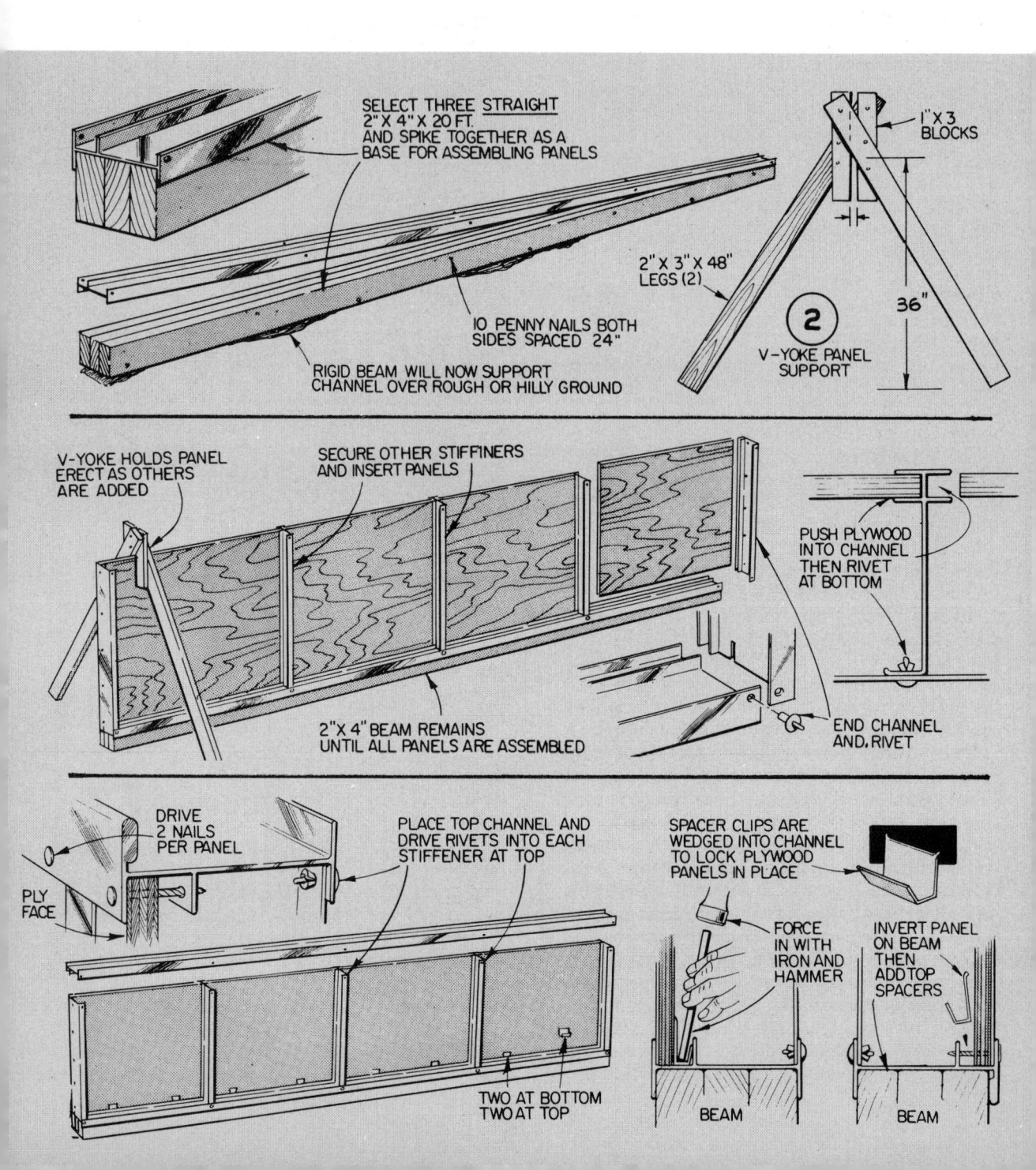

SELECT THREE STRAIGHT 2" X 4" X 20 FT. AND SPIKE TOGETHER AS A BASE FOR ASSEMBLING PANELS

1" X 3 BLOCKS

2" X 3" X 48" LEGS (2)

36"

② V-YOKE PANEL SUPPORT

10 PENNY NAILS BOTH SIDES SPACED 24"

RIGID BEAM WILL NOW SUPPORT CHANNEL OVER ROUGH OR HILLY GROUND

V-YOKE HOLDS PANEL ERECT AS OTHERS ARE ADDED

SECURE OTHER STIFFINERS AND INSERT PANELS

PUSH PLYWOOD INTO CHANNEL THEN RIVET AT BOTTOM

2" X 4" BEAM REMAINS UNTIL ALL PANELS ARE ASSEMBLED

END CHANNEL AND RIVET

DRIVE 2 NAILS PER PANEL

PLACE TOP CHANNEL AND DRIVE RIVETS INTO EACH STIFFENER AT TOP

SPACER CLIPS ARE WEDGED INTO CHANNEL TO LOCK PLYWOOD PANELS IN PLACE

PLY FACE

FORCE IN WITH IRON AND HAMMER

INVERT PANEL ON BEAM THEN ADD TOP SPACERS

TWO AT BOTTOM TWO AT TOP

BEAM

BEAM

POOL • 2163

Here all wall panels are in place. Exterior braces are now added and the panels checked so they are plumb.

solutely level, you should also have a transit or builder's level, a 16' rod (or 2 x 4) to be used as a "story pole" to determine when you have reached the exact level of excavation at various points along the bottom. In addition, you will need an assortment of long-handled pointed shovels, two 50' tapes, masons string, a tamper, a 50 pound bag of garden line and ten 18" lengths of ½" reinforcing bars (referred to as rebars) which are used when staking out the pool outline and forming the hopper.

Even before your excavator arrives you should lay out the dimensions of the pool, noting that the excavation will be about 18" wider on all sides than the finished pool. Of course, before determining the exact pool location make certain your installation conforms to your local Building Code.

The elevation of your pool is just as important as the location. If your land is absolutely flat, your depth should be such that the coping will be about 6" above the surrounding terrain so you can gently grade the adjacent patio or side walk area to slope away from the pool to prevent surface water from flowing over the cop-

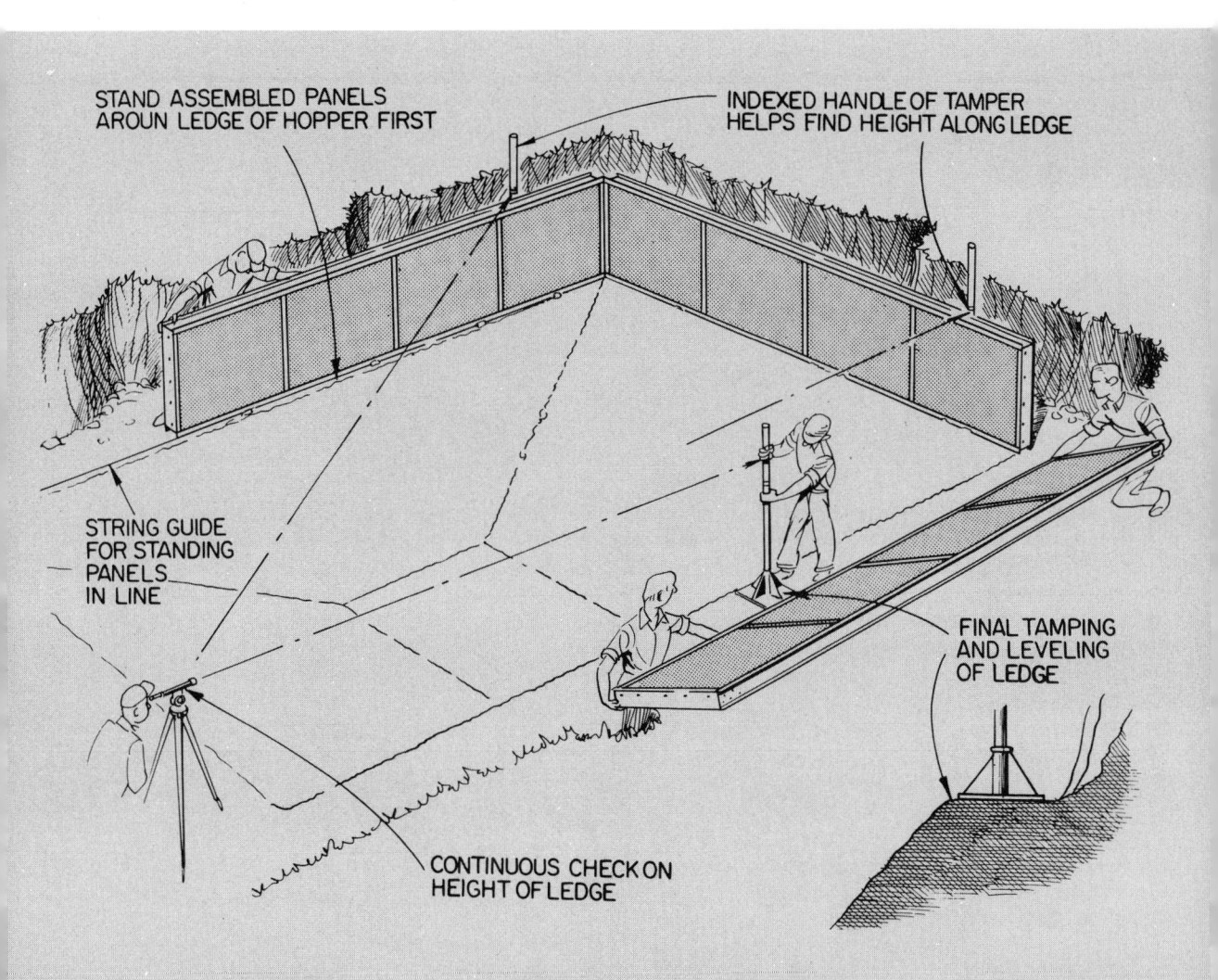

of the hopper. Once the backhoe is on the jobsite, before starting the actual excavation, first dig a test hole in the hopper area to again check the presence of water. If some water is present, you should plan to line the lower hopper area with gravel (1" to 1½" size) and run a 1½" line to a sump to permit pumping out the hopper during construction.

The ideal machine for pool excavation is a hydraulic backhoe with a 12' or 14' boom. Since the pool walls must be ab-

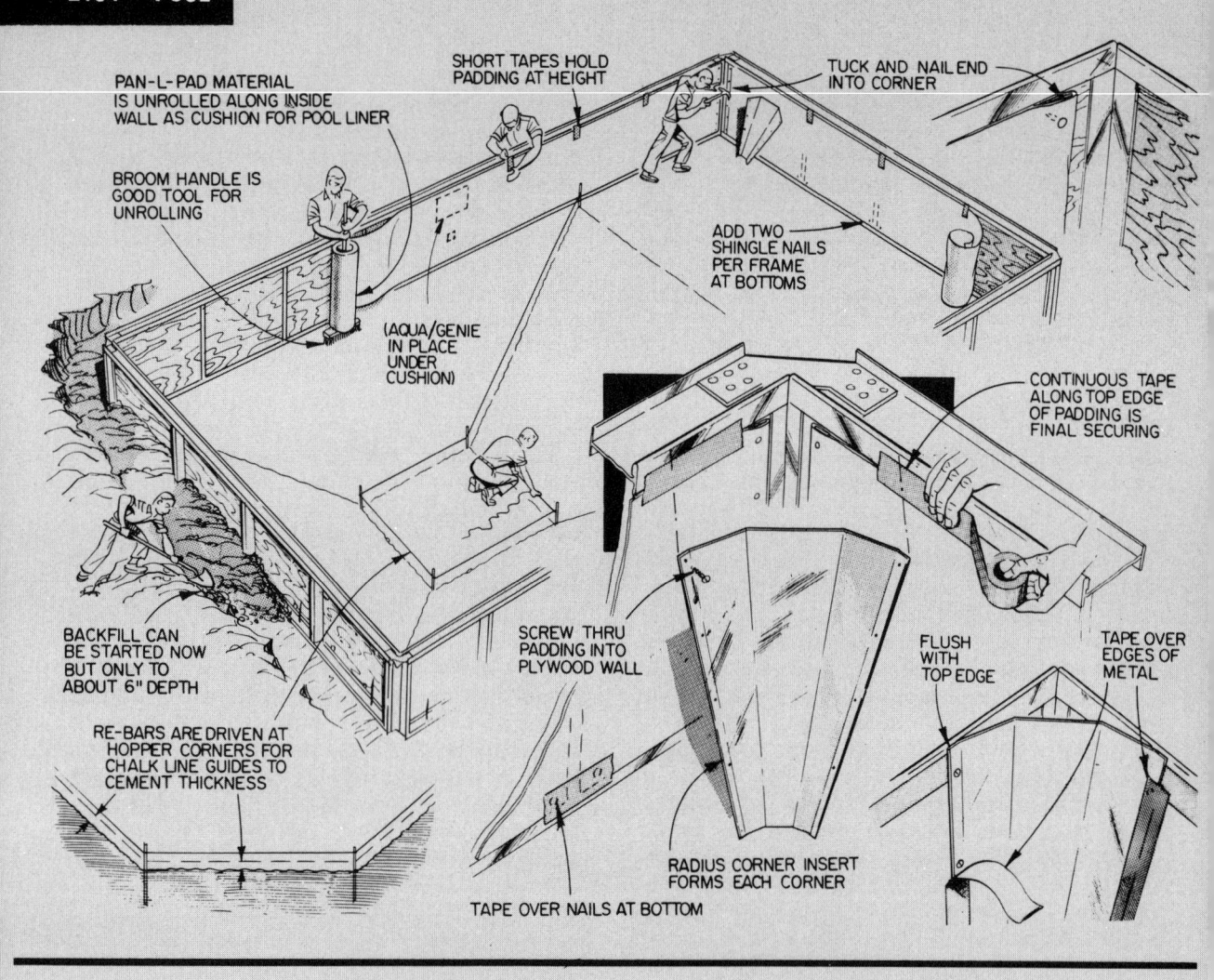

2164 • POOL

PAN-L-PAD MATERIAL IS UNROLLED ALONG INSIDE WALL AS CUSHION FOR POOL LINER

BROOM HANDLE IS GOOD TOOL FOR UNROLLING

SHORT TAPES HOLD PADDING AT HEIGHT

TUCK AND NAIL END INTO CORNER

ADD TWO SHINGLE NAILS PER FRAME AT BOTTOMS

(AQUA/GENIE IN PLACE UNDER CUSHION)

CONTINUOUS TAPE ALONG TOP EDGE OF PADDING IS FINAL SECURING

BACKFILL CAN BE STARTED NOW BUT ONLY TO ABOUT 6" DEPTH

SCREW THRU PADDING INTO PLYWOOD WALL

FLUSH WITH TOP EDGE

TAPE OVER EDGES OF METAL

RE-BARS ARE DRIVEN AT HOPPER CORNERS FOR CHALK LINE GUIDES TO CEMENT THICKNESS

RADIUS CORNER INSERT FORMS EACH CORNER

TAPE OVER NAILS AT BOTTOM

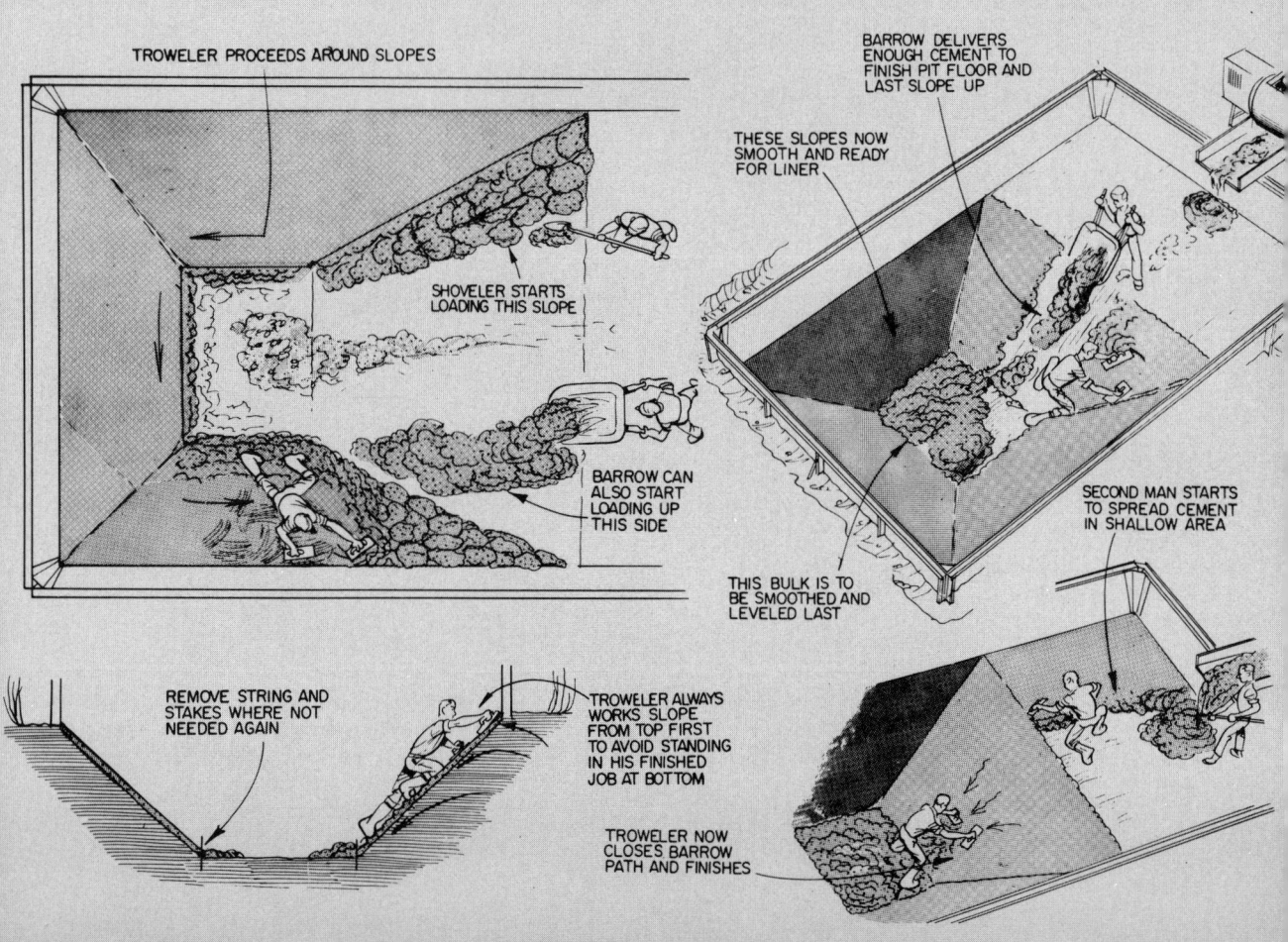

TROWELER PROCEEDS AROUND SLOPES

BARROW DELIVERS ENOUGH CEMENT TO FINISH PIT FLOOR AND LAST SLOPE UP

THESE SLOPES NOW SMOOTH AND READY FOR LINER

SHOVELER STARTS LOADING THIS SLOPE

BARROW CAN ALSO START LOADING UP THIS SIDE

SECOND MAN STARTS TO SPREAD CEMENT IN SHALLOW AREA

THIS BULK IS TO BE SMOOTHED AND LEVELED LAST

REMOVE STRING AND STAKES WHERE NOT NEEDED AGAIN

TROWELER ALWAYS WORKS SLOPE FROM TOP FIRST TO AVOID STANDING IN HIS FINISHED JOB AT BOTTOM

TROWELER NOW CLOSES BARROW PATH AND FINISHES

ing. If you have a hillside area work carefully with your excavator to develop a height that (1) Will not result in surface water entering the pool during a driving rain and (2) The wall section should always rest on virgin soil and not on fill.

Once you have determined the depth you desire, stake out the pool with garden lime. Then take several readings with a transit or builders level to determine the exact slope of the area. Calculate the finished height of the pool wall by adding 42" to the lowest reading, and then subtract the number of inches you wish to have the pool elevated from your total. This is the measurement to which your initial trench will be dug. Once your excavation is complete and you have checked and tamped the ledge on which the walls will rest, you can start assembling and positioning the wall panels.

The pre-engineered wall panels can be easily assembled by two men in less than 10 minutes per panel. Six panels are required. All the necessary drive rivets, top and bottom rails and the vertical stiffeners and panel clips are packed separately. You require only a 16 oz. hammer and a ¼" taper pin to help locate the holes in the vertical stiffeners where they join the horizontal top and bottom rails. All panels are identical with the exception of the panel in which the Aqua/Genie is mounted. This has a cut out area and should be located in the side wall closest to the pool center, near the filler location and preferably facing the prevailing wind.

A flat surface is required to assemble the panels and we recommend spiking three 16' 2 x 4s together to form this building base. The aluminum rails and stiffeners are cut, notched and drilled so all you need do is put them together in erector-set like fashion. After each panel is finished, set it aside in a position convenient to the pool so it can be lifted in place. A panel can be easily handled by two men.

The end stiffeners differ only in that one is notched at the base for right hand use, and the other for left hand use so when they are assembled the sides are flat and the groove to to accommodate the plywood faces forward. The top and bottom rails look similar but upon close examination you will note they are different extrusions. The top rail has a pronounced lip over which the coping fits; the bottom rail can be recognized by the holes in the flat area thru which re bars are driven after the panels are set in the excavation.

As previously emphasized, the wall panels must rest on a level surface and the best way to make the base level is to tape a ruler to the tamper handle then tamp and sight the measurement at 1' intervals as you proceed around the perimeter of the excavation where the panels will rest. If the level is too low, add a shovel of dirt and tamp it down. If too high, cut away the excess. This base area should be level to within ⅛".

Start erecting the hopper and panel first; then set the adjacent wall panels. After the hopper end panel is set in place and the two adjacent panels loosely bolted, add the wall braces and make the walls temporarily perpendicular so you can check the diagonal measurement (which should be equal) to make certain the panels are square. With these panels in place, and square, install the three remaining panels in the same manner.

The wall braces are set at the prescribed intervals and are adjustable to make certain the panels will be absolutely perpendicular. Once all wall sections are bolted and riveted together, drive the rebars in the bottom channel holes and

Finishing a vermiculite bottom requires teamwork, and muscle. Lines outlining hopper are removed last.

2166 • POOL

Clever way to exit finished pool hopper is via a ladder and gravity tamper. By Westdyk Pools, New Jersey.

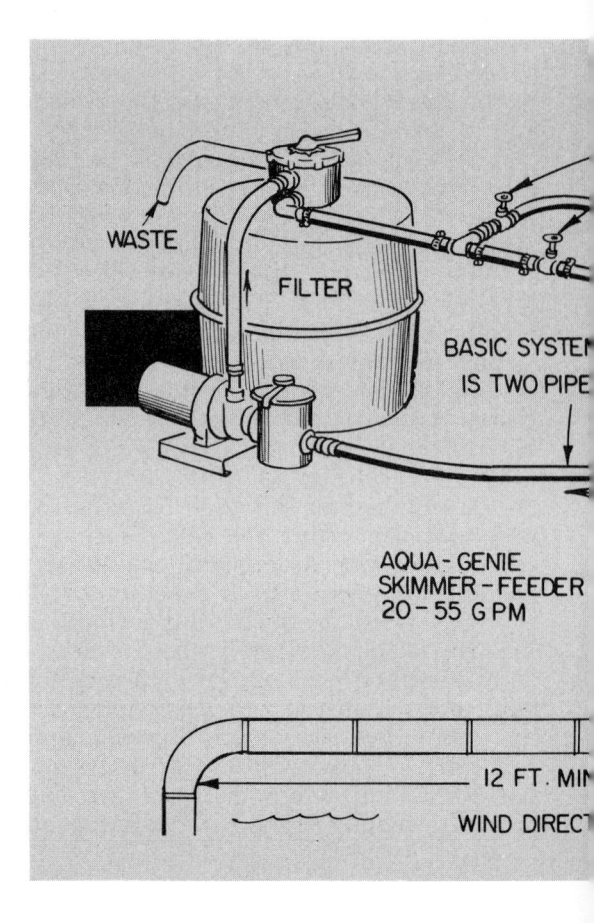

TROWELER NOW IN HOPPER FLOOR SPREADS BULK CEMENT TO A LEVEL DEPTH ALL AROUND HIM

TROWELER IN SHALLOW AREA LEANS IN TO FINISH EXIT CORNER

TO GET THIS MAN OUT —

3/4" PLYWOOD TAMPER IS LOWERED ACROSS PIT FOR HIS USE

LONG CURVE RADIUS IS FORMED IN CORNERS

3" RAD.
18"
12"
ROUND EDGE

TROWELER FINISHES FLOOR HUNCHED ON PAD ONLY

LASTLY TWO MEN PULL TAMPER ABOUT TO SMOOTHE BOTTOM

EXIT IS UP LADDER WHICH RESTS ON PAD

WASTE
FILTER
BASIC SYSTEM IS TWO PIPE

AQUA-GENIE SKIMMER-FEEDER 20-55 GPM

12 FT. MIN
WIND DIRECT

tighten the wall braces permanently so the walls are perpendicular. Then backfill over the bottom rail extrusion with about 6" of dirt around the entire outside perimeter of the pool.

Your pool kit comes complete with filter, which should be assembled as directed. Since only two lines come from the Aqua/Genie—one returning filtered water to the pool and the other delivering water from the pool to the pump—the pipe hookup with stainless steel clamps is simple.

Locate the filter as close to the pool as possible, but allow sufficient space for possible maintenance and installation of a heater, if desired. The filter and motor rest on a cement slab, which can be either precast or poured in place. A special moulded rubber base is provided so the tank can be shifted to make it absolutely level. Also, note the motor is bolted to a special mount which merely rests on the slab surface. It need not be bolted to the concrete slab.

Your filter will require an electrical line; we recommend a direct line equipped with a Ground Fault Interrupter as per the requirement of your local Electrical Code. Since your pool will probably require local approval of your building department—with whom you should check BEFORE you even contemplate construction—it is important that all electrical, plumbing and construction rules and regulations are followed. Remember, your pool is a PERMANENT addition to your home!

The combination skimmer and feeder, appropriately called the Aqua/Genie, not only simplifies the plumbing system but makes maintenance (including chlorinating) virtually automatic.

In the case of Aqua/Genie equipped pools, all filtered water returning to the pool comes through the lower nozzle and this powerful downward thrust of water in a sheet-like jet, creates counter currents that produces a skimming action that is by far more effective than the conventional skimmer. As mentioned, the Aqua/Genie is also an automatic chlorinator, using Vinylchlor cartridges that fit into its feeding tray. Drop in the chlorine cartridge and you chlorinate automatically for weeks!

As shown in the drawings, run the main suction line from the sump of the Aqua/Genie before the walls are backfilled. Tape the other end of the pipe closed to prevent any dirt from entering during the backfilling operation and mark this end "TO

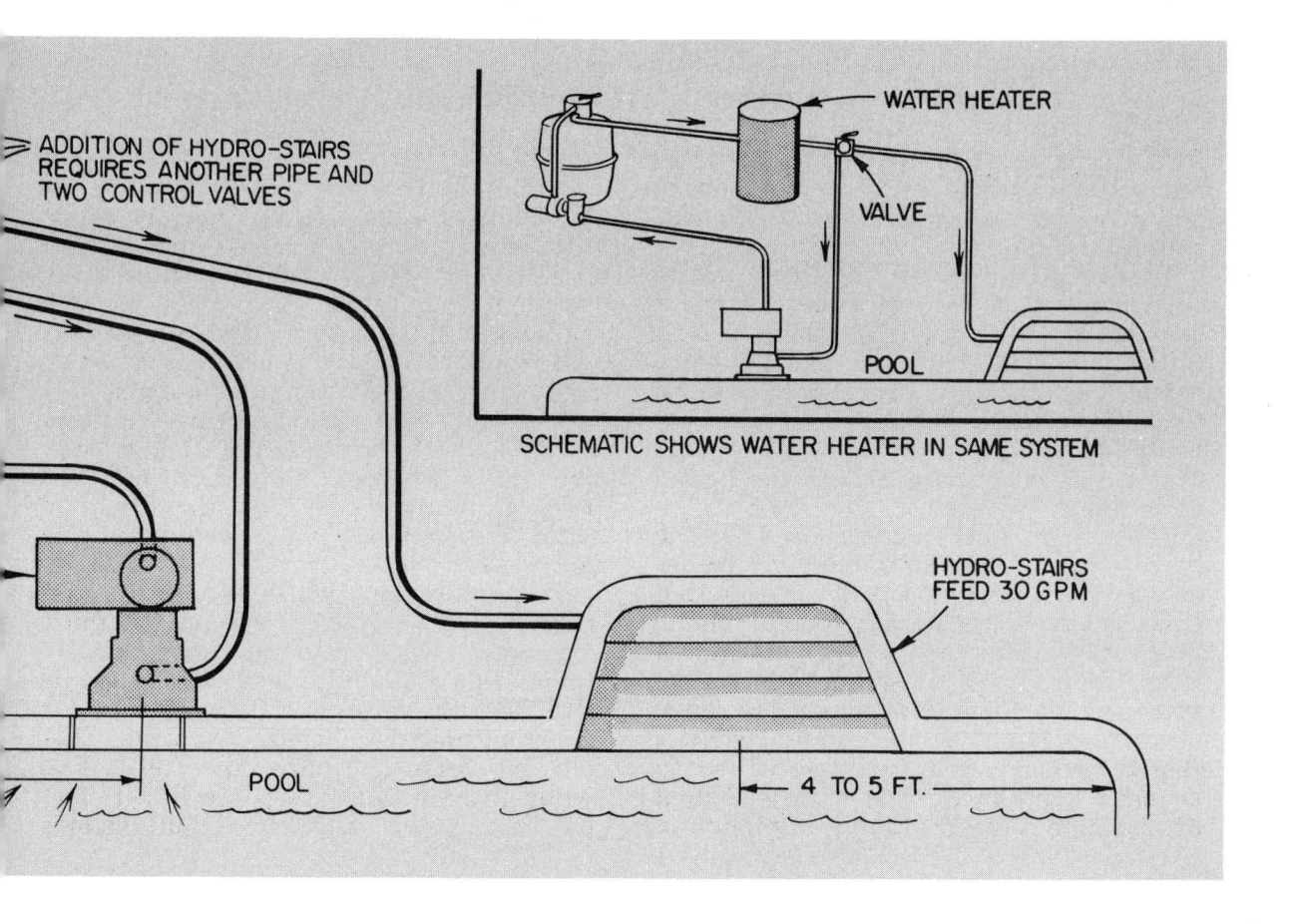

2168 • POOL

AT FIRST ALL CLAMPS ARE APPLIED AT OUTER EDGE OF TOP CHANNEL

CLIP FIRST END TO SHALLOW WALL OF POOL

CLAMPS MUST BE APPLIED RIGHT BEHIND UNROLLERS AS THEY MOVE TO SUPPORT LINER

UNROLL TOWARD HOPPER

AVOID PINCHING VINYL LINER ON POOL EDGE BY PIPE

DEEP AREA DROPS INTO HOPPER FLOOR

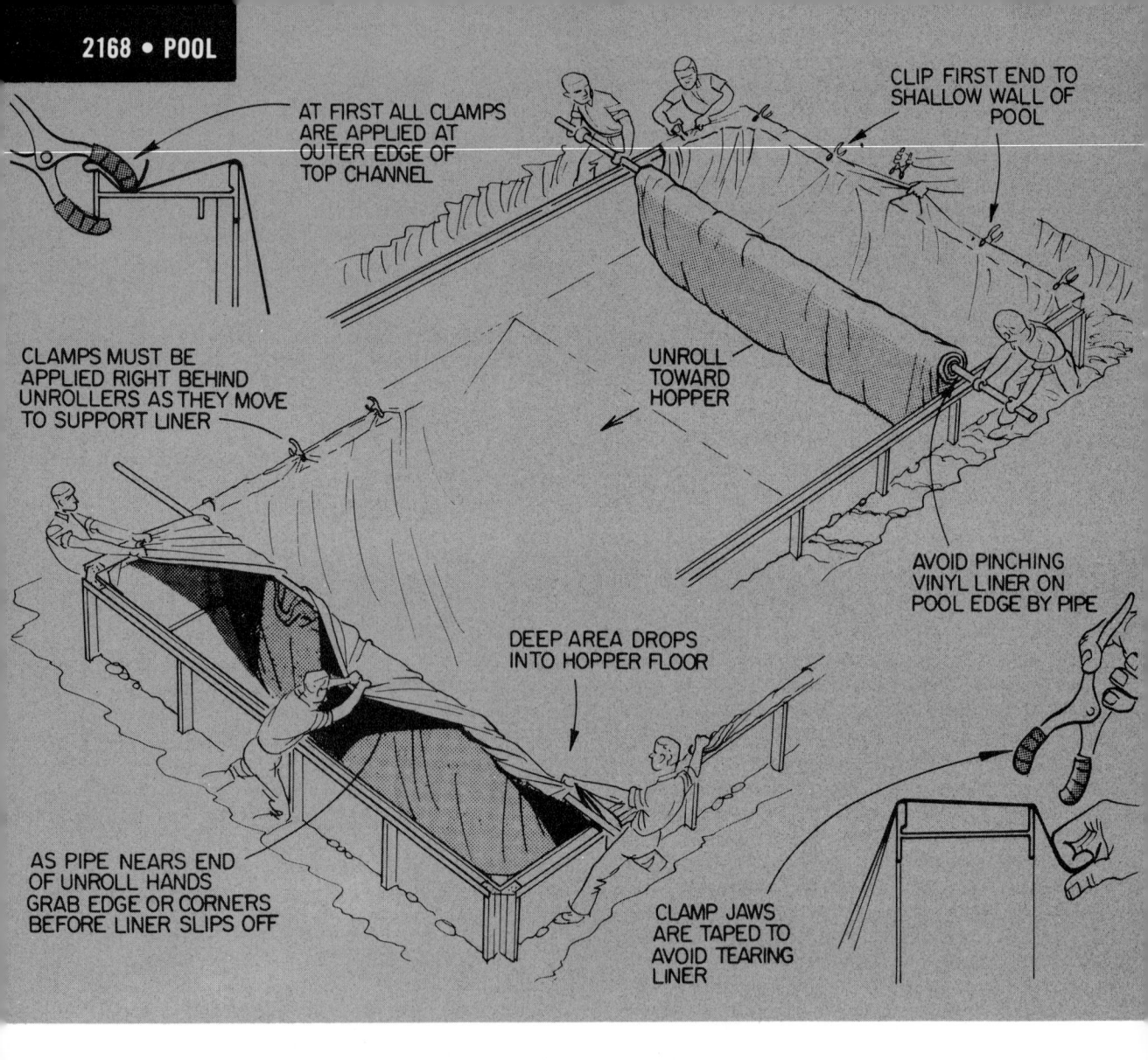

AS PIPE NEARS END OF UNROLL HANDS GRAB EDGE OR CORNERS BEFORE LINER SLIPS OFF

CLAMP JAWS ARE TAPED TO AVOID TEARING LINER

PUMP". Incidentally, make sure all pipes rest on undisturbed earth free of stones, and other sharp objects in that settlement could cause failure.

The second line feeds the lower nozzle compartment of the Aqua/Genie and is connected with a 1½" plastic-to-thread fitting with TWO stainless clamps. Once connected, the other end should also be temporarily taped closed and labeled "TO FILTER." If you elect to install Hydro-Stairs or a pool heater, adapt the piping accordingly.

After your lines are attached to the Aqua/Genie, cover them with six inches of backfill, making certain you do not exert any harmful pressure on the piping that sweeps into the Aqua/Genie connections. Tamp this layer of backfill level so you have a smooth walking surface when the liner is hung and the coping installed. Backfill should be granular material (sand) or bank run gravel with a clay content of not more than 25% and a minimum of organic material.

It is absolutely imperative that the backfilling be done as the pool is being filled with water. If you add the backfill in 3" layers, normal walking will produce excellent compaction. And if the backfill is dampened slightly better compaction will result. When you reach the top of the pool bring the fill about 2" above the coping level to allow for settling. You can always expect some settling so it is best not to plan a poured patio deck immediately. If you do not allow the earth to settle the concrete will eventually sag and crack.

To provide the vinyl liner with the best possible wall surface, a special ⅛" thick expanded foam material appropriately called Pan-L-Pad is taped to the walls BEFORE the bottom is prepared for our recommended vermiculite surfacing. Staple one corner and unroll the Pan-L-Pad while it is vertical. Keep the Pan-L-Pad flat against the wall with small sections

POOL • 2169

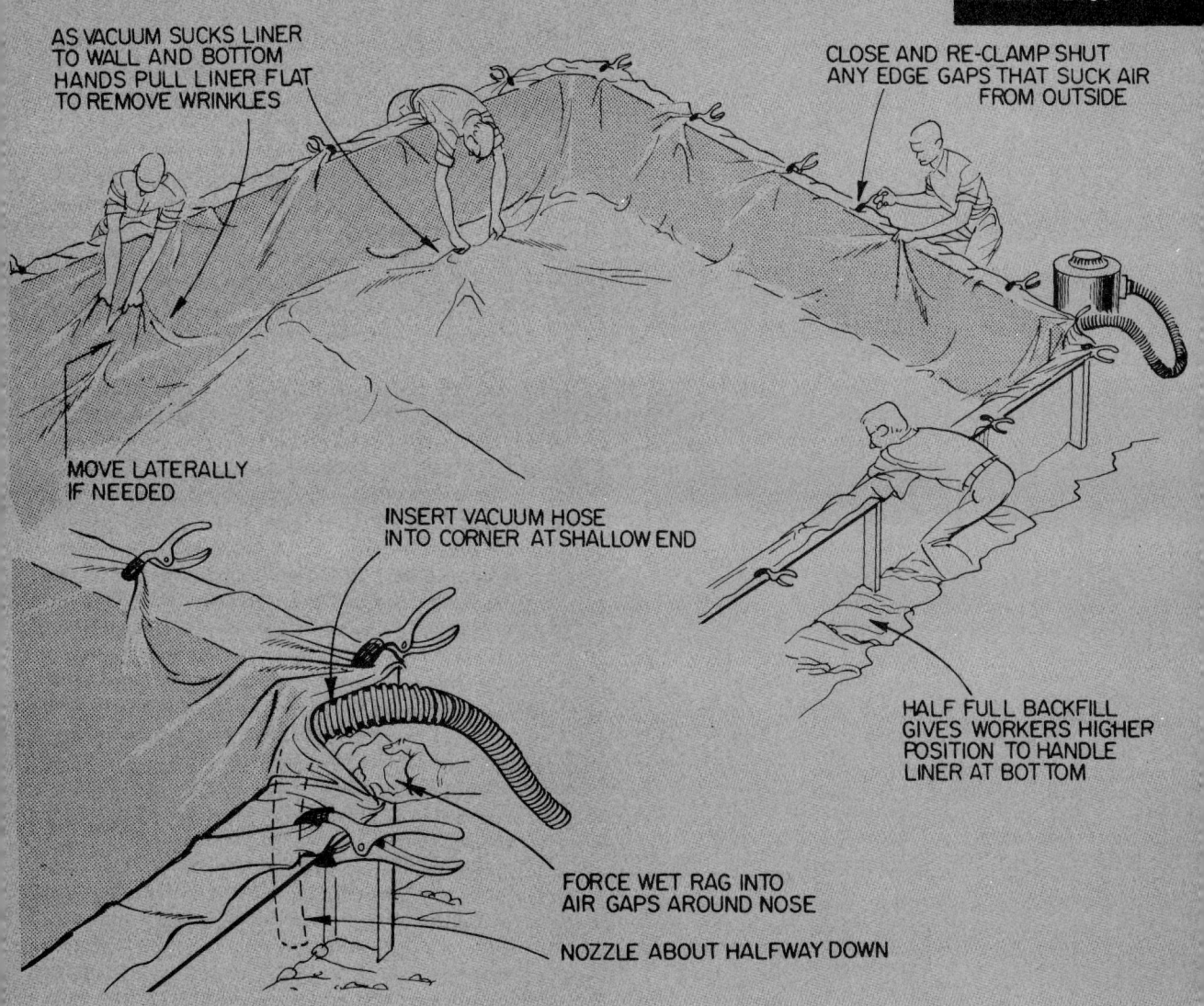

AS VACUUM SUCKS LINER TO WALL AND BOTTOM HANDS PULL LINER FLAT TO REMOVE WRINKLES

CLOSE AND RE-CLAMP SHUT ANY EDGE GAPS THAT SUCK AIR FROM OUTSIDE

MOVE LATERALLY IF NEEDED

INSERT VACUUM HOSE INTO CORNER AT SHALLOW END

HALF FULL BACKFILL GIVES WORKERS HIGHER POSITION TO HANDLE LINER AT BOTTOM

FORCE WET RAG INTO AIR GAPS AROUND NOSE

NOZZLE ABOUT HALFWAY DOWN

of tape placed at regular intervals along the top and bottom. The Pan-L-Pad should be flush with the top of the wall sections. After all four walls have been covered, screw the Corner Inserts in place as shown and add a strip of tape over the vertical edges. Also, cut out the Pan-L-Pad covering the Aqua/Genie and the lower wall suction fitting; then tape the edges to hold the Pan-L-Pad secure.

Although a regular sand base has been popular with vinyl liner pools over the years, vermiculite mixed with portland cement to make a lightweight concrete results in a superior bottom. It provides a firm "footprint free" base for swimmers and is sufficiently porous to cope with possible exterior water conditions. Also, the vermiculite concrete makes it much easier to form the hopper walls because it "stacks" better than sand on the 45° hopper walls.

The pool excavation dimensions allowed approximately 2" for the vermiculite base, and in the case of the typical 16' x 32' pool you will require approximately 50 bags of vermiculite (4 cubic feet each) and 25 bags of portland cement, depending upon how accurately your bottom was hand trimmed, the exact length of mixing time, etc.

Mixing and placing the vermiculite is a testing operation and requires a one bag paddle type mortar mixer, used by masons and available at most industrial equipment rental shops. DO NOT USE A REGULAR CONCRETE MIXER because it will not mix the vermiculite properly. This is a job that requires quick action and some experience with concrete.

Once you establish the correct mix (usually two bags of vermiculite and one bag of cement or as stated on the bag of vermiculite you use) the placement of each load is steady and hard work. For best results, follow these basic rules:

(1) Mix a full bag of portland cement and two bags of vermiculite at a time

AND NEVER MIX MORE THAN ONE MINUTE after vermiculite has been added to the mix. In fact, you will ruin the mix if you tumble it in excess of one minute! Experiment initially with the water content to keep the mix firm and then adhere to your established proportions. You will use about 16 gallons of water per mix, depending upon the weather.

(2) Quickly dump the mix in a wheel barrow and start placing it in the shallow end. Work rapidly, because it will set up fast. Wood float it first, and if you have the time you may top it with a steel float although an absolutely smooth surface is really not necessary because over troweling will bring cement to the surface.

Of course, the hopper end requires the most care because the tendency of the mix is to slide down the sloped sides. Shovel a batch of vermiculite concrete to the top area, to extend about 2" above the Pan-L-Pad and work down. Push it in place, and always keep the hopper lines and stakes shown in the drawings in place to guide you as to the exact placement and finished thickness. Work all four sides of the bottom as shown, and then climb out after the flat base section of the hopper is complete. Completion of the shallow section is identical.

In placing (or dumping) the vermiculite concrete near the wall panels, you may splash some mix on the panel surface. Brush the mix off so it will not show when the liner is in place.

The installation of the liner and unique Cas-Lok coping follow a tested procedure. Most importantly, install the liner on a warm day by first unpacking and spreading it out on a smooth, rock and twig free area so the packing wrinkles will be eliminated. Above 65° temperature is ideal and to further simplify this operation keep the liner carton indoors for a few days if the possibility exists that the outdoor temperature will be less than 65° at installation time. Once the liner is spread out flat, allow it to rest for about three hours.

The best way to "drop your liner" is to roll it on a piece of pipe that is at least two feet longer than the width of the pool. Start rolling the hopper end of the liner first, so it will unwind last, and then rest the pipe (with the rolled-up liner) over the shallow end of the walls as shown in the accompanying drawing. Unroll the liner from the shallow to hopper end and, as you move, clamp the edges of the vinyl to the Cas-Lok channel. Heavy duty spring clamps shown in the photos do an excellent job.

Once the liner is resting on the bottom you will require some tugging here and there to smooth out obvious wrinkles.

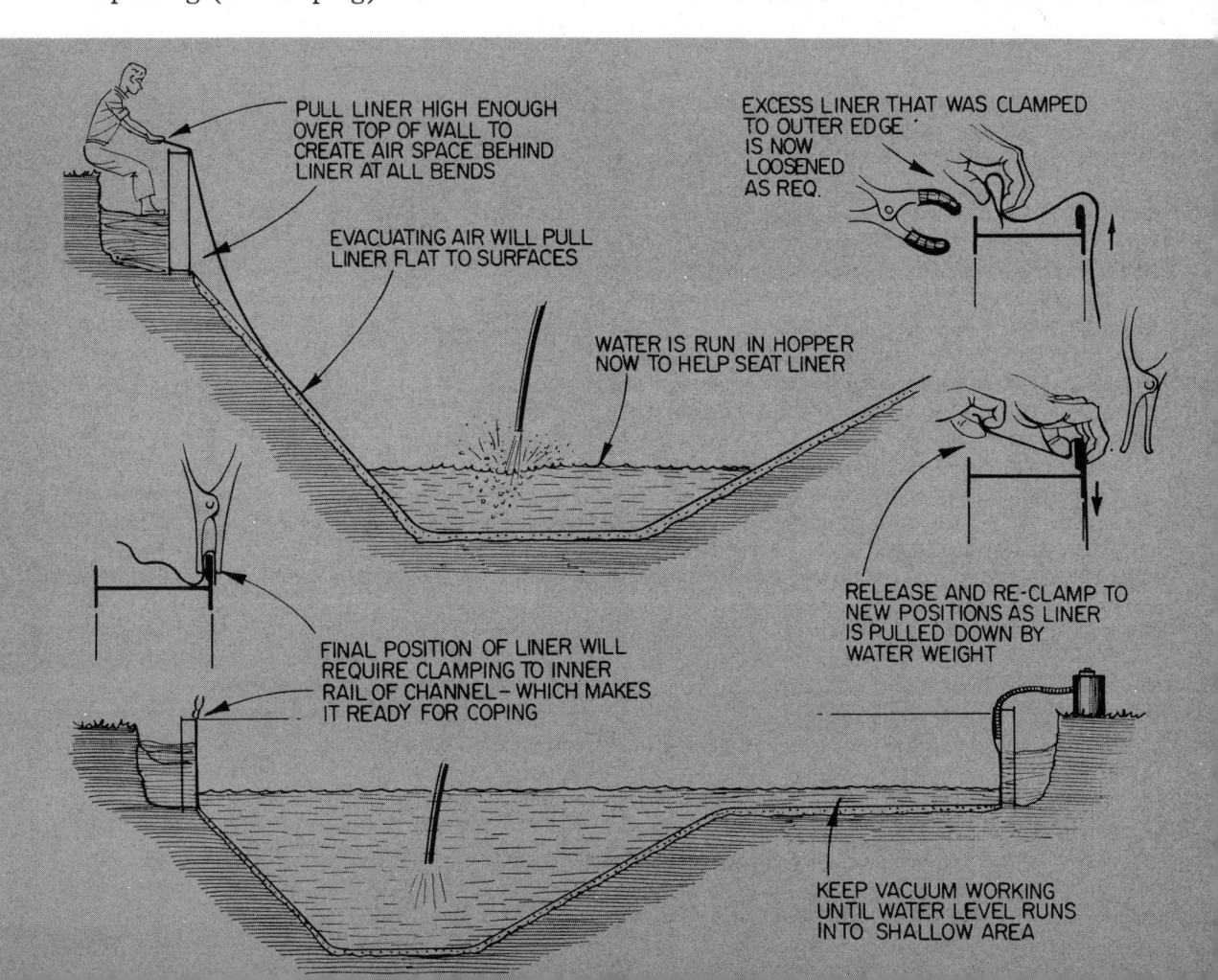

Since the liner is designed and fabricated to form a PERFECT FIT with the pool bottom and sides if the excavation was dug to specifications and the vermiculite bottom installed as directed. When it looks good to the eye with the corners square and the perimeter around the top absolutely even, insert a vacuum (an industrial type, not the common home tank type) hose into a corner. The vacuum will remove most of the air behind the liner and atmospheric pressure will flatten the vinyl against the bottom and the sides. If the vacuum does not remove an obvious wrinkle, shut it off, tug where required. Start the vacuum and if it does not remove an obvious wrinkle within 5 minutes, air is rushing behind the liner from around the edges where the hose is inserted or through the Aqua/Genie opening. When the bottom fits perfectly, check to make certain the liner rests on both the bottom and sides and does not span the corner where the floor meets the wall. If you note an arc along the base on the wall where it meets the bottom, the liner is unsupported at this point. To correct this condition, turn off the vac and remove the clamps temporarily to permit more of the liner to extend into the pool.

Once you are satisfied with the fit, keep the vacuum running (even if it takes a day to two) and start fiilling the pool.

Once you reach the level of 6" up the pool wall you can turn off the vacuum. At this point, install the coping. Start at one side just beyond a corner, remove the clamps and press the special vinyl strip over the lip of the Cas-Lok channel, after you are cerain the liner is seated evenly along the bottom. When you reach the corner, the special nylon clips are pressed in place. After the complete circumference is perfectly fitted you can screw the Radius Corner Coping in place, followed by inserting section by section 2' lengths of Cas-Lok coping. Use a spacer between each section so the plastic joint covers will fit after all sections are secure.

At this stage your pool will start to look as if it were part of the house. You will require a patio area, and this should be done after the earth has had time to settle. One good recommendation is to tamp the filled area, add a layer of sand and set patio blocks around the perimeter. When they have fully settled, just before the swimming season next year, you can pick them up, add more sand and place them in place permanently using one of the techniques described in another volume of this encyclopedia. Of course, you can pour a concrete deck but unless you followed the tamping and backfill recommendations you will have some settling in future years.

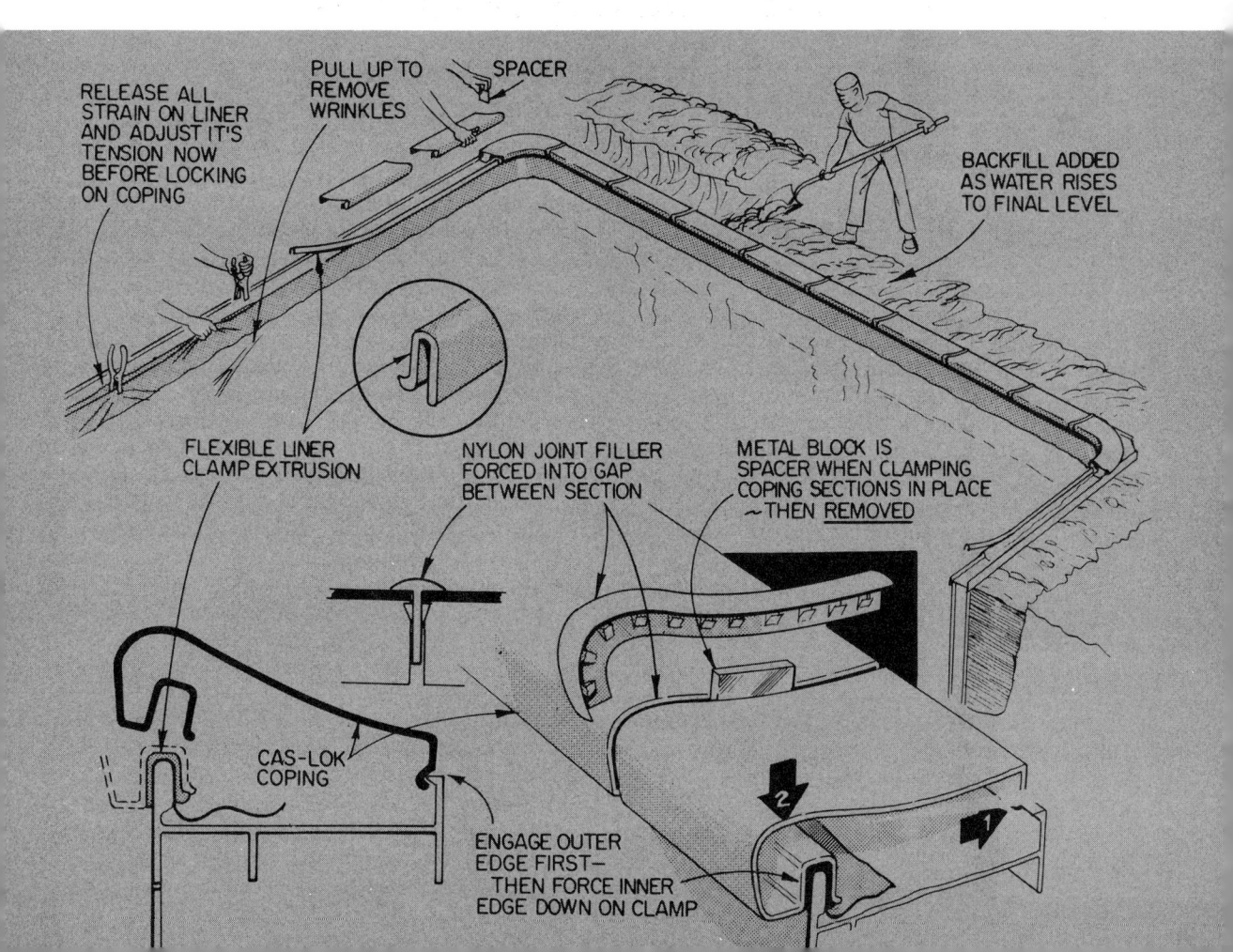

"SWIMMER" POOL
with Built-in Deck

Here's a unique half-in/half-out pool designed for smaller yards. It is available in three sizes.

Here's a unique backyard pool, a permanent structure that differs slightly from the regular vinyl liner in-ground pool in that it extends just 18" out of the ground so the surrounding redwood deck can be used as a handy lounging or conversation seat. It is much smaller than the popular 16' x 32' in-ground pool in that the swimming area ranges anywhere from a compact 10' x 16' to 12' x 24', depending upon your yard and which size kit strikes your fancy.

Another unusual feature is that the bottom does not have a "deep end," as we usually refer to a pool with a "hopper," in which case the "deep end" is nearly eight feet. The pool described on these pages has what is called a "swimmer's bottom"; the depth gradually slopes from three feet at one end to four feet at the other. Since many homeowners, especially older folks and non-swimmers, look upon a pool as a place for good exercise and body refreshing rather than an area for aquatic challenges, this half-in/half-out concept has the added advantage of (1) Being able to be located in a smaller yard area than the conventional in-ground unit, (2) Does not require as much earth removal (which can be a big plus in certain yards where heavy equipment is difficult to use, (3) The bottom is much easier to shape than a hopper pool, (4) The decking, which is a structural part of the pool wall, cuts down if not eliminates, the usual concrete or flagstone patio area of the typical in-ground pool, (5) The filter system is mounted underneath the decking, thereby eliminating considerable plumbing, (6) The redwood deck makes possible extending your lawn right up to the edge, preventing grass clippings and other debris from blowing into the pool, (7) The pool requires less water which can mean a smaller pump and therefore slightly lower operating costs.

While the kit costs slightly less than an in-ground pool, when you consider the

POOL • 2173

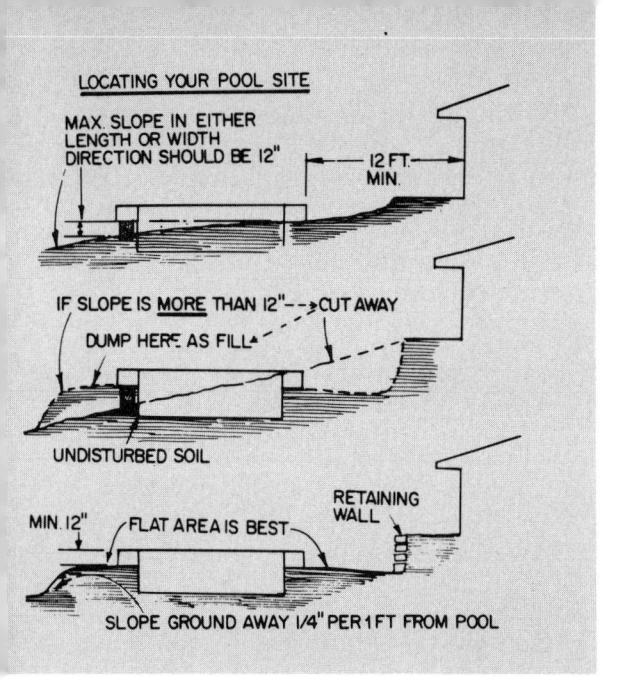

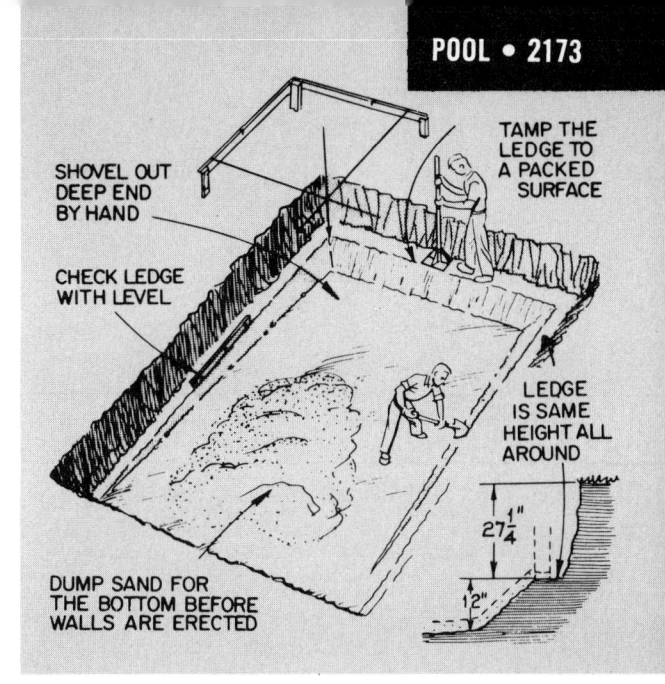

fact that you can virtually eliminate the entire patio area because of the built-in decking, the overall cost will be substantially less than a 16' x 32' in-ground pool.

Pools like these have their place in the market and it may be just the type for your particular use. If it is, here is how you can build one in your yard.

The construction is basic; the walls are built up from panels of pressure-treated plywood that does not rot, the bottom is shaped from sand or vermiculite and cement, the liner is vinyl, the coping is aluminum and the decking is made of pre-cut redwood boards.

As is the case with all pools, it is best to check your local building department when planning an installation in that you should comply with the codes as they relate to the backyard site, fencing, disposal of back-wash water, possible drainage and electrical connections. The latter is especially important since the pump motor is located beneath the decking in about

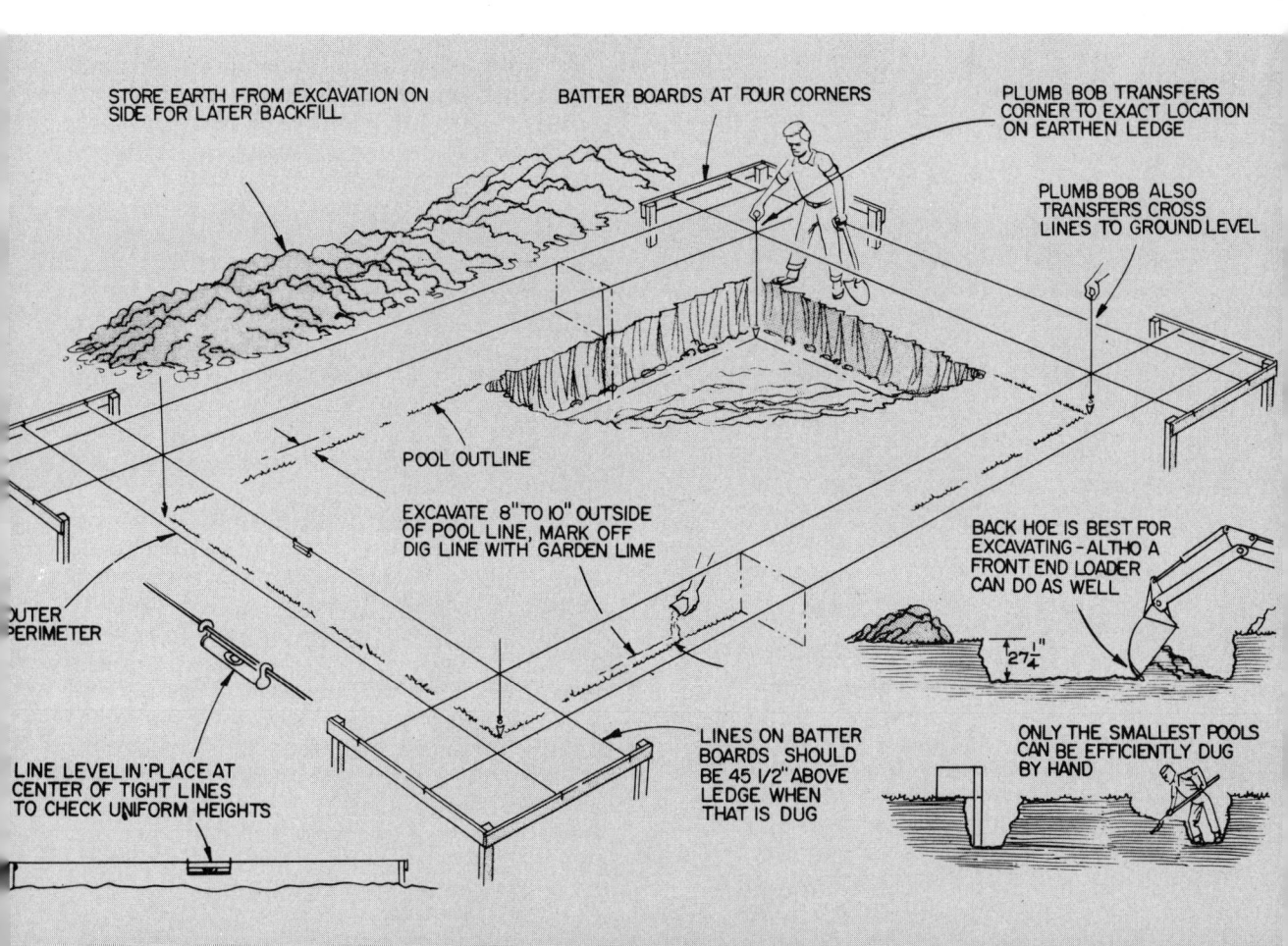

ASSEMBLY OF GUSSETS

- 5/8" PLYWOOD GUSSET PANELS
- 3/8" X 1 1/4" CARRIAGE BOLTS INTO JOINERS
- ASSEMBLE LIKE PRODUCTION AND STACK UNTIL ALL COMPLETE
- ALUM. JOINER
- PANELS FOLLOW LINES
- DRILL FOR RIVET INTO METAL AND PLYWOOD
- NAIL SET
- SPLICE PLATE IS PRESS FIT THEN DIMPLED TO LOCK IN PLACE
- SAW BEVEL AT INNER JOINT

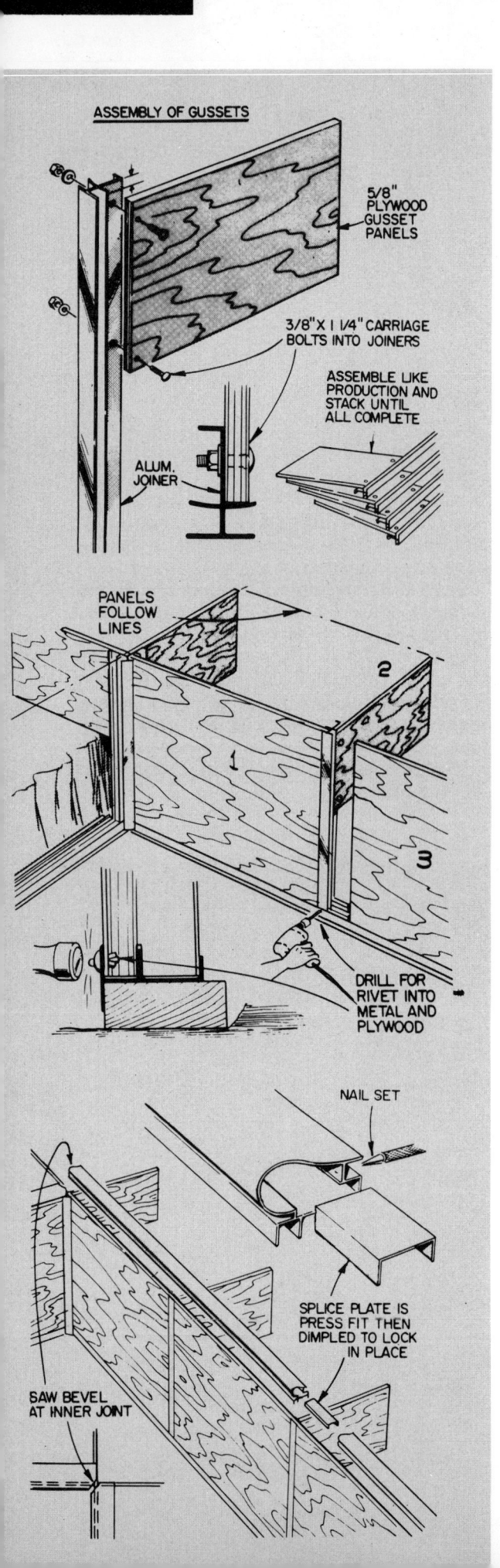

the same proximity as the millions of pump motors of the popular above grade pools.

While each yard area is different, here are a few essential rules you should follow when determining the exact location of your pool. Ideally, you will gain best use of your pool if it faces south and southwest. Keep it at least 12 feet from your home; 20 feet is preferable in that it will permit more tasteful and efficient arrangement of a patio and sun bathing area.

As mentioned previously, one of the unique features of this pool is the fact that the deck extends just 18" above the finished grade, which in turn not only provides you with a very attractive and functional bench, but also greatly simplifies the excavating. Once you have decided upon the location, with a simple line level or builder's transit, note the slope of the area in both the width and length direction of your pool. Most yards are not absolutely level and if your area has a slope of more than 12" in either length or width direction you should plan to grade the land to make it level.

If your slope is greater than 12" you do have some leeway to grade the area to fit your pool but always keep in mind that the 42" high walls *MUST* rest on virgin or undisturbed earth. Under no circumstances should any of the four sill plates be rested on fill.

A rubber tired backhoe with a front end loader bucket is used for excavating, although if you have a tree or rock problem the same type of equipment on tracks is a more practical choice. Note that the bottom is not flat but has a slight slope; one end is just 12" deeper. Unlike many pools, construction of the walls is easily done from *INSIDE* the pool area, so your excavation need be only slightly larger than the final dimension of the pool. Since the sill plates are 2" x 4", a final width and length excavation 8" or 10" larger than your pool will make it possible for you to provide a level ledge for the sill with a minimum of backfill.

If your excavator has a transit (and most do) he can leave you with an absolutely level ledge; if not, position the batter boards as shown and use a line level to make certain the ledge is level as it is being dug. With your pool outline marked with lime, start digging at the "deep" and proceed toward the "shallow" end but always make certain the ledge is undisturbed. After your excavation is trimmed and the ledge checked and tamped to make certain it is level and will provide an even base for the sill plate, dump sand in the center which will be used later to smooth out the bottom.

With your ledge absolutely level, mount the aluminum channel to the 2" x 4" base sill with roofing nails. When you find it necessary to join two lengths of 2" x 4" to make a complete sill plate length, lap over the channel to form a splice. After all four base sills are complete, drill a 5/8" hole through the 2" x 4", using the holes in the aluminum base channel as a guide. When the sill is positioned on the ledge, after it is level and square, the 1/2" rebars are driven to hold the sill secure while the wall is being assembled.

Erecting the walls will proceed more rapidly now, and with your sill plate absolutely square and level, your pool will begin to take shape. Your four corner extrusions, the aluminum joiners and the plywood gussets are clearly marked and pre-drilled to simplify construction. First assemble all the gusset panels on the joiners with the 1 1/4" carriage bolts. Keep the washer on the aluminum side and draw the nuts tight with a ratchet wrench. Stack them in place inside the pool area and proceed to assemble the four corners. Examine each side carefully and place the side that is smoothest and has the fewest number of knots facing the inside.

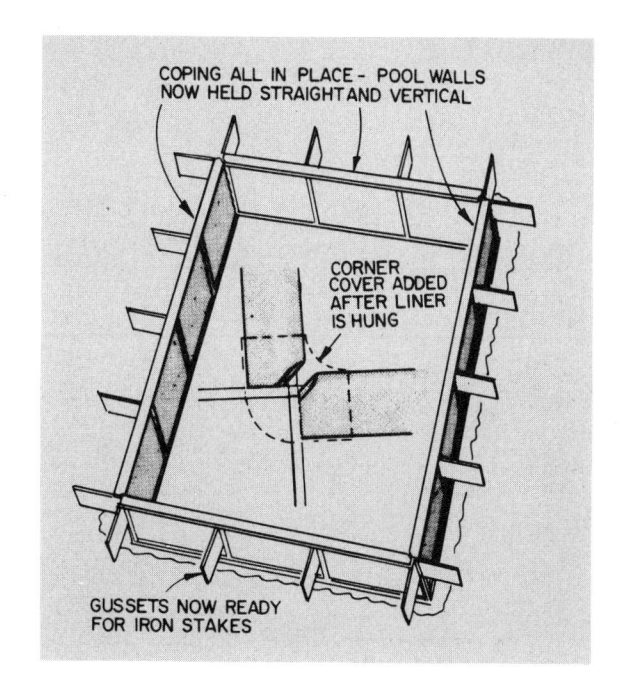

After the gussets are joined, press one corner extrusion into the base channel and proceed to add the wall panels. The corner extrusion will stand erect and once the first plywood wall panel is in place, drive nails through the rear of the aluminum corner flange and into the panel. Make certain the plywood is seated before you drive the nail home with a nailset. Pro-

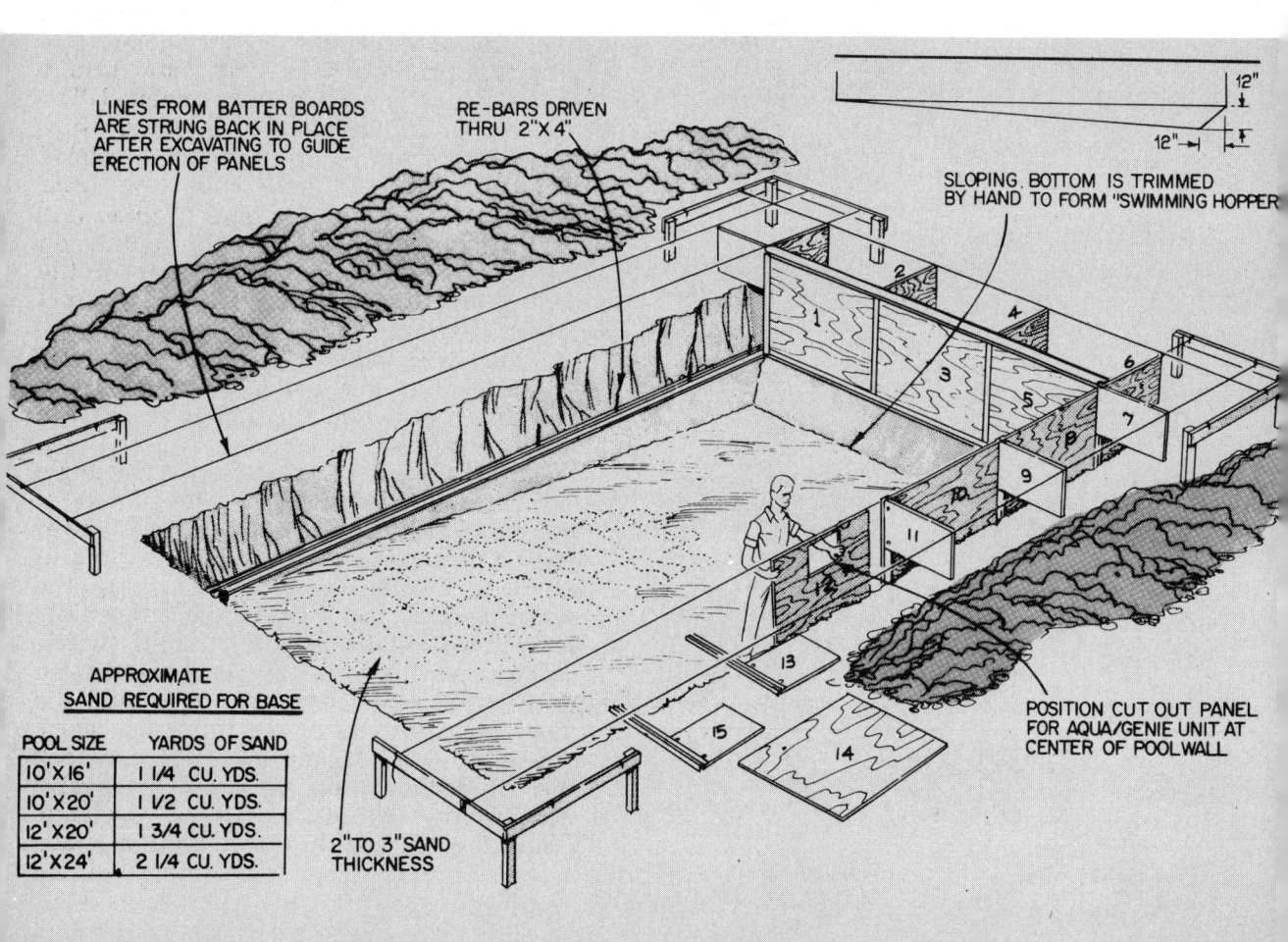

POOL SIZE	YARDS OF SAND
10' X 16'	1 1/4 CU. YDS.
10' X 20'	1 1/2 CU. YDS.
12' X 20'	1 3/4 CU. YDS.
12' X 24'	2 1/4 CU. YDS.

APPROXIMATE SAND REQUIRED FOR BASE

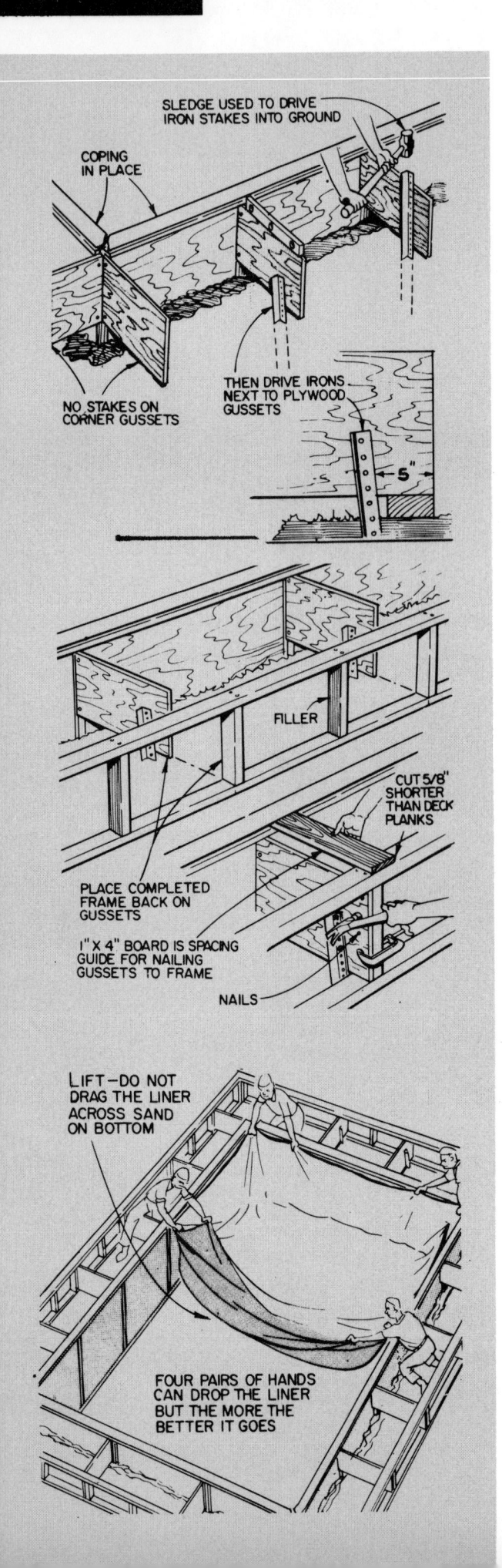

ceed by adding the wall panels and panel dividers in one direction around the entire perimeter until all panels are in place and the corner nailed. Note that one of the wall panels will have the cutout for the Aqua/Genie Feeder-Skimmer-Filter and this panel should be located in the center of the long wall and preferably nearest the house. The pump is mounted in the deck compartment, so keeping the power line as close to the house as possible will cut your electrical installation costs.

After all panels have been seated in both the corners, drill through the face of the base channel extrusion, through one side of the aluminum joiner and into the plywood. Then insert a drive rivet and drive it home.

At this point all your walls will be in place and they may appear to be waving. To secure them further before each gusset is bolted to a steel stake, the coping sections are added. Set the coping sections in place and note that where they meet at the corner some trimming will be necessary. When installing a length of coping, work from one corner around the pool and where two pieces of coping join, press the special splice plate into position.

Push the coping down so it seats over the panel dividers and then drill a ¼" hole through the back of the coping into the aluminum panel joiner. Then insert a ¼" drive rivet and drive it home. Repeat this procedure with all four corners so the coping is permanently attached. The vertical aluminum panel dividers are further secured to the base channel extrusion by drilling a ¼" hole from the front through the face of the base channel and into the panel divider. At this point add the drive rivet through the rear of the coping and into the flange of each panel joiner. The walls will now be fairly rigid but they will still bend in or out slightly at the center. This will be eliminated in the next step when the angles are driven into the ground.

With the coping in place, drive the angle stake anchors adjacent to the gussets of the short side of the pool. Keep them at least 5" from the end to permit sliding in the 2 x 4 stringer which make up the lower part of the exterior deck framing. Keep these angle stakes as straight (vertical) as possible so the gusset will not twist excessively when the bolts that hold the gussets to the stakes are tightened. Once the short wall stakes are driven, check the top with a level and hold the gusset next to the iron stake with a C-clamp. Using the top hole in the stake as a guide, drill through the plywood gusset and insert a carriage bolt and nut. The shank of the bolt digs into the face of the gusset. Tighten and then drill and insert a second bolt at least 3" lower than the top bolt.

Now that both short walls have their anchors in place repeat this procedure along the long walls. Drive the stakes next to the gussets, and true up the side wall by sighting down the coping. Then C-clamp the gusset and stake nearest the center splice after the coping appears to be absolutely straight.

At this point, before the 2 x 4 framing is up, screw the Aqua/Genie Skimmer-Filter in place from the rear.

Spread the sand in the bottom with a shovel and rake to a point meeting the top of the base rail extrusion. Tamp and spray the sand lightly with water so it can be worked and troweled with a mason's float. Or, if you prefer, you can install a hard vermiculite bottom as described in the in-ground pool article in this volume.

Now your carpentry skills come into play with the construction of the 2 x 4 frames that make up the side walls. First prefab the long wall by marking the lower and upper stringer to locate the 2 x 4 vertical members. Make the side in one piece by splicing the 2 x 4 and drive 16 penny nails through the face of the 2 x 4 and into the precut vertical members. Set the complete frame on the gusset and, using a length of 1 x 4 exactly ⅝" shorter than the deck planks, slide the 2 x 4 to the gusset as shown.

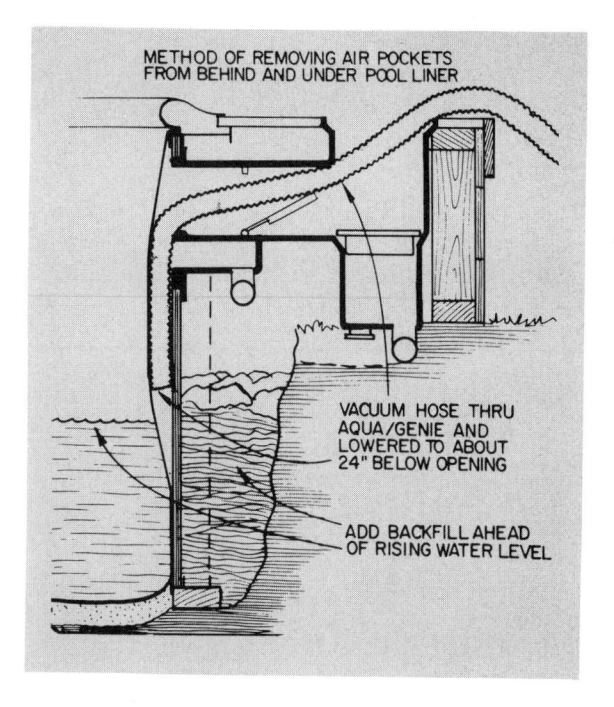

The pump and filter assembly is mounted

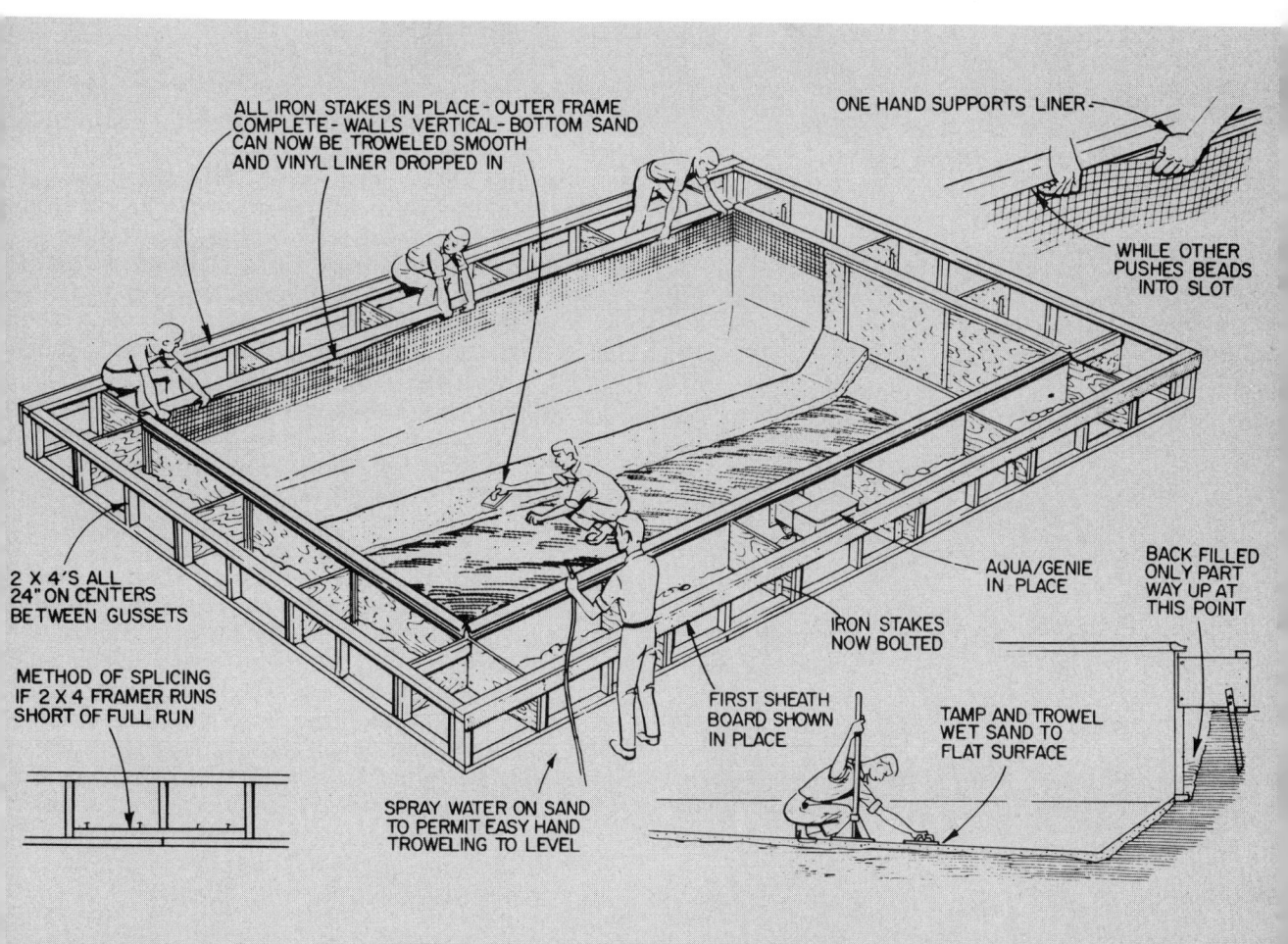

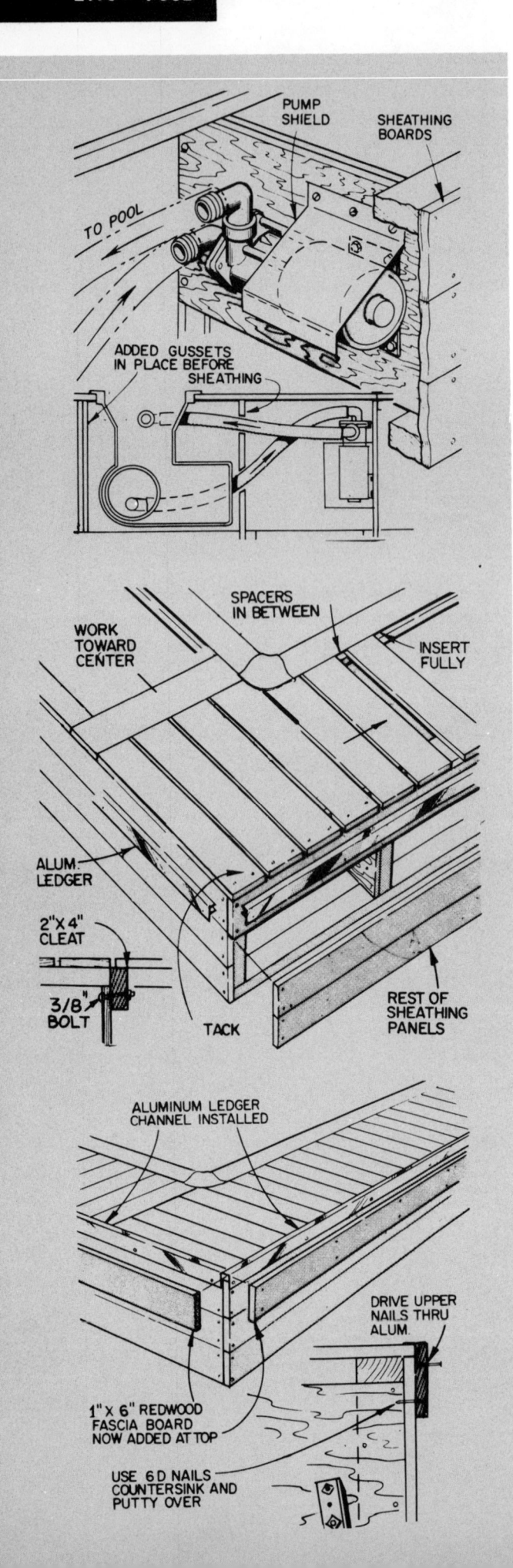

on a bulkhead underneath the decking so merely run the two short flexible plastic lines from the Skimmer-Filter to the pump. At this time install the underground electrical line from the motor to your power source within the house. If your power line extends directly to a branch panel box the connection should terminate in a GFI (Ground Fault Interrupter). Your electrician will have the type properly sized for your motor. The GFI is a relatively new development specified by the National Electrical Code. Basically, it is a transistored device that is so sensitive, if as little as 5/1000th of an ampere goes the wrong way—such as to a body of a bystander—the current is automatically flipped off!

With the exterior deck framing walls in place you can install the liner. Note the deep end of the liner and have four men (or women) grab a corner and set it in place. Locate one of the corners first, pull the liner in place and press the solid lip of the liner into the groove provided in the coping. The liner will appear to be wrinkled at this point, and the technique to remove these wrinkles prior to filling with water is to insert an industrial (or heavy duty) vacuum through the top of the Skimmer-Feeder-Filter and extend the hose down about 24" below the opening. Pack wet rags in the top and the lower suction fitting to seal off the openings as much as possible. Turn the vac on and watch the atmospheric pressure virtually paste the vinyl liner against the bottom and sides. If you encounter a stubborn wrinkle, turn the vac off and, leaning over from the side and work out the wrinkle with a soft-bristled broom. Start the vac again and, after you are satisfied with the fit start filling. But keep the vac running while you fill the pool.

As the pool is being filled you can backfill by hand. Keep the backfill a few inches above the water level and tamp lightly.

When the water level reaches about 18" below the top, remove the vacuum hose. Allow the water to reach just below the lower opening of the Skimmer-Feeder-Filter; then install the face plates.

Before the precut decking is set in place, cut the polyethylene sheeting to size and spread over the backfilled area between the gussets. You will note the redwood boards for the corners are slightly longer than the regular decking, and these should be installed first. Each corner has five of these boards *nailed* in place. Once the corners are covered, work from each end toward the middle, setting the planks into the slot in the rear of the extruded coping. Press a spacer in place as each plank is added, and when you reach the center, cut the last plank to fit. Then slide the aluminum ledger strip underneath the ends of all deck planks and nail the ledger to the sides. Finally, nail the 1" x 6" redwood fascia board so it is flush with the top of the ledger. Repeat this process with the remaining three sides of the deck.

Since it may be necessary on occasion to gain access to both the pump and the Aqua/Genie, the decking that covers this equipment should be trimmed and a batten screwed to the underside connecting the boards. Note the hatches rest a shade less than halfway into the ledger and the coping extrusion, and each hatch can be removed by pushing it forward so one end bottoms in the slot while the rear edge lifts up. Note that two extra bulkheads are needed to provide a firm support.

With the decking in place, installation of the white brick panels just about completes your pool. Note the corners are formed at right angles. Start with one corner and nail it in place, using anywhere from six to ten nails per panel. The upper edge of the panel touches the underside of the fascia board. Nail only in the joint lines and make certain the fit is tight where two panels meet. These brick panels are molded from white styrene and the heavy duty thickness makes them impervious to the elements; they will never require painting.

Grading your area will add the final touch to your installation. Grass up to the base of the brick or use any of the many patio materials available to make your pool the most functional and attractive pool in the neighborhood!

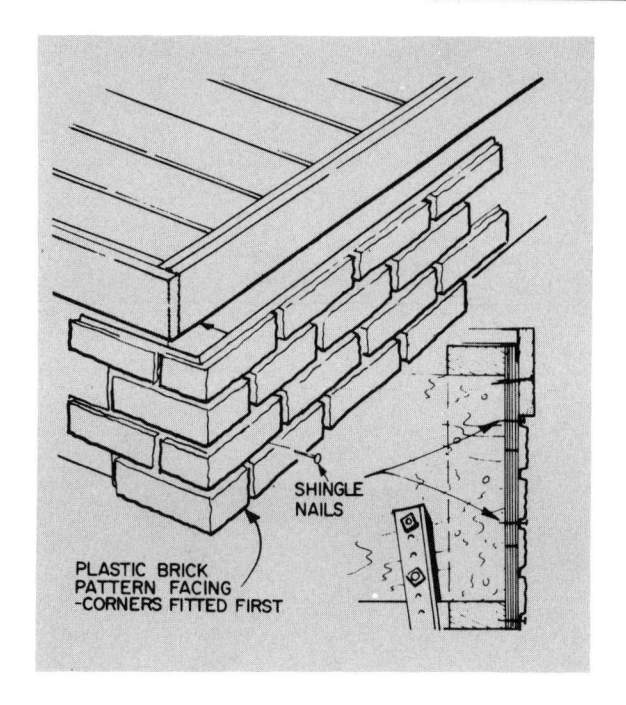

This pool concept is relatively new so if you need additional information, please contact the Cascade Industries, Inc., Talmadge Road, Edison, New Jersey 08817, Attn: Robert West, Chief Engineer. Cascade is one of the oldest manufacturers of quality pools carrying the famous Buster Crabbe endorsement.

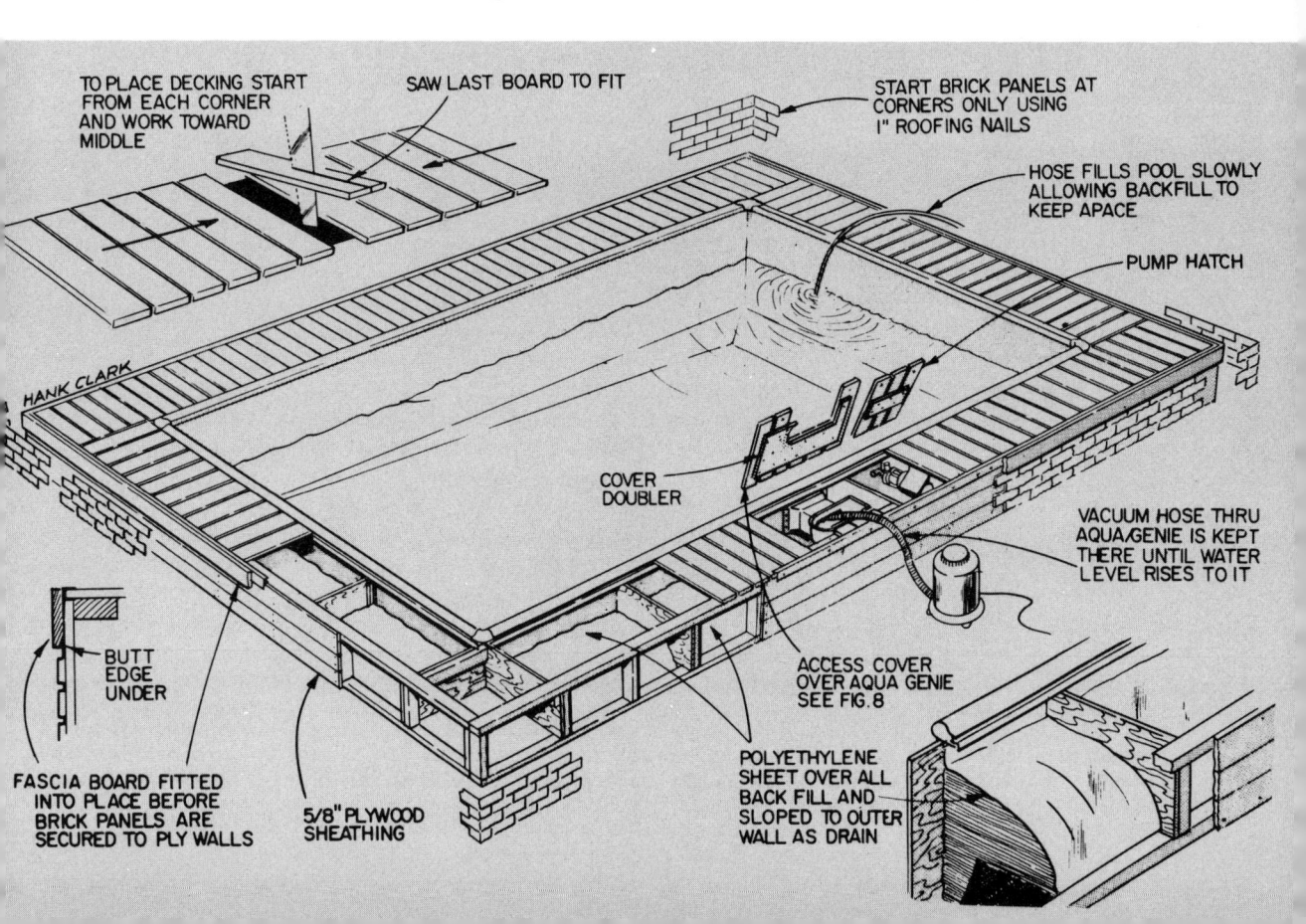

2180 • POSTS

Putting Up Posts

Need posts for lights, patio roof or clothesline? Here's how to do it

Patio roof (above) was built after slab; holes were drilled in concrete slab with carbide-tipped bit so L-shaped clips which hold posts could be bolted down. Other methods are shown in drawings opposite. Construct post lights as shown page 2268; use burial cable and check your local regulations.

THERE ARE many jobs around a house that involve posts of one kind or another. Posts for a wooden fence are the keystones of the project; weakness here and the fence will eventually lean, sag or just fall. A cover over the patio slab (you will surely want to erect one some day to provide shade) requires sturdy posts for support. You need posts for tetherball, a swing, clotheslines, a volleyball net, a driveway light and so on. Regardless of the types of posts you build or install, masonry materials play an important part in providing a strong foundation.

How do you install posts on concrete, a patio slab for example? The method used here will depend largely on whether you plan for the posts before you pour the slab or decide to put them up after the concrete work is done. You can provide an adequate foundation for a post that must bear a heavy load by digging a footing for it (see sketch) as you prepare the ground for the slab pour. The foundation hole should be about 1 ft. square and 1 ft. deep. The form for the concrete is provided by the earth itself, which should be well tampered and cut vertically on the sides. If anything, the sides should slope outward toward the bottom of the hole. Since the post footing will have more weight than adjacent slab areas, you can guard against cracks by using reinforcing steel, bent 90 degrees, to tie footing and slab together. The post can be tied down with masonry fasteners, or by setting a piece of steel vertically in

Methods of erecting posts on slab. Work must be done before pour unless L-clips are used.

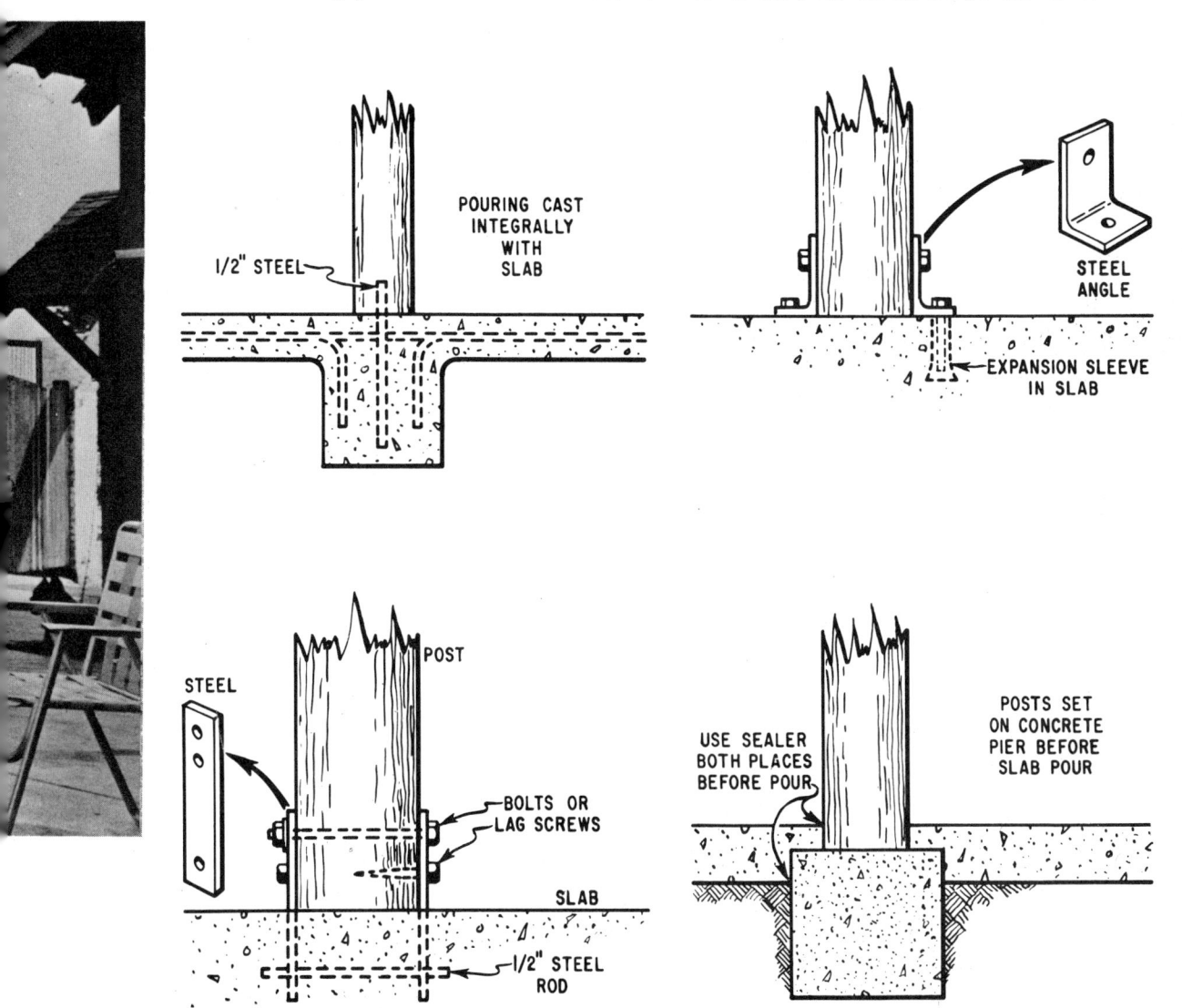

the center of the footing before the pour so that it projects about 3-4 in. Drill a matching hole in the bottom of the post, and set the post over the steel.

Another method of providing a post foundation is to precast footings and set them solidly in place before the pour. Here, you can use ready-made piers which are available for use in crawl spaces and foundations.

Still another way of erecting a post is to use strap steel bent into a U-shape (or two pieces tied together with steel to form a U) which is imbedded in the slab pour so that the arms project about 5-6 in. After the slab sets, the post is placed between the arms and secured with bolts or lag screws. You must be careful about the distance between the legs of the "U"; use a scrap piece of post to establish the dimension.

Where the slab is already in, you can use any number of masonry fasteners to secure posts. More information will be found in the chapter on this subject.

Holes for fence posts should be 5 to 6 in. deeper than the depth the posts will be buried. This is so the bottom of the footings can be lined with gravel or small stones. Most fence posts are 4x4s, so the diameter of each hole should be a minimum of 6 in. Digging is easy if you work with a "clam" post hole digger or with a powered auger. There's nothing wrong with digging larger holes except that it involves unnecessary labor and you'll need more concrete fill. If you must work with a shovel, select a scoop type with a small blade and long handle.

After each hole is dug and the bottom 6 in. filled, set the post in place and use a level to see that it's plumb. If you use a stiff concrete mix, it's possible to keep the post plumb without further juggling. If you should have trouble, however, set up temporary braces to keep the post in place until the concrete hardens. Use a short length of 2x4 to tamp the concrete and slope the top to provide a runoff for water. Some professionals will dig all holes and actually construct the fence before cementing the posts on the basis that the fence assembly

Wrought iron posts have preformed mounting brackets. Matching holes are drilled in concrete, or mounting bolts placed in concrete before pour.

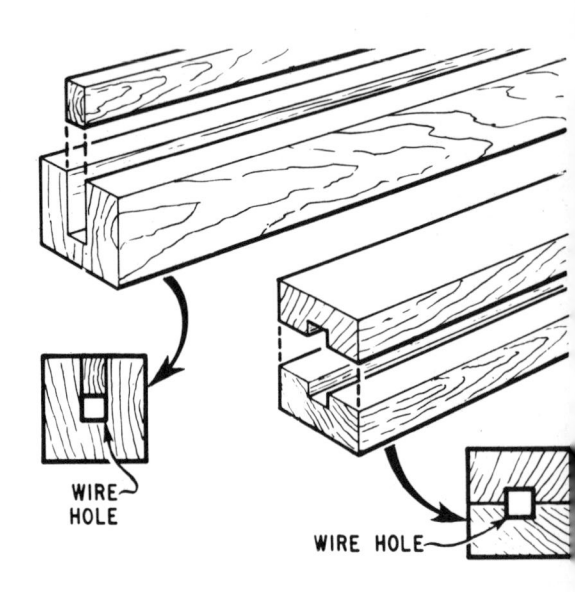

Two ways of making wire hole in post are shown above. Run deep dado in post and partially fill, or put together two 2x4s, each with shallow dado.

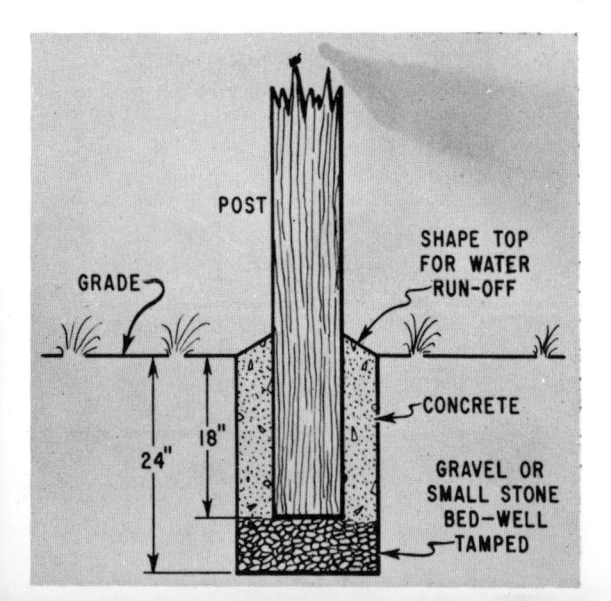

Sturdy fence posts are made as at left. For 4x4 post, 6 in. diameter hole is minimum; 8 in. is better. Treat the buried section with preservative.

will keep the posts plumb and in alignment without temporary bracing.

For a post light, you can form a center hole for wires in one of two ways. Run a deep dado (a rectangular groove) down the center of the post and partially fill it with a strip of wood. The opening that remains should be at least ½ in. square. The other method is to use two 2x4s to make a 4x4 post. Run a ½-in. dado down the center of each post and glue and nail the halves together.

Removable and Portable Posts

To make a post that you can remove, a tetherball or a clothesline post, for example, use a 5-gal. drum as a form and a length of pipe to serve as a sleeve. The drum is buried a little below grade level and the pipe centered in the concrete used to fill it. Put the post in the sleeve pipe when you pour the concrete—this will make it easy to keep the sleeve plumb. Use a wooden plug in the pipe to keep it from filling with dirt or water when the post is not being used. Be sure the plug doesn't project above grade for people to trip over.

A post permanently imbedded, yet possible to move from place to place, can be constructed in a similar manner. Again, use a 5-gal. drum, but set the post directly in the concrete. The drum can sit above ground or it can be buried. Another method is to use an old automobile tire as a permanent form. Tire posts are good for tetherball and volleyball and badminton nets, especially when the back yard will not permit a permanent installation. Rest the tire on firm, level ground or on a piece of plywood and center a sleeve in the concrete that you pour to fill the tire. A post constructed this way has ample rigidity yet is easy to move since you can tip it over and roll it about on the tire.

Posts can be constructed of brick, masonry units or stone using the same construction techniques you would employ in building a wall. Posts of this type are, of course, more time consuming, but time is on the home craftsman's side since he doesn't have to pay for his own labor. •

"Portable" post (left). Post and base can be left above ground or reburied in new location. Removable post (right) is handy for game nets, etc.

Ideas for brick posts: method of casting top; hollow post for light wiring; large post with rubble center; solid post; post to take fence rails.

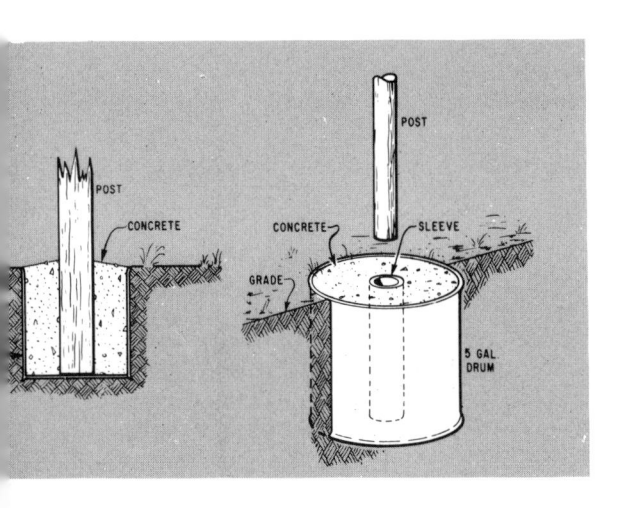

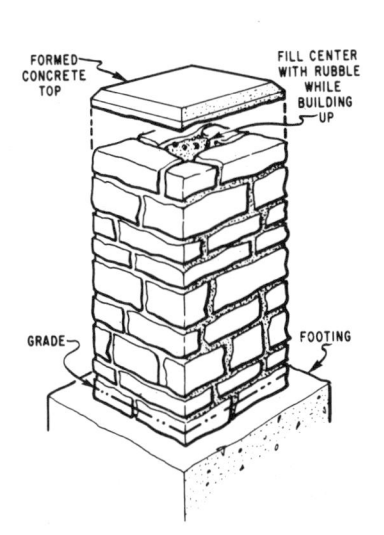

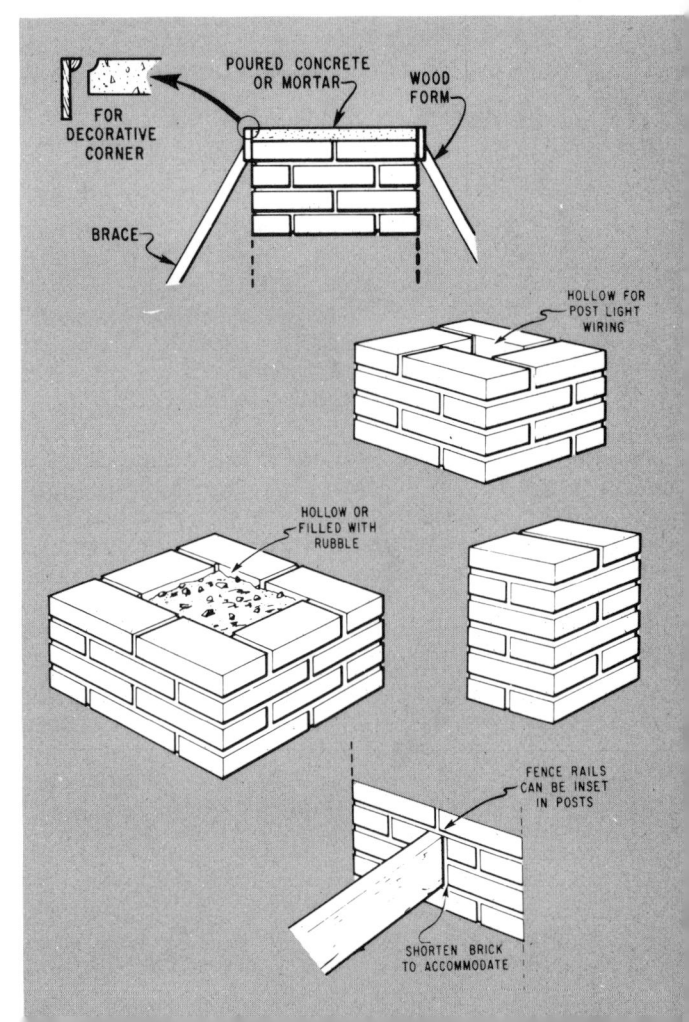

Build a Potter's Wheel

Whether foot-powered or electric, your pottery efforts will revolve around an efficient wheel.

IT HAS been said that our civilization revolves on "the wheel." In a larger sense this is true, since without the wheel as a basic part of all machinery, whether ground to an eccentric or cut into a cog, basically it still is a wheel. In pottery, too, the wheel has always been of extreme importance.

The reference wheel refers to a circular disc, free to revolve on an axis placed exactly at the center of the disc and at right angles to the disc. The shaft upon which the disc revolves should be absolutely vertical. It should be supported by smooth-running bearings or sleeves.

There are many uses to which a wheel may be put. It is customary to employ a wheel for the purpose for which the particular wheel is designed. The simplest type of wheel is a whirler, or banding wheel. This wheel is used for designing or sketching a design in regular thickness completely around your ware. The gold band around the edge of a plate or the stripe of color around the base or mid-section of a lamp or cup are just a few of the uses of a banding wheel. An incised design may be cut with extreme regularity into your piece by the use of a banding wheel or whirler.

In building a piece of ware by the coil method, a whirler will save walking around the piece. In glazing, too, a revolving table or whirler is useful since all sides may be glazed or decorated without moving from your original position. All sides are equally exposed by revolving your wheel.

In sculpting it is necessary to view your piece and work your ware from all sides. A whirler eliminates the necessity of moving around the piece to work. It also permits building an arm or hand rest on one side next to the wheel and working on all sides without shifting your arm rest

An inexpensive potter's wheel or whirler can be made from a wire-spool, pipe and fittings.

An ordinary nipple used by the plumbing profession is put in the spool to serve as an axle.

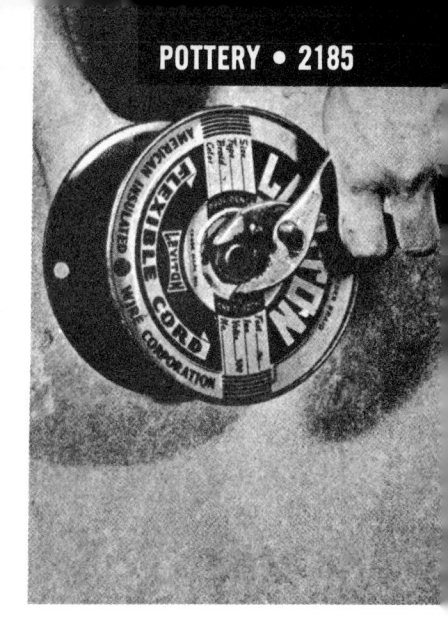

Locknuts are used to tighten the ends of the nipple. Make one end flush to plaster bat.

As at left, axle is extended to desired height, then is placed in shaft for free rotation.

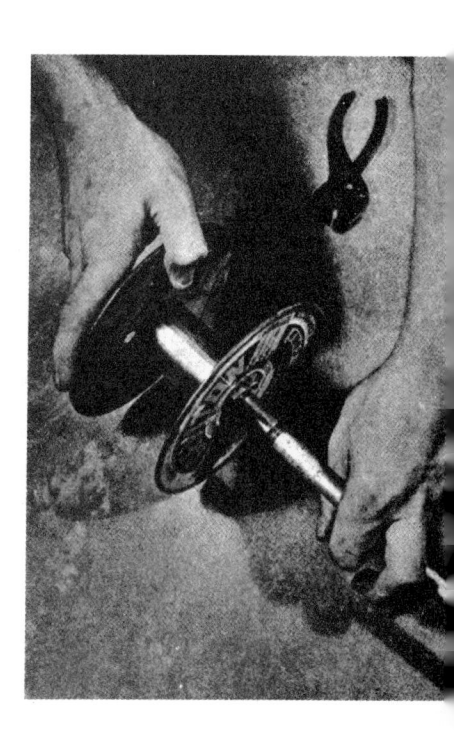

A sleeve, or bushing, of approximately the same diameter as shaft serves as bearing.

How to Make a Whirler

A simple whirler can be made from a spool. Obtain a spool with flanges not less than 6" in diameter. The spool should be wood or metal. Metal is preferable. Such a spool is usually used for winding or dispensing wire or ribbon. This spool will have a hole through the axle. Place a short piece of pipe (threaded on both ends) through this axle. Secure a bushing on top of the spool, tightening it on the pipe. Secure a coupling on the bottom of the pipe to draw up tight to the bottom of the spool. Affix into the other end of the coupling a two-foot piece of pipe. Insert this two-foot pipe into another piece of pipe just large enough to allow the spool and the two-foot piece of pipe to revolve freely. Use strap iron to secure the outer pipe in a vertical position at a convenient height. Upon the top of the spool drill three holes at irregular positions. Drive a Parker screw point up through each of these holes. Take a plaster bat, drill a hole part way through from the bottom for the bushing on top of the spool, and drill three small holes for the Parker screw points to fit snugly. This procedure will hold the plaster bat level on the spool and will keep it from shifting.

2186 • POTTERY

In constructing a kick wheel, the first step is to build a sturdy table to support wheel arrangement.

Below, the top of the table is made to fit type of wheel you plan to use. Note reinforcing at the top.

The legs of the table are braced all around to give it maximum stability. Bolts are unnecessary.

With wheel and pulley all set up, kick wheel is set for operation. Foot pedal should be hinged to floor.

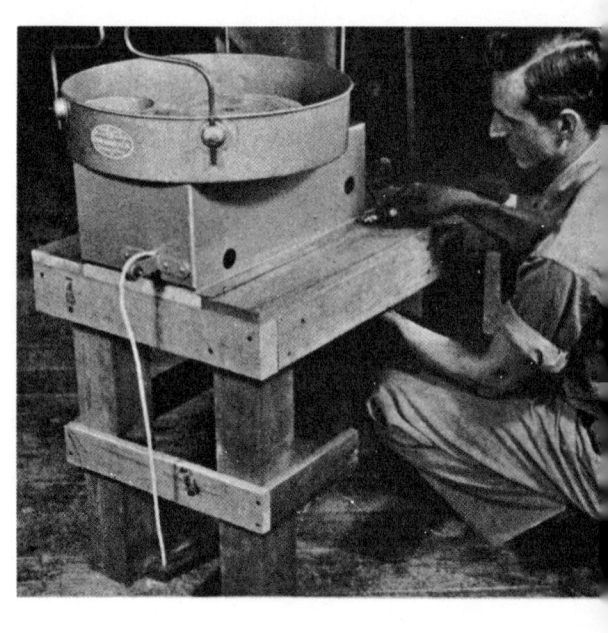

How to Construct a Kick Wheel

To construct a kick wheel, it is necessary to understand that the power is supplied by foot. Hence, for convenience and comfort it should be built with a seat for the operator. His feet may dangle comfortably so that one foot may kick out to revolve a larger floor wheel. The construction is not involved. Erect a narrow table 36" high, 12" wide, and 30" long, well braced and cross-braced to insure rigidity. Obtain an old grinding wheel or similar wheel which is heavy. This wheel should be between 22" and 26" in diameter. Obtain a small wheel for the head or working wheel; this wheel should be between 8" and 12" in diameter. The working (head) wheel will have to be flanged on the underside to permit the securing of an axle. This axle will then penetrate through the center of the table 4" from the side on which the operator will be seated. The axle will extend through the table and through the large heavy wheel. It will continue to the floor, where there should be a flange to keep the axle from end thrust or shifting. The female portion of the flange may receive a marble or steel ball upon which the solid axle may float. The large heavy wheel should be secured rigidly to the axle so that a kicking action on this wheel will revolve the axle and operate the working top.

Underside of the wheel shows the reduction pulley and speed control system. A motor may be attached.

The Power Wheel

The foregoing may be used as basic designs for a power wheel. Add a pulley to the shaft and set up an electric motor with a pulley. A belt between these pulleys will provide power drive. The smaller the driving pulley and the larger the driven pulley, the slower the speed. Most power wheels, however, are equipped with variable speed devices. Variable speed may be achieved by several methods. Arrange your motor with a loose belt and add in the path of the belt another pulley on a free axle. The axle bearing should be secured in slots so that pressure exerted by the foot pedal shifts the axle to increase tension on the belt, or by releasing pressure on this axle, belt slippage permits slower operation. Another arrangement of speed control is achieved by movable shivs on a split pulley. This automatically varies speed by changing the ratio of the pulleys. Another wheel manufacturer employs a sewing machine type motor where a foot-controlled rheostat diminishes power and hence speed, at will. Still another design employs a geared motor for speed control. •

How to Figure Motor Size

To determine the size of electric motor needed for a given job, the formula may be used:

$$\frac{\text{HP Output Reqd.}}{\text{ME} \times \text{PF} \times \text{LE}} = \text{size of motor needed}$$

Where:
HP Output Reqd. is the power required to move the loaded machine
ME is the motor efficiency.
PF equals power factor.
LE is line efficiency, or voltage output divided by voltage input.

For example: An electric motor is required to operate a shale planer which when under load puts a demand of 50 horsepower on the power source. Power at the plant's connection to a nearby public power line is 440 volts, but due to the resistance of the No. 2 wire used to span the 2,000 ft. distance to the shale planer, the power at the motor is only 410 volts. With a motor of 85 per cent efficiency, in a plant where the power factor is 85 per cent, the formula becomes:

$$\frac{50}{.85 \times .85 \times \frac{410}{440}} = \text{size of motor needed}$$

$$\frac{50}{.723 \times .93} = \text{size of motor needed}$$

$$\frac{50}{} = 74.6 \text{ or a 75 HP motor is needed}$$

volts. With a motor of 85 percent efficiency,

2188 • POWER BOATS

KEEPING A BOAT SHIPSHAPE

Regular, routine maintenance keeps up appearance and performance.

YOU might as well face it, there is no such thing as a maintenance-free boat. Don't confuse low maintenance with no maintenance, for no matter what type of material has been used in the construction of your boat, its looks will gradually deteriorate and its performance will become sluggish.

No one wants to become a slave to his boat, and one way to prevent it is to be sure that effort and money expended aren't wasted. You don't have to be a professional painter, joiner or a shipwright to keep your outfit up to snuff.

As a kid, I used to be sent to a church bake sale. One day, because I dallied too long, most of the choicer-looking cakes had disappeared, so it was quite by accident that I discovered that the best baker in town always covered her oven masterpieces with a messy icing. The slick, fancy-looking jobs sold right off, but those terrific chocolate cakes I learned to spot by their saggy, lumpy-looking frosting were always mine just as though I had reserved one in advance.

That theory of ignoring finish may be fine with cakes—at least if you want one just for eating and not a showy type for a wedding or an important company dinner—but finishes on cakes and boats are different. That chocolate icing I talked about covered some really tastily put together ingredients even though the finish looked

Often boats will have this much marine growth after a few months without antifouling paint.

Bottom of fiberglass hull wasn't coated with an antifouling paint, so barnacles must be scraped.

as though it had been smeared on with a piece of cedar shingle. But who wants the exterior of his boat or its brightwork to look as though it had been slopped on with an old hairbrush or dabbed on with a burlap sack? Marine varnishes and paints are expensive, far more expensive than house finishes because they are expected to withstand considerably rougher treatment by the elements. Three basic things are required of any marine finish job: painstaking preparation of the surface, proper choice of finish material and care in the final finish. What follows should make these three basics easier—but always remember that good results are based on a well-prepared surface.

PREPARATION OF SURFACES

• **To flow expensive varnish** over a sloppily-prepared surface is as disappointing in its result as to stuff an overweight old burlesque queen into a Dior evening gown. If old varnish is crazed, alligatored or shows fine cracks, no amount of fine quality varnish will hide the blemishes. If wood is badly stained, bleaching is necessary. In either event, old varnish must be removed.

• **One method** used to remove old varnish is to scrape with a hook-type cabinet tool. Trying to work with a dull scraper is as ineffective as attempting to do figures on skates with dull blades. The scraping tool must be in good condition which means that the edge must be filed sharp. When filing, be sure to follow the original bevel angle of the blade edge.

• **When using paint remover,** be lazy and let the remover do the work for you. Don't rush the job. Apply remover heavily over an area that you can scrape in about 15 minutes time.

Wait about 15 minutes, then apply remover to another patch the same size as the first. In about 15 minutes, the varnish will start to wrinkle, but lay the scraper down! In about a half an hour the surface should be ready. Apply a third patch of remover and then go to work on the first. By the time you have removed this, the second area should be ready to work on and you can progressively keep treating new sections. If you haven't fought the clock, you can rub the old varnish off with a cloth or push it off with a putty knife. Don't fight small patches to which hard varnish clings. Apply another dab of remover, go on with the next section and return to the stubborn patches in half an hour.

• **If tiny bits of varnish** cling to the pores of wood, rub them with bronze wool saturated with lacquer thinner. Never use steel wool in preparing a surface of a boat. Steel particles may remain and later cause rust spots.

• **To neutralize** paint remover, follow instructions on the can, since different brands call for different flushing liquids. Some require turpentine, others alcohol and still others benzol.

• **To bleach** and remove stains after finish has been removed from wood, make up a saturated solution of oxalic acid crystals and warm water. Apply the solution with a clean cloth. Wear rubber gloves to protect your hands. As the dark areas become lighter and smaller, dab additional acid solution until the stained area is completely bleached. When the saturated area is nearly dry, swab it with a neutralizing solution consisting of one quarter cup borax to a pint of hot water. After the area has dried, dust or preferably vacuum. Always bleach before sanding, since the bleaching process will roughen the wood.

• **A good finish** calls for a dust-free surface. Brush or use a vacuum cleaner first, then follow up by rubbing surface with a tack cloth. The latter is made with a section of cotton sheeting about a yard square.

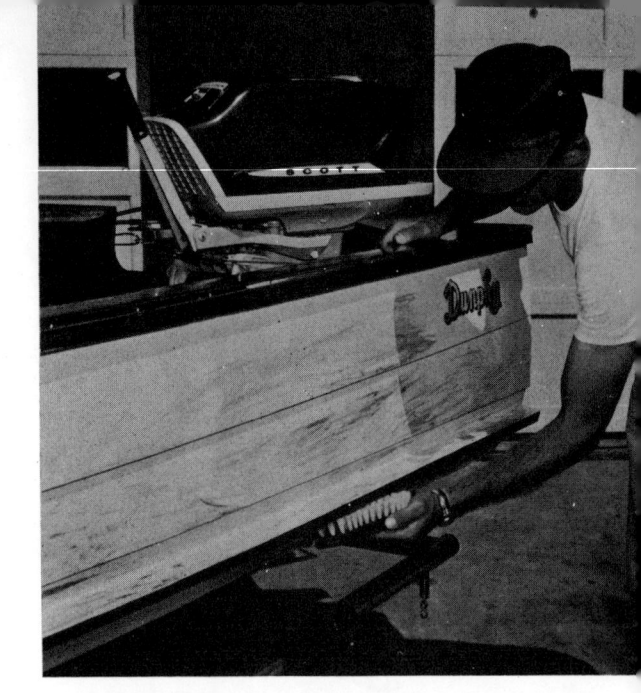

Trailboat operator can save a big clean-up job by scrubbing off grease and dirt after each use.

Soak the cloth thoroughly in hot water, then wring out. Sprinkle the damp surface with turpentine, then trickle a thin crisscrossing of varnish over the surface. Roll the cloth into a tight wad and knead it so that the turpentine and varnish are evenly spread over the entire cloth. This forms a sticky rag which, when rubbed over a surface to be varnished, will pick up most particles of dust. If the tack cloth becomes dry, simply moisten it again with warm water, squeeze it and its tackiness will be restored so that one tack cloth will serve for the entire job.

• **Always do varnish** finishing using two cans, one containing varnish, the other empty. Punch a couple of nail holes opposite each other near the top of the empty can. Push a section of wire (coat hanger) through these holes and bend over the ends. Don't shake the can containing varnish, for this will create air bubbles that later will cause pock marks. Dip the brush deeply into the fresh varnish, letting it drip into the spare can. Varnish dripping into the filled can will create air bubbles. The varnish-saturated brush will also contain air. Release the air bubbles from the brush by striking the brush gently against the wire suspended across the drip can.

• **When applying varnish,** ignore the direction of wood grain and stroke vertically on vertical surfaces. Varnish will flow and obliterate brush marks. Brush marks remaining in varnish are an indication of an insufficiently thick coating. Don't be a

Varnish finish lasts longer if swabbed regularly with fresh water. Salt water spray harms it.

Patch small blemishes or gouges immediately; it will prevent development of major deterioration.

pennypincher and attempt to work with too little varnish on your brush. Never apply a gloss finish over a gloss finish. Let a finish thoroughly dry then sand lightly to knock down the gloss. Go over the surface with a tack cloth and apply another coat.

• **Paint is unnecessary** to protect an aluminum boat, but if you prefer a painted surface, aluminum is no more difficult to paint than any other material. All grease, scale and marine growth must be removed. Scrape first then scrub the surface with a commercial de-greasing solvent. Sand the clean surface with medium-grit abrasive paper. Flush the clean and sanded surface with a prime wash, an etching liquid specially made for aluminum hull preparation and designed to assure good adhesion of paint to nonporous metal. Apply a coat of zinc chromate and follow up with two coats of good quality marine paint, preferably of a type specially formulated for use over aluminum.

• **Minor dents** in aluminum boats, actually stretched areas, may be worked out by hammering from the outer periphery of the dent inward with a rubber or plastic hammer. Deep dents or gouges should be filled with plastic aluminum. Holes and tears are most simply repaired by applying a riveted patch. Before riveting the patch, coat the damaged section liberally with plastic aluminum.

• **Never apply** an antifouling bottom paint directly to an aluminum boat without first applying a prime coat to the metal surface. The antifouling paint may contain copper or a metal oxide that will react with the aluminum to cause damaging galvanic corrosion.

• **Bare fir plywood** should never be sanded or the grain will lift. Apply a prime coat of Firzite and then sand.

• **Since the first coat** of finish applied to any boat will largely determine the life of the job, painting should only be done on dry surfaces, during dry weather and only on surfaces that are free from oil and grease.

• **A smooth surface** will result only if all nail and screw holes, gouges and splits are filled prior to painting. Apply a prime coat before filling imperfections with putty, seam cement, glazing compound or plastic wood; otherwise the oil in the filler compound may be wholly absorbed into the dry wood, leading to crumbling of the filling compound.

• **Painting** should be done only when the temperature ranges between 45 and 90° F, varnishing at 60° F or above. The colder the day, the slower will be the drying time. Overly hot temperature may cause blistering or wrinkling.

• **Fiberglass** may be painted but, prior to painting, the surface should be thoroughly scrubbed with a detergent to remove wax

2192 • POWER BOATS

When calking cotton has been tamped in place it should be primed. It's best to use round brush.

After calking and priming, the seams should be filled with a compound made for this purpose.

or any residue of grease film, then a fiberglass neutral primer should be applied. Sand within four to six hours of application. Two prime coats are usually recommended, followed by any good grade marine enamel.

- **To remove heavy coats** of paint from canvas surfaces, liberally coat the area with varnish remover and then cover the varnish remover with newspapers or damp rags to reduce the evaporation rate of the active ingredients. Keep this cover in place for about 45 minutes.

- **Scrape softened paint** with a scraper on which the corners have been rounded to prevent cutting. As a final step in removing paint from canvas, rub with a stiff bristled scrub brush.

- **Marine grass,** barnacles and other marine growth are more easily removed when they are still wet, just after the boat has been hauled. Use a long-handled garden edging tool, a hoe or an ice scraper for the job.

HINTS ON BUYING MATERIALS

- **Simplify the color scheme** of your boat as a first step in painting economy. Three or four contrasting colors may give your boat a gay, circus wagon appearance, but each time you introduce a new color you pave the way for extra maintenance costs. There's less waste overestimating on two colors than on three or four.

- **In estimating** amount of material, assume that one gallon of marine paint will cover 500 square feet of already painted surface or 325 square feet of unpainted surface. A gallon of varnish will cover approximately 750 square feet of surface previously varnished, about two thirds as much when applied to bare wood. Expect to remove about 200 to 250 square feet of old paint per gallon of paint or varnish remover.

- **To figure** the number of square feet of bottom surface, the design of the boat must be considered. For an outboard of semi-planing type, multiply the overall length of the hull in feet by the waterline beam at the stern. Deduct 20% of this total for taper toward the bow.

For deep keel boats, multiply the waterline length by the draft in feet, then multiply this figure by 3.5.

The bottom surface of a sailboat of centerboard type is figured by multiplying waterline length by draft in feet times three.

- **The area of the sides** of a boat in square feet is approximated by multiplying the length of the hull measured around the gunwale in feet by the maximum freeboard in feet and multiplying this result by 1.5. The deck area of a boat may be approximated by multiplying the length of the gunwale in feet by the maximum beam in feet, then multiplying the result by .75. Since the superstructure is rectangular in shape, there's no trick to figuring its square footage

After cleaning the bottom, cover minor scrapes, etc., with surfacing putty; then sand and paint.

The easy way to keep track of removed hardware is to mark up separate envelopes for all parts.

- **In choosing colors**, keep in mind that white or brightly-colored foredecks may create an annoying glare to the helmsman in bright sunlight. White or light-colored hulls will look longer and lower than dark hulls and will be more visible at night.

- **The proper choice** of color for a cabin interior is a personal matter, though a strongly recommended selection is a lighter tint of the deck color.

- **High gloss finishes** are easier to maintain, but softer-finish, nonreflective paints are recommended for modern craft that have a broad expanse of glass. Otherwise, annoying flashing reflections from sunlight on the water will dart about the cabin's interior.

- **A professional finish** calls for suitable brushes. A cheap brush can make an enamel finish look as though it had been given a treatment of hair restorer, guaranteed to make bristles grow on a billiard ball. Cheap brushes have horsehair, which does not have flagged ends. Resulting paint jobs look as though they had been laid on with a comb. Better brushes are made of tapered animal bristles that have split ends, known as flags. Look for them, for the flagged ends help paint adhere to the bristles and spread paint evenly.

- **Synthetic bristle brushes** should not be used with any paints containing lacquer solvents or alcohol as thinner. The bristles may dissolve or kink like a bad permanent. Nylon brushes require break-in and should

Wear gauze face mask when sanding fiberglass or a paint containing arsenic or any other poison.

be suspended in linseed oil for a day or two before they are used.

- **The complement of brushes** for a boat paint job should include a narrow sash brush for finer work and boot topping, a three-inch or four-inch flat wall brush, a double-thick, chisel-pointed bristle brush for varnishing only and a painter's duster.

- **Dust from certain paints** can cause irritation to mucous membranes. When sanding prime coats containing lead or zinc chromate or antifouling bottom paints containing arsenic or mercury, it is recom-

2194 • POWER BOATS

mended that ... use a gauze face mask.

• **Since ever**... f boat construction material (me... ss and wood) calls for a marine finish specially blended for that material, consult with your marine dealer. Be sure before you buy that the selection of a finish is the proper one for its intended job.

• **Plastic marine coatings,** epoxies or polyurethanes, cost considerably more than conventional finishes, but they are claimed to stand up far longer than conventional paint, adhere better on wood, metal and fiberglass, resist marring, scratching and staining and remain unaffected by alkalies, acids and common chemicals. These claims are largely true. There are both two-component systems and one-package systems. The two-component systems give the toughest and more chemically-resistant coating. The one-package systems are less expensive and easier to apply.

• **Can you apply** epoxy finishes over old paint or varnish? You can, provided it is not recently applied paint that will be softened by the epoxy solvent. However, it is foolish to apply epoxy over an old marine finish. One of epoxy's greatest assets is its tremendous adhesion. If the old paint, which has lesser adhesion to the surface, fails, contact with the under surface is lost and the new paint will peel.

• **Epoxies are self-primed** and do not require an undercoat or primer. In fact, a prime coat is undesirable. You want epoxy to bond directly to the surface.

Marine dealers can offer many time savers such as clear aerosol spray that protects hardware.

MAINTENANCE AND REPAIR TIPS

• **Painting the inside** of a centerboard trunk is difficult. This and other confined areas may be handled by tacking a piece of carpeting around a flat stick and using the carpeting as a paint applicator.

• **Breaks in steel** hulls should never be welded with an arc or electric welder. The heat is too intense and may buckle the sheet steel. Instead, insist that steel boat patching be done, using a coated welding rod and acetylene torch.

• **If you are planning** to refinish striping on a wooden deck, always apply the striping after the final varnish coat has been given to the planking. This will prevent seam striping from turning yellow. Striping is easily accomplished with a striping wheel carried by any hardware store. This is a handy, simple-to-use little gadget, a plastic tube containing paint of the right consistency and a ball point wheel arrangement that feeds the paint as the wheel is run down the seam.

• **If you remove** trim molding and deck hardware, I recommend that you draw a sketch of your boat and identify by numbers or letters the location of each item as it is removed. Place each item, along with its screws or bolts, in a separately-numbered envelope. Repair or fill enlarged or stripped screw holes.

• **Name plates** and control panel labels often combine colored enamel with metal. White or colored paint often is applied to

Firzite is good to use as a sealer and a base before applying a paint finish to new plywood.

the recessed lettered areas. To refurbish, polish the raised, exposed metal first, then paint to match original color or letters. Before the paint sets up, carefully wipe the polished surface so as not to disturb recessed, painted areas.

• **When possible, avoid hauling** a wooden boat during extremely warm weather, for the water-saturated underwater planking, exposed to the air, will dry partially and offer ideal temperature conditions for fungi to make a start. Wood decay fungi multiply fastest between 75° and 85° F and decay is more rapid in fresh than in salt water. Decay requires dampness and will not take place when the moisture content remains below 20% and will not occur in completely submerged planking, since decay fungi must have air.

• **Periodic buffing** of fiberglass boats with a good quality auto body wax will keep the finish from deteriorating.

• **Sand is an enemy** of marine paint and varnish. Thoughtful guests wipe their feet and brush sand from bathing suits before boarding.

• **When beaching** a boat, some skippers place a shallow pan of water in the cockpit so that passengers in boarding can rinse their feet.

• **Secure anchors** in chocks both as a safety measure and to prevent abrasion. To help preserve the deck, rinse anchors before bringing them aboard. Grit underfoot is easily ground in.

New polyurethane calking compound for decks is good since it holds up longer than many others.

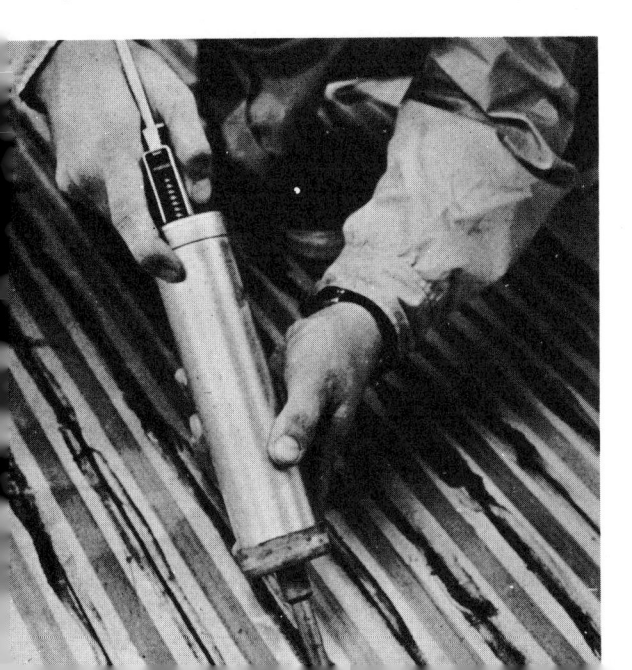

• **Often when hardware** is removed for painting, the fresh coats cover screw or bolt holes. To avoid delay in locating holes when replacing fittings, put match sticks in screw holes after the final brush strokes have been made.

• **When recalking** a carvel-planked boat, do not drive calking in too tightly or apply too much compound, for planks will swell appreciably. Seams should be hollow when the boat goes overboard, otherwise swelling will push calking or seam compound out and may draw planking away from frames and ribs. At best, it will bulge out and create extra drag. •

Check steering cables periodically and tighten up the fastenings for the pulleys and hardware.

Minor fiberglass hull damage is easily repaired with a kit of resin, catalyst and glass cloth.

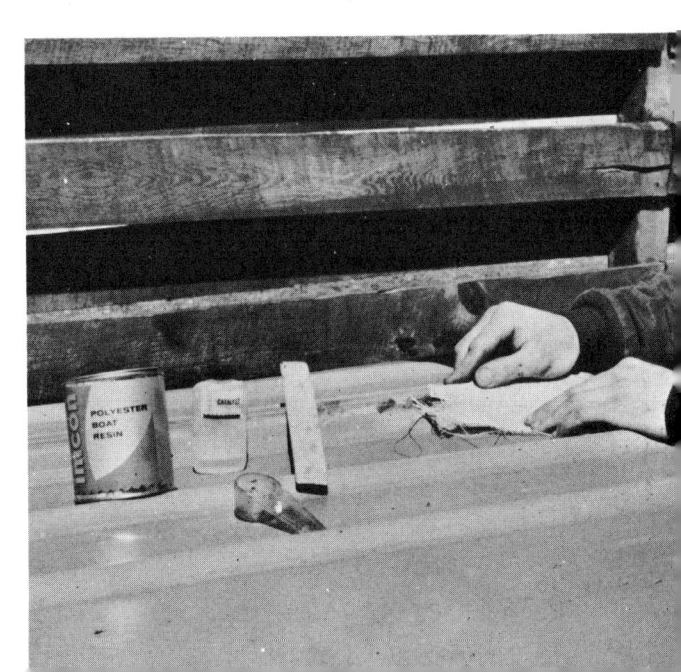

Hotei

By Hal Kelly

Here's a 23-ft. family boat with three bunks, two cockpits, all conveniences.

HOTEI is 23 feet long with an 8½-foot beam and every inch a family boat. Menfolk can ride in the forward cockpit where the helmsman has a clear view. Youngsters can sleep or amuse themselves safely in the large cabin which has 5-foot 11-inch headroom, bunks for three, galley and marine toilet. The gals can sun themselves in the roomy aft cockpit. All are well distributed, not crowded together near the stern. And with passenger weight shifted forward, Hotei levels off for speed under power of a Merc 800. The 80-hp motor drives her at 25 mph with six aboard!

With only two aboard, Hotei does better than 27 mph—and she gives a comfortable ride at this speed even in a three-foot chop. She also banks into a turn like a fine runabout—not digging in on the outside to throw passengers all over the boat like

POWERED with an 80 hp outboard motor, Hotei will do over 25 mph with six passengers.

TRANSOM FRAME is almost complete here as last notch for batten is chiseled out.

CLAMPS and more clamps are required in building up the laminated stem on the rig.

many a small cabin cruiser. Nor is she a wet boat. We've been out in five-foot waves and stayed dry.

A lot of thought went into storage space construction. There's a large compartment in the forward cockpit for charts and other items. The cabin has several shelves for small items and storage under the bunks for water skis, life jackets, etc. The aft cockpit has a 19x24-inch storage bin over six feet long that doubles as a seat. On each side of the motor well there's storage for battery, bumpers, line and spare props with six-gallon gas tanks below. The well itself is designed to take two Merc 800's or 500's if you wish and there's room for a 25-gallon long-cruise gas tank below it.

Needless to say, you can't build Hotei in a couple of weeks. Our building time was slightly over 400 hours—but the total cost for the hull with Fiberglas bottom, sink, head and hardware was under $800. A comparable manufactured boat would cost close to $3,000. Consider what you have to earn to be able to spend the $3,000 and your building time is well worth it. A Gator trailer, Model 565, is used to transport the boat to the waterways. This piece of equipment costs a little over $600 but it will save you that in mooring and hauling fees in a few years.

All framing in Hotei is one-inch mahogany which, in the dressed state you buy it, is about the $\frac{13}{16}$-inch thickness specified in the drawings. Therefore, the lumber is bought in planks and ripped to size for battens, etc., on a table saw. Besides flat-

PLAN LAYOUT

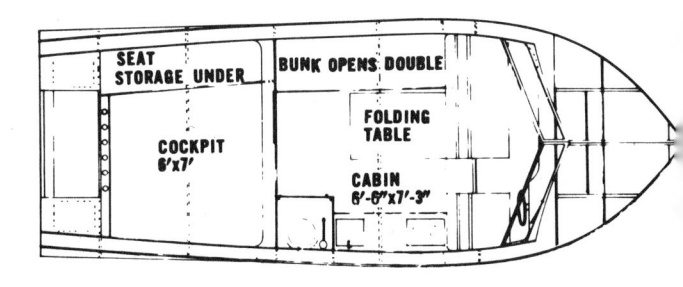

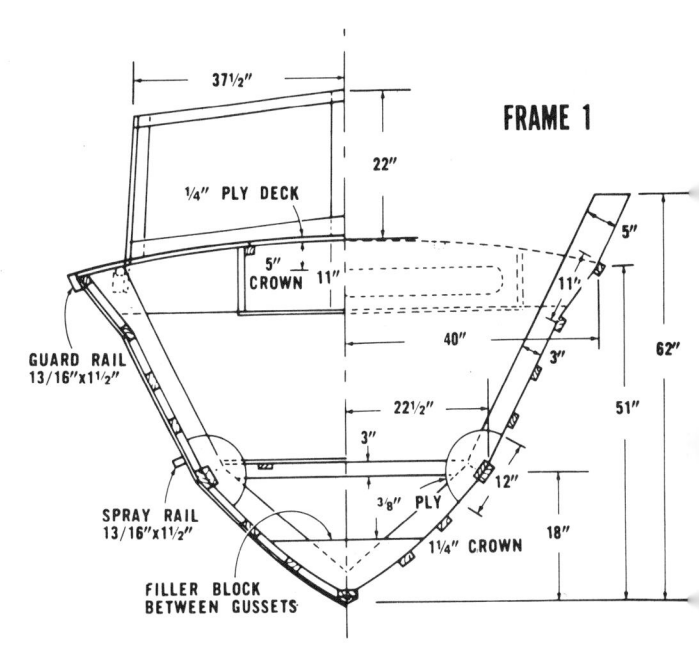

FRAME 1

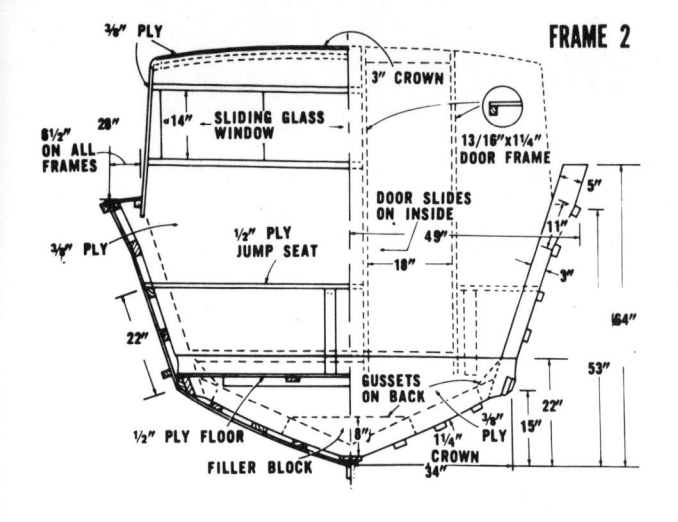

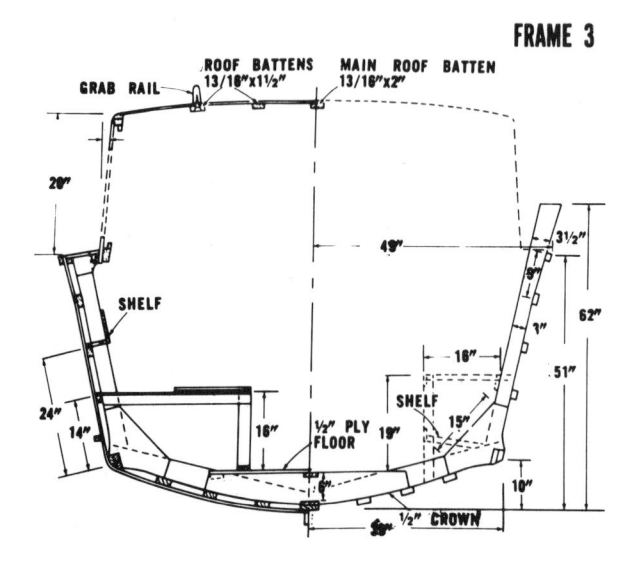

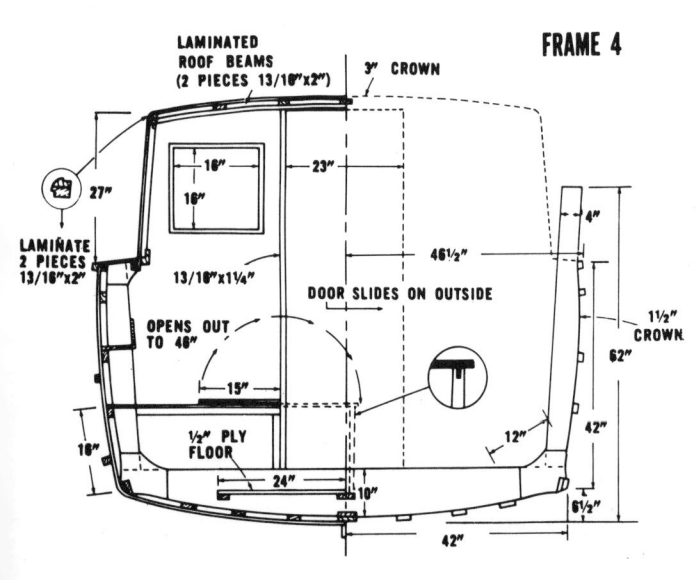

head bronze screws, silicon bronze Stronghold nails (made by Independent Nail & Packing Co., Bridgewater, Mass.) are used extensively in assembly and Weldwood resorcinal glue is used in all the joints.

Construction follows a thorough study of the drawings. Start by laying out the six frames and the transom on a level floor. Draw each outline in a different-color chalk, one on top of the other. In this way you will be able to detect any obvious mistakes.

The transom frame is made first with the joints lapped, glued and fastened with one-inch, No. 12 Stronghold nails. After notching it for the keelson, chines and battens, the half-inch plywood transom is secured to it with glue and the same type nails. All frames are butted at the joints and 3/8-inch plywood gussets are glued and nailed on each side of each joint, again using the one-inch, No. 12 nails. The frames are notched only for the keelson and the chines. If notched for the battens, they would require more work, be weakened and limber holes would have to be bored so that bilge water could flow through. Nowhere in the boat do the frames come in contact with the plywood planking.

The jig is erected after the frames and transom are complete. This is an important step because any misalignment would cause progressively worse misalignment in the hull as you advance in construction. Be sure all members are parallel, vertical and level as required.

After the frames and transom are set up on the jig and temporarily braced, a piece of three-inch-wide mahogany (only widths will be given since the $\frac{13}{16}$-inch thickness is used throughout) is butted between frames one and two below the line of the keelson. The frames are glued and screwed to this piece. The joints are also reinforced on each side with small blocks set in resin-saturated Fiberglas cloth and nailed. It is over this piece that the laminated stem and keelson are spliced.

The keelson, made of two three-inch widths, is next installed. The first piece is glued and screwed to the frames and transom and the piece butted between frames one and two. The second piece is in turn glued and screwed to the first. Note, however, that it is six inches shorter at the forward end. One-inch, No. 10 screws are used in both cases.

A stem jig is next cut to the proper shape

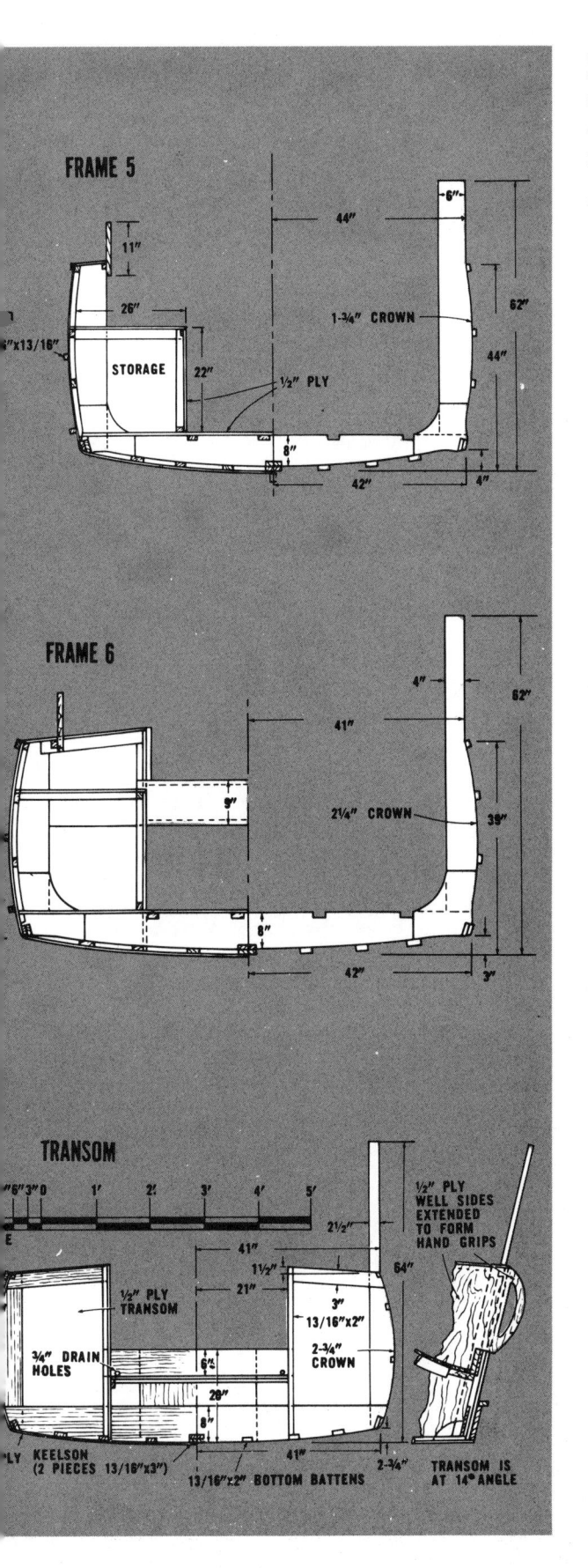

and temporarily fastened to frame one. The stem is laminated from four pieces. Take two three-inch-wide pieces and rip them down the center of the thickness to make the four. Then spread a generous amount of glue on the four pieces and bend them into place on the jig. The first two pieces butt against the inner member of the keelson and are glued and screwed to the brace between the first two frames. The second two pieces lap over the inner member of the keelson and butt against the outer member. They're glued and screwed to the inner member of the keelson. A number of C clamps hold the pieces together on the jig until the glue sets.

All bottom battens are two inches wide. The side ones are a half inch narrower. The battens are carefully fastened in place after some necessary fairing on all frames. Glue and 1½-inch No. 10 screws are used. Placement is important because the rear seat, bunks and front jump seats rest on or are fastened to many of the side battens. With the exception of two battens, all run to the stem where they are glued and screwed after careful beveling. The chines go in the same way except that they are made of two pieces of two-inch wood for strength and easier bending.

Fairing is always a tedious job but the work can be cut down considerably with a Skill planer and a simple jig. I clamped a 30-inch piece of aluminum to the base of the planer with a pair of Sure Grips. The aluminum, flush against the battens, acted as a fairing stick and enabled me to plane the chines and keelson to the proper bevels easily. If you don't own a planer and don't want to buy one, it's well worth renting.

The planking is five-ply, ⅜-inch-thick Weldwood Royal Marine plywood. This can be obtained in 42-inch widths 24 feet long. The 42-inch width leaves very little waste. Four pieces are used. Plank the sides first, using glue and one-inch No. 12 Stronghold nails at all battens, the stem and the transom. Another person inside with a weight against each batten will help in the fastening. The best procedure is to have a few friends hold the planking in place while you mark it off. Then trim the excess. I used a Homemaster Routo-Jig made by Porter Cable for this job. It's good for cutting all the planking because it cuts with a bit-like blade at high rpm and does not chatter the plywood like a saber saw.

When cut, the planking is clamped in

2200 • POWER BOATS

LENGTH of right-angle aluminum clamped to planer makes good chine fairing guide.

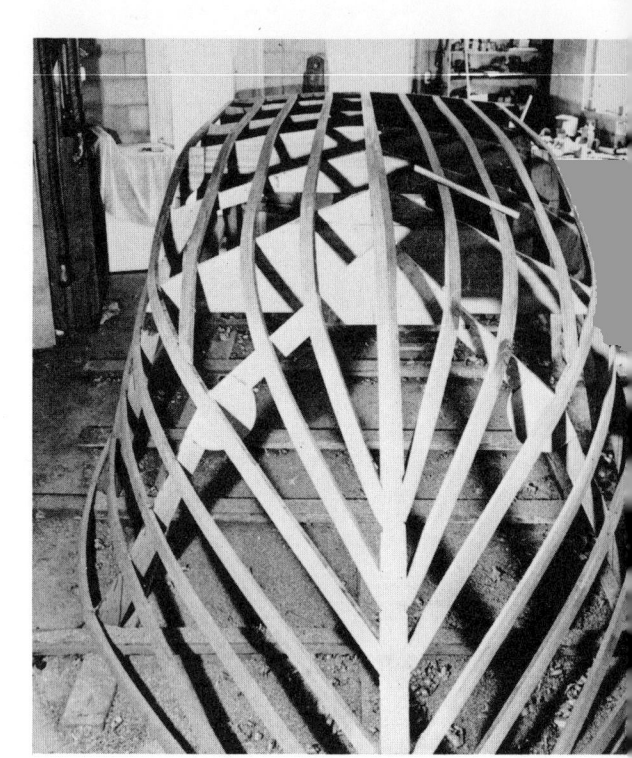

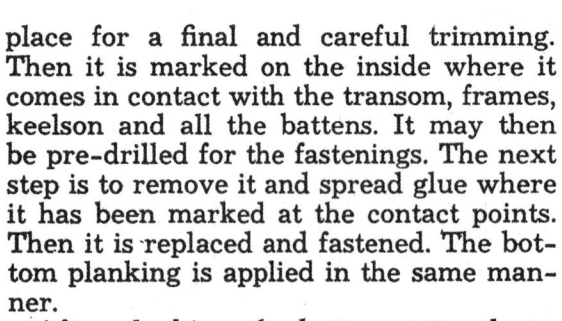

FRAMING faired and ready for planking. Note gussets on each side of frame joints.

place for a final and careful trimming. Then it is marked on the inside where it comes in contact with the transom, frames, keelson and all the battens. It may then be pre-drilled for the fastenings. The next step is to remove it and spread glue where it has been marked at the contact points. Then it is replaced and fastened. The bottom planking is applied in the same manner.

After planking, the bottom gets a layer of Fiberglas. The spray rails are first glued on the outside and fastened from the inside with screws. Then the chines are rounded off and the bottom is rough-sanded in preparation. Since the sides are also rough-sanded in that area. The cloth is laid on one half of the bottom at a time. A 50-inch width is used on each side and it laps the keel line by about three inches. Lay the cloth in place and trim it to size. Then remove it and give the whole bottom

FIBERGLAS covers the bottom up to the spray rails. Work from stern toward bow.

HULL turned upright on trailer for topside finishing. It shouldn't be allowed to twist.

POWER BOATS • 2201

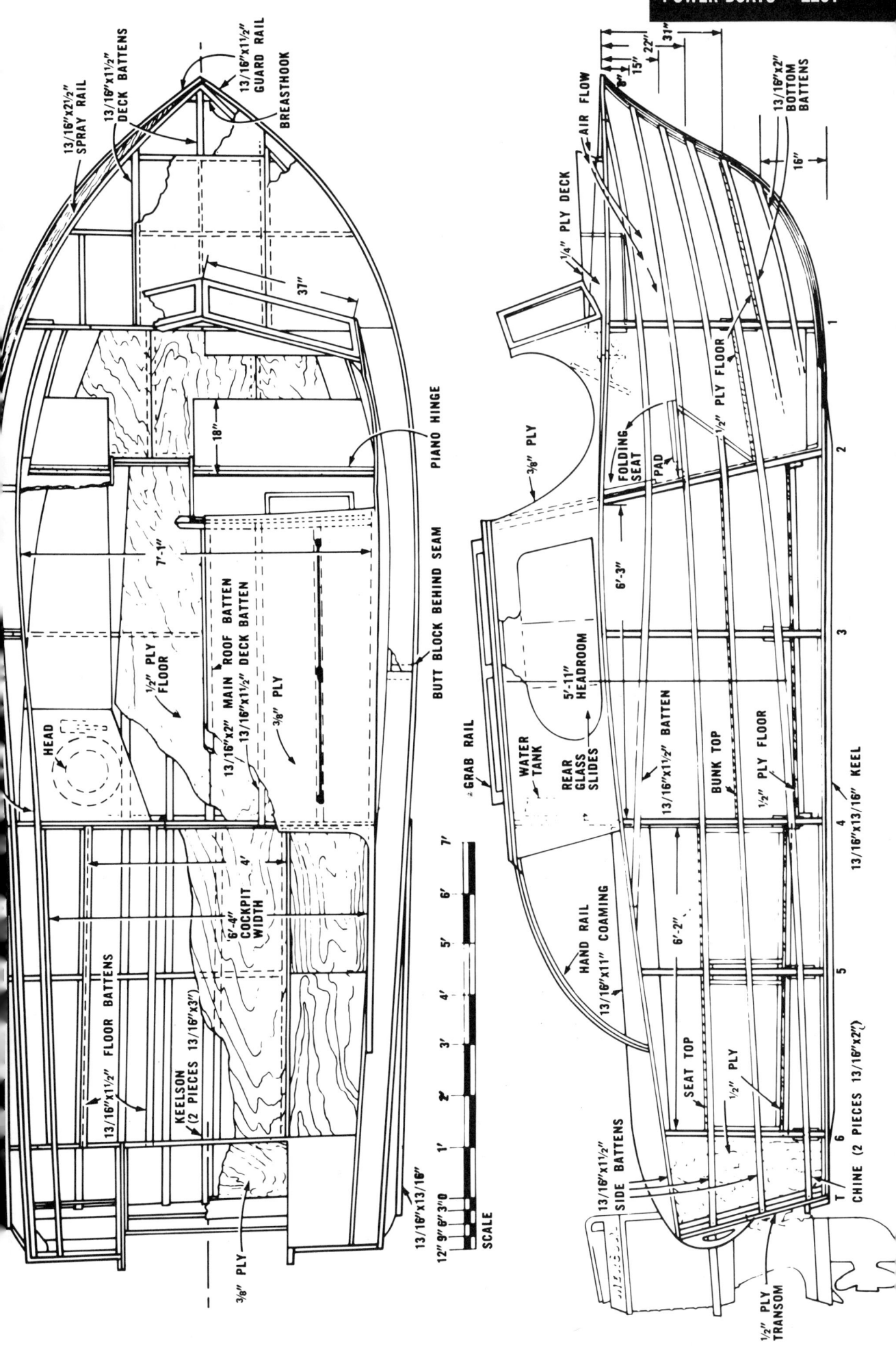

2202 • POWER BOATS

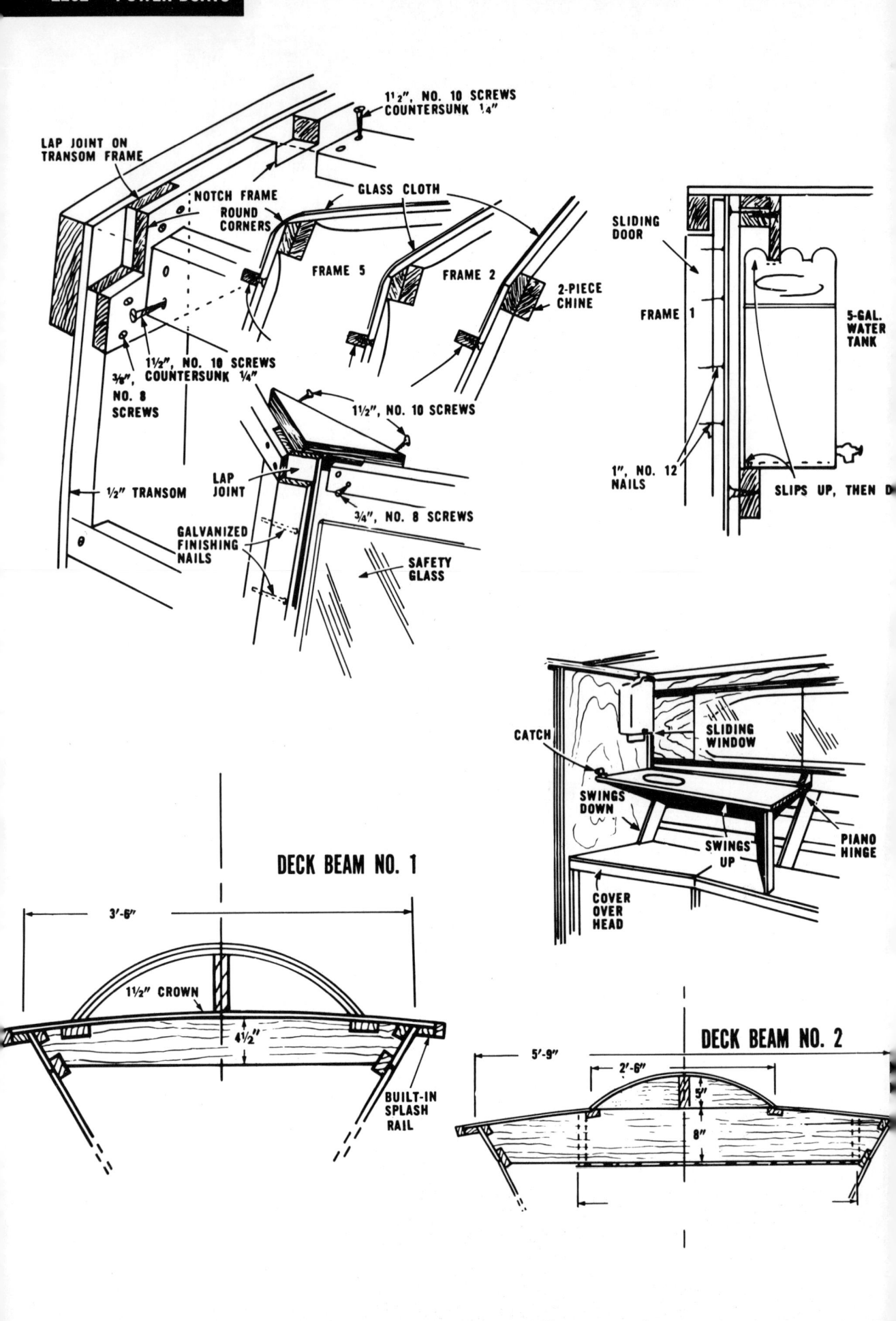

POWER BOATS • 2203

FORWARD DECK, including the curved air scoop, is applied in four separate pieces.

BLOCKS are set in Fiberglas and nailed to reinforce frames at all batten points.

BILGE is vacuumed before painting. Note framing of well and compartments at stern.

CABIN SIDES are installed after decking is in place. Cabin front follows the sides.

a coat of resin. When the resin has hardened, mix up another batch with a pigment added if you wish. I used bright red, mixing the pigment in thoroughly before adding the hardener. Using a cheap brush, coat one side of the bottom with the resin and then apply the cloth. When the cloth is smooth, apply another coat of resin, spreading it with a paint roller. Be sure it is well saturated and then allow it to harden.

When the whole bottom has hardened, use a disk sander to feather the edges of the cloth at the keel line and near the spray rail. Then lay a three-inch-wide strip of cloth along the keel line from the transom to the point of the stem. Before the resin has hardened, screw a one-inch mahogany keel strip along the centerline. This protects the bottom in beaching. Fiberglas materials are available from Glass Plastic Supply Co., 1605 W. Elizabeth

2204 • POWER BOATS

FRAME, TRANSOM, AND STEM PLACEMENT ON JIG

NOTE: FRAMES 1, 3, 4, 5 AND 6 ARE 90° TO JIG

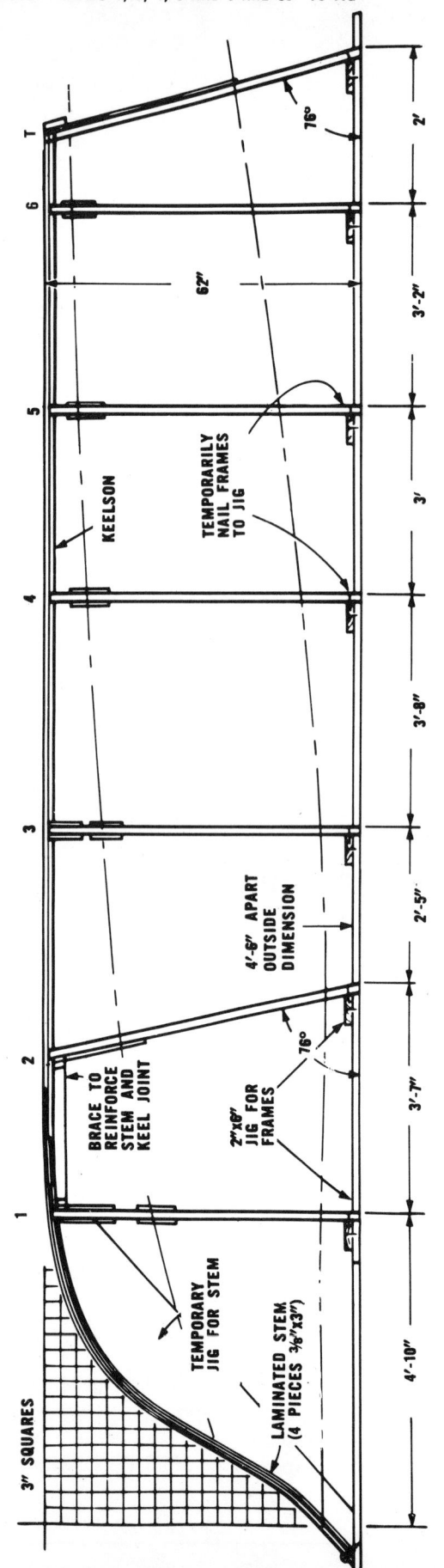

- 76°
- 2'
- 3'-2"
- 62" KEELSON
- TEMPORARILY NAIL FRAMES TO JIG
- 3'
- 3'-8"
- 4'-6" APART OUTSIDE DIMENSION
- 2'-5"
- 76°
- 2"x6" JIG FOR FRAMES
- BRACE TO REINFORCE STEM AND KEEL JOINT
- 3'-7"
- TEMPORARY JIG FOR STEM
- LAMINATED STEM (4 PIECES ⅜"x3")
- 4'-10"
- 3" SQUARES

ROOF BATTENS fit into notches in the cabin roof beams and are screw-fastened.

STEERING WHEEL is secured to box on forward deck beam. Note chart compartment.

SINK is mounted in hinged panel which drops to allow use of single bunk below.

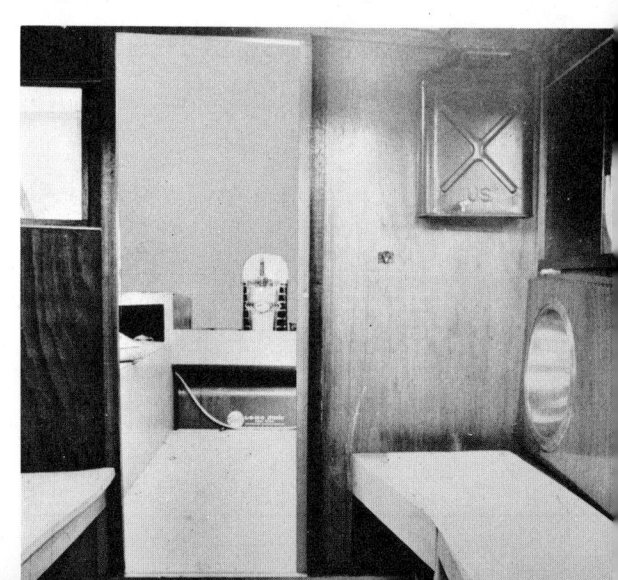

LAUNCHING from the Gator trailer. Note: the bed tilts and wheels aren't in the water.

Ave., Linden, N. J. They will also supply literature on application.

The hull is now turned over (with the help of about seven friends) and placed in a level, well-braced position. I set it on the Gator trailer. I laid three layers of glass cloth on the inside of the stem, also installing a bow eye at this time. For added strength, I also fastened a small block on each side of every frame and batten joint. Again, these blocks were set in resin-saturated glass cloth and nailed.

After trimming off the excess on the frames and transom which was used to fasten them to the jig at a working height, the top of the side planking is installed. This is made up of scraps left over from the sides and bottom. These flaring parts really help to keep the boat dry. When they're on, the top edges are planed even with the sheer batten.

The sides of the motor well run from the bottom battens to the top and from frame six to the transom, forming a real strong transom brace. Note that another piece of wood six inches wide is fastened to the transom between these pieces.

The decking is quarter-inch mahogany marine plywood. All the flooring and the storage bin is half-inch exterior fir plywood. Most floor battens are glued and screwed to the flooring. The exception is where the flooring butts. These battens are glued and screwed to the frames.

With all deck battens in place, the bilge is cleaned and painted up to the floor line. Use one coat of Firzite and one coat of marine paint. Bottoms of the floorboards are also painted and the flooring is then screwed in place.

After the decking is on, the cabin sides are installed. They're followed by the front and rear bulkheads as illustrated. The windshield glass is shatterproof and Plexiglas is used in the cabin.

Inside, bunks are framed up and installed as indicated. A head is a handy thing to have and I installed one under a removable section of the port bunk. The sink in the hinged panel above the bunk drains into the head and a five-gallon water tank is mounted on the bulkhead above the sink. For padding the seats and bunks, I used Ensolite, Type M. Lightweight, non-absorbent, fire resistant and dimensionally stable, it is easily bonded to the wood with contact cement. Available in 5x7-foot sheets, it costs about a dollar a square foot.

After painting with marine enamel and applying an anti-fouling paint to the bottom if you're going to leave the boat in salt water, all that remains to finish the boat is to install the deck hardware and lights, a compass and a fog horn. •

LARGE SCALE PLANS

will greatly simplify construction of this boat, HOTEI. Please consult your PLANS REFERENCE LISTING for the exact source and price. Refer to Plan Number 109.

2206 • POWER BOATS

Ski Tow

Stylish and sturdy, this fine boat can be built from plans or frame kit—with ease.

By Glen L. Witt

Wide cockpit can "sleep" two when seats are removed—providing an eight ft. long flat floor space.

THE "SKI TOW" is a modern-styled outboard runabout intended for construction by the amateur builder. The overall center line length of 14' 8" combined with a 6' 6" beam makes the hull capable of handling almost all of the larger motors. For all around general usage, such as water skiing, use about a 50 HP outboard motor. An unusual feature is the large flat cockpit floor. Since the seats are removable they can be shifted to any position and the flat area be utilized for sleeping. With the seats removed a full 5' wide by 8' long flat area is available. An excellent safety feature of this boat is the self-bailing well that separates the motor from the cockpit area and also provides self bailing for any water coming over the transom cutout.

Plans and Patterns as well as Frame Kits, Fastening and Fiberglass Kits are available from "GLEN L" at the address noted in the box that accompanies this article.

Lumber for building should be first grade, free from shakes and knots. All plywood used should be edge stamped EXT-DFPA to insure that the material will stand up in marine conditions. All joints throughout the construction should be glued with the plastic resin type considered satisfactory although the rescorinol type is preferable.

When the term "nails" is used it refers to the annular ring type boat nails. Bronze or hot dipped galvanized screws are used in other points and are preferable to the brass which is rather weak and tends to fracture under stress.

The frames are constructed from standard 1" material with corner gussets on either side of ⅜" plywood. Throughout these instructions the term 1" material will refer to "four quarters" lumberyard material. Such stock will usually result in finished lumber about ¾" to ⅞" in thickness. The bottom frame member at the transom frame No. 1, No. 2, and No. 3 are all in single width from chine to chine. At the No. 4 frame, however, the bottom frame is made in two halves joined together over a backing member called floor timber. Note that a slot is left so that the stem will mate to the floor timber while fitting between the side frame members, in this instance. The stem, breasthook, chine blocking, and transom knee are all made from laminations of ¾″ plywood. The chine blocking is that member that rests in the ledge on the stem to accurately position the chine log. The upper portion rests on the ledge while the lower part lock notches around the stem. The breasthook is similar in nature but rests on top of the stem to accurately position the sheer clamps. The stem, as noted, in the drawings is merely two layers of ¾″ plywood laminated together. In all cases coat the laminations with glue and fasten together with 1¼″ nails or 1½″ No. 8 screws. The transom knee reinforces the junctions from the keel to the transom and is built up from three laminations of ¾″ plywood glued and fastened as the aforementioned laminated members.

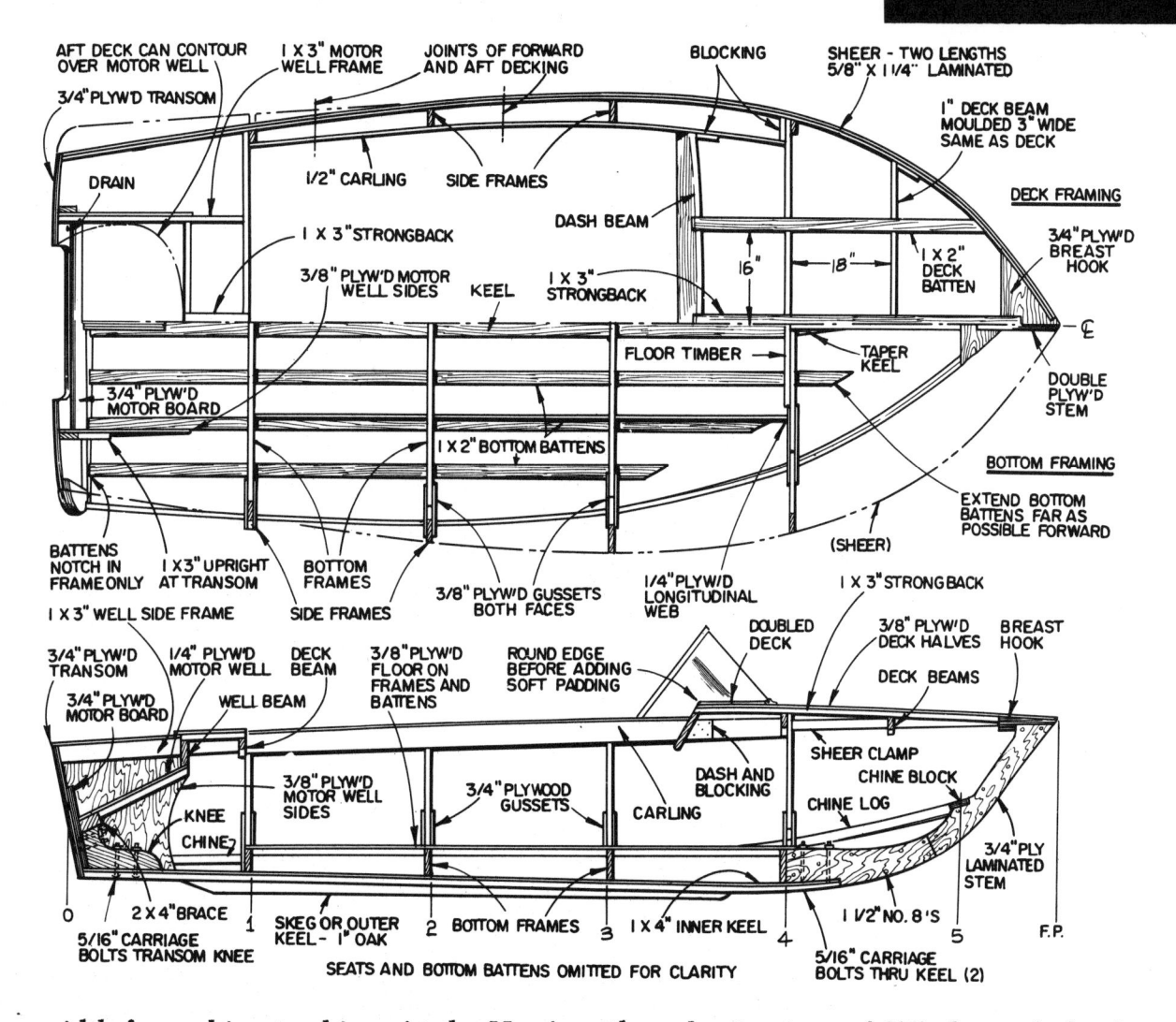

The hull is built bottom side up on a simple building form consisting of two longitudinal members. Each of the frames is aligned carefully in position and the stem breasthook assembly located accurately the required distance below the form. The keel member of 1″ x 4″ laminated on the inside with ⅜″ plywood is then sprung into position and bolted to the stem. The sheer clamps are put on in a vertical plane in two laminations of ⅝″ x 1¼″ material. The 1″ x 2″ chine logs are sprung in from the bow starting aft anchoring at the chine blocking first and fitting into beveled notches in each of the frames with 2″ No. 10 screws.

All of the members must be faired or beveled so that the planking will lie flat to all members. It is best to install the 1″ x 2″ battens after the fairing is accomplished so they may be set in ex-

POWER BOATS

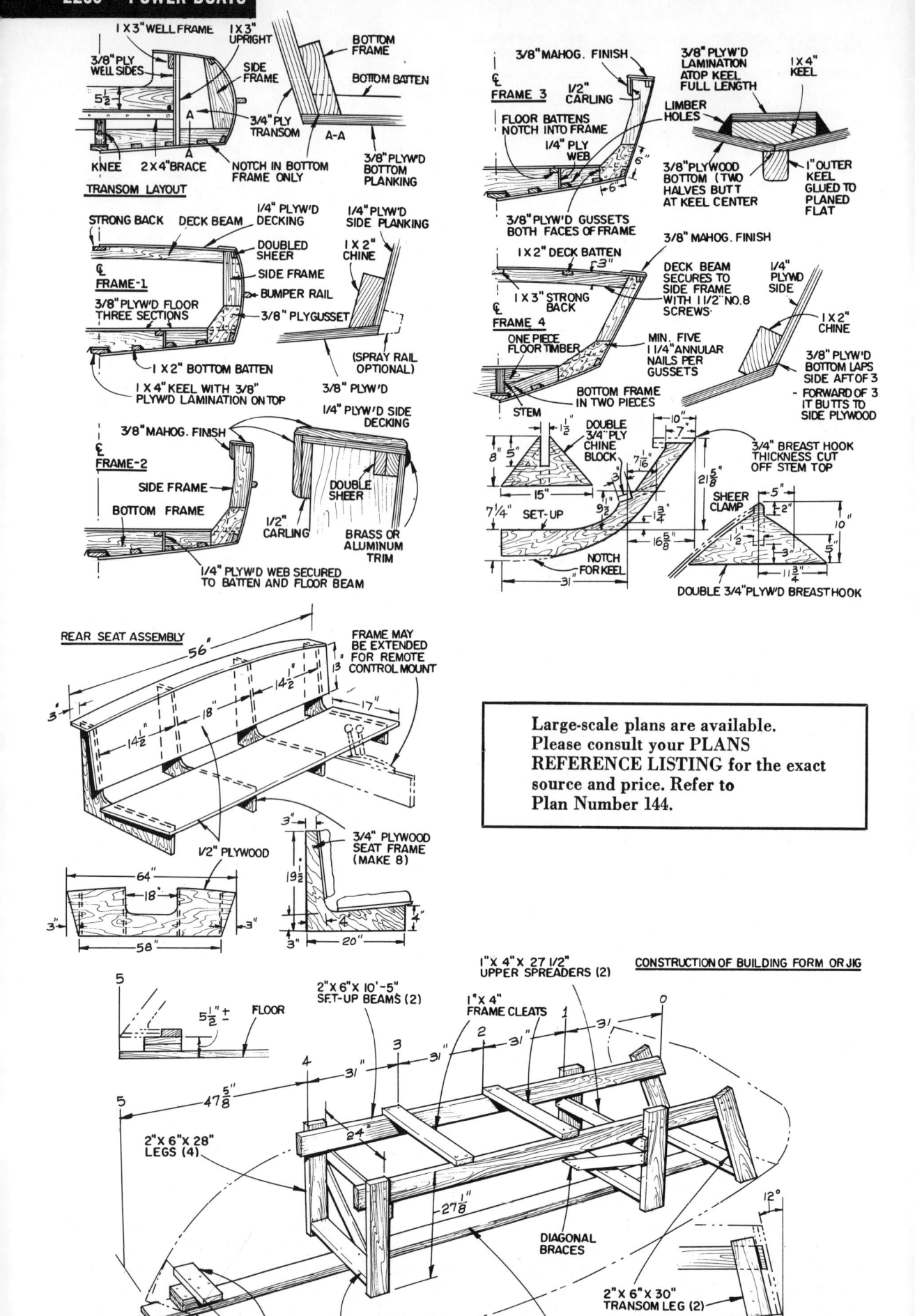

Large-scale plans are available. Please consult your PLANS REFERENCE LISTING for the exact source and price. Refer to Plan Number 144.

Framing is beveled for a perfect fit, then checked with short piece of scrap as shown.

Putting finishing touches on bumper rails that extend around sides and transom area.

actly the thickness of the material to be used. Take care in the fairing that the lines are all smooth and even without humps or bumps.

The side planking of ¼" plywood, preferably in full length, is leaned up against the side of the boat and roughly marked to fit. The only part that is necessary to fit closely is that portion forward of frame No. 4 that will butt join with the bottom planking. Aft of this point, along the chine, the stem, transom, and sheer, the planking may overhang to be trimmed off after application. In applying the planking coat the mating surfaces with glue and fasten the planking in place with 1" No. 8 screws starting at midpoint. Position the area that will butt to the bottom planking first then roll in the curved aft section progressively to the transom.

The ⅜" thick bottom planking is installed in similar fashion. Again it will be necessary to fit the panel to the side planking forward of frame No. 4 and also along the keel and stem area. After fitting all the planking in place trim the overhanging areas, putty the holes, and sand smooth. The hull may then be righted preparatory to the installation of the interior.

The decking area is faired smooth and the carling members as well as the intermediate deck beams and dash beams fastened into position. The fore and aft strongback and deck beams notch into each of these beams and end either at the breasthook or taper to fit against the chine.

The motor well is ruggedly constructed with uprights from the second batten outward from the keel with ⅜" sides. These sides form the motor well area and also provide reinforcement for the transom. Athwartships across the top of the transom knee a 2" x 4" lumberyard member is used for additional reinforcing for the tray bottom.

The floodboards are ⅜" thick plywood put on in three pieces and are 8' in overall length. The seats are intended to float free on this structure and can be moved from point to point, placed back to back, or even removed entirely for a flat sleeping area. The seats are constructed of ¾" plywood with ⅜" plywood backs and seats. Upholstery can be to the builders own desires or life preserver cushions used to pad the seats.

The "SKI TOW" is intended for outboard motors, however, a small lightweight inboard/outboard type unit, not to exceed 500 pounds, could be installed. When an inboard/outboard is used the motor should be mounted on longitudinal stringers extending as far forward as possible. These will bear on top of the frames and be blocked and bolted to each with a 2" x 2" oak upright. Space the stringers to suit the particular motor to be used. Minor deviations will be required at the transom depending on the type of inboard/outboard used. Controls and fittings are optional with the builder.

The hull may or may not be fiberglassed as the builder desires. If the fiberglass and resin is applied, only a paint intended for use over this material should be used. Needless to say good marine paints and primers should be used according to the manufacturer's directions throughout the construction.

2210 • POWER BOATS

Length is 7 feet 9 inches, beam is 4 feet, depth is 14 inches. Weight is about 79 pounds.

Ring-a-ding

Even an amateur can do a professional job on this fine design.

By C. P. and E. D. Burgess

Plan revisions by Edwin Monk

HERE'S AN IDEAL all-purpose plywood dinghy. Handy for the yachtsman who needs a strong seaworthy craft or the sportsman who needs a lightweight cartop boat. It is easy for youngsters to row, yet sturdy enough for a small outboard motor. With all these features this little dinghy is simple enough in design for even a beginner to tackle—by following these simple instructions.

Before you begin work, study this plan until the details of each step in construction are clear in your mind.

Layout: First draw full-sized outlines of the bow and transom panels on the ½" fir plywood. To lay out the curved bottom of the transom, tack brads at dimension points. Then spring a ¼"-thick batten around these brads and draw the curve along the batten.

Either cut out the panels with your saw angled to cut the bevels shown in the plan, or cut the panels slightly oversize and bevel to the outlines with a plane.

Note that the notches for the chines are cut in the hardwood frames only, not through the plywood bow or transom. Assemble the frames to the panels with waterproof glue and 1" No. 8 flat head wood screws, bronze or brass.

It's not necessary to bevel the edges of the molds. Notch them for the chines,

POWER BOATS • 2211

SIDE PANEL PATTERN

Dimensions along top (left to right): 3/8", 3/4", 1/4", 1/8", 3/8", 5/8", 13/16"

Vertical measurements: 10 7/8", 12 1/2", 13 5/8", 14 3/8", 14 5/8", 14 1/4", 13 1/8", 11 1/4", 8 3/4"

Horizontal spacing: 12", 12", ETC.

Labels: TOP, FWD

Construction Horse Set-up

Labels: TRANSOM, STA. 2 FORM, 3/4" STOCK BRACES NAILED TO 2 x 4" STRINGERS AND FORMS, STA. 1 FORM, BOW, CHINE LINE, 2" X 4" SET UP STRINGERS, SHEER LINE, SAW HORSES

Dimensions: 2 1/2", 21 1/2", 22", 48", 20 1/4", 21 5/8", 6 1/2", 1"

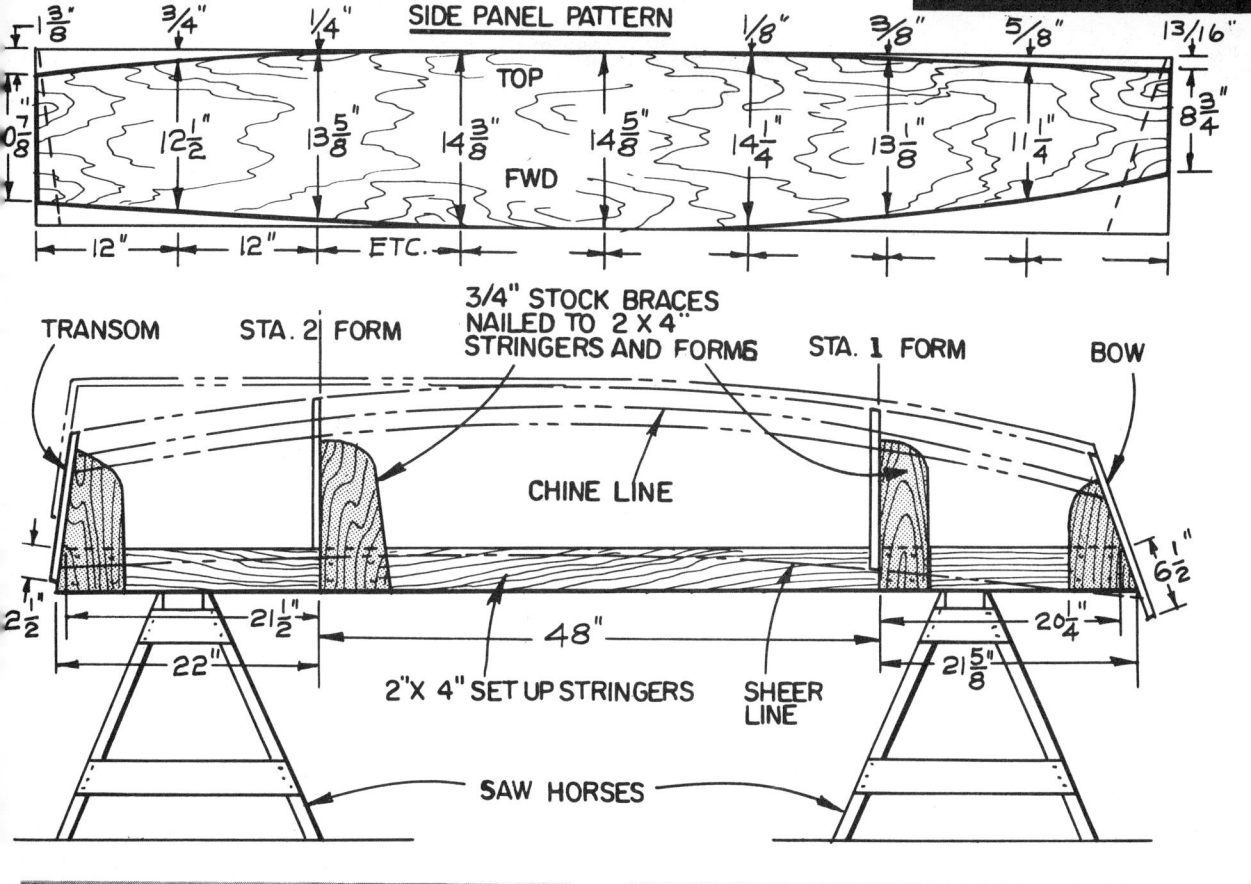

Set-up jig, parts and pieces for the pram dinghy are shown here. Assembly is simple.

Bow end of construction horse set-up. The solid frames allow the chines to be bent on.

Photo shows chines fitted into notches in frames and transom. Frames will come out.

With sides installed, 1x2" framing members are now fastened in place as shown below.

2212 • POWER BOATS

Bottom piece is clamped, braced and set in candlewicking and glue for watertight fit.

Amidships and stern seat frame detail. The solid frame molds are now no longer needed.

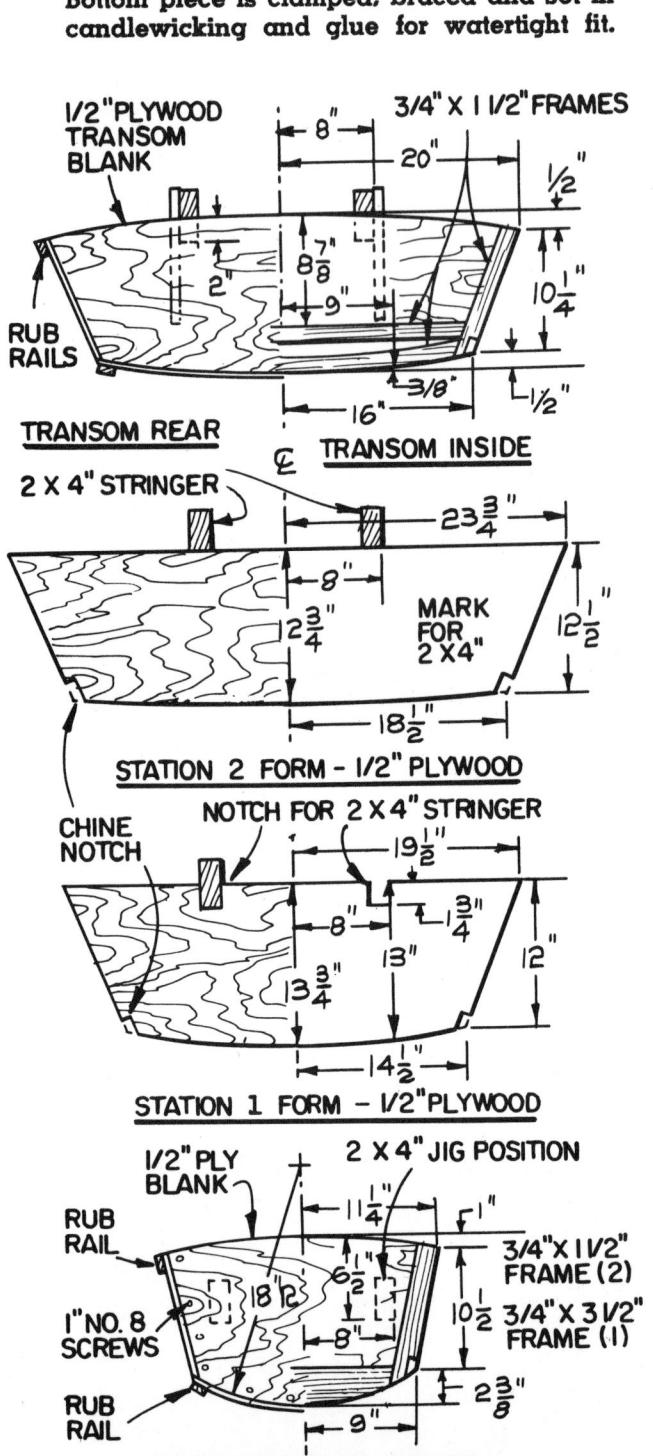

TRANSOM REAR / TRANSOM INSIDE
- 1/2" PLYWOOD TRANSOM BLANK
- 3/4" x 1 1/2" FRAMES
- RUB RAILS
- 8", 20", 1/2"
- 2", 8 7/8", 9", 10 1/4"
- 3/8", 16", 1 1/2"

STATION 2 FORM – 1/2" PLYWOOD
- 2 x 4" STRINGER
- 23 3/4", 8", 2 3/4", MARK FOR 2 x 4", 12 1/2"
- 18 1/2"

STATION 1 FORM – 1/2" PLYWOOD
- CHINE NOTCH
- NOTCH FOR 2 x 4" STRINGER
- 19 1/2", 8", 1 3/4", 13", 12"
- 13 3/4", 14 1/2"

BOW FRONT / BOW INSIDE
- 1/2" PLY BLANK
- 2 x 4" JIG POSITION
- RUB RAIL
- 1" NO. 8 SCREWS
- RUB RAIL
- 11 1/4", 1"
- 18 1/2", 6 1/2", 3/4" x 1 1/2" FRAME (2)
- 8", 10 1/2", 3/4" x 3 1/2" FRAME (1)
- 2 3/8", 9"

however, and notch the mold for Sta. 1 to fit over the setup stringers.

Setup: Assemble these stringers—the temporary backbone on which you'll build your dinghy—as shown in the plan. Mount them across sawhorses or solid crosspieces. When you've checked to see that they're parallel, level and ends lined up exactly, nail them down securely. Then measure off locations for the two molds and fasten cleats to the outer sides of the stringers at these marks. Nail the molds to these cleats.

When you fasten the bow piece and transom to the ends of the stringers, nail through scrap wood "washers." This will make it easy to pull the nails later.

Now you're ready to fit the 5/8" x 1 1/4" chines. Mortise the ends of these strips carefully into the blind notches at bow and transom. Glue the ends, and screw them to the hardwood frames with 1 1/2" No. 12 screws. Countersink the screw heads deeply.

Plane each chine to fair with the bow and transom, and also fair up the bevels on the frames. Springing a strip of 1/4" plywood across the framework will show you the exact bevels required. Working carefully with your plane, take off high spots and correct the bevels until you're sure the side and bottom planks will lay up tightly against the framework at all points.

Side and Bottom Planks: Side planks are fitted first. Saw them to the approximate shape shown in the plan, allowing enough material for trimming, and clamp them temporarily in place to check the fit.

Before fastening them permanently,

POWER BOATS • 2213

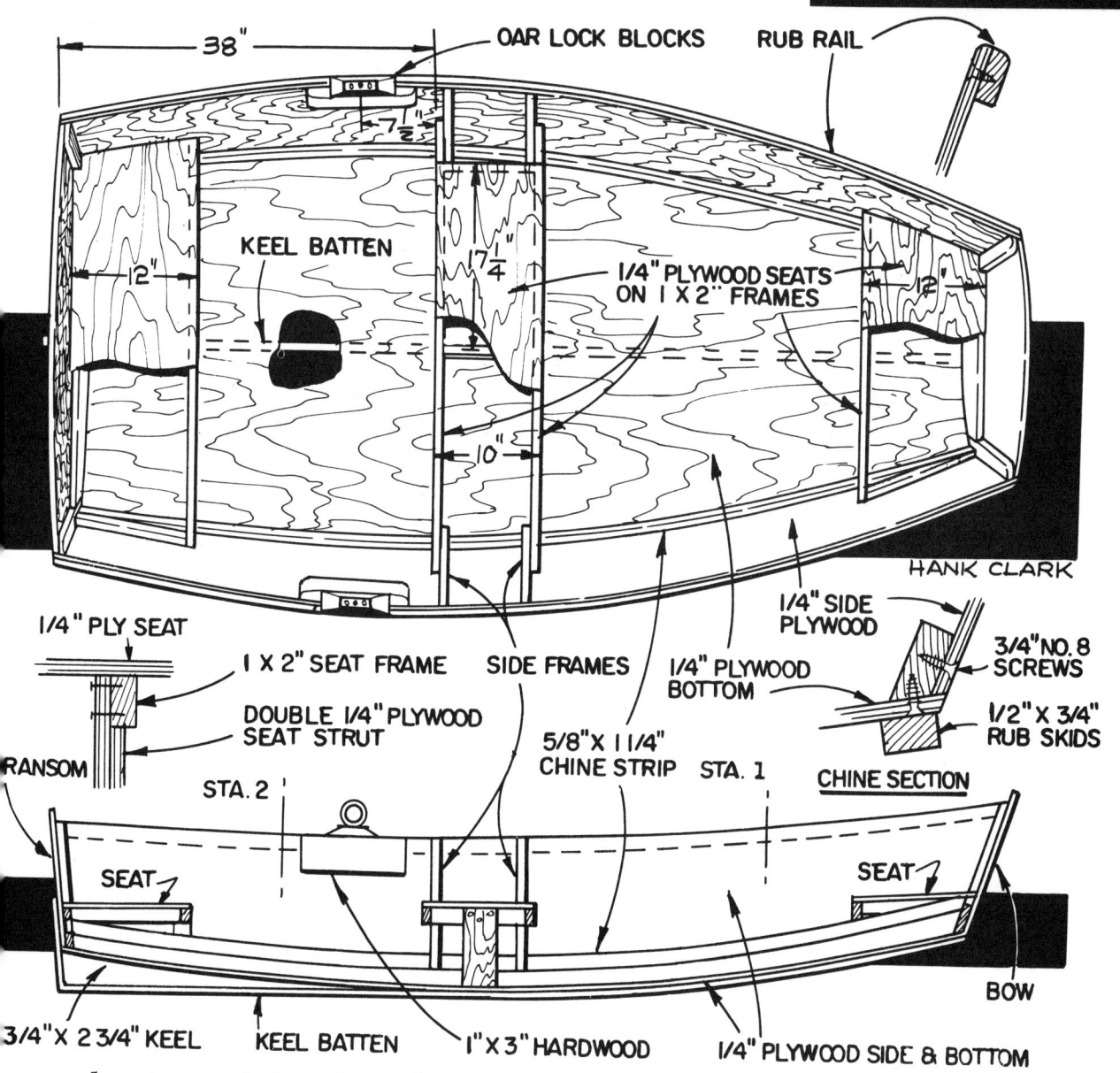

spread waterproof glue along the bow and transom assemblies and the chines —not along the edges of the molds, of course. It's wise to lay in lengths of glue-soaked candlewicking or string along the frames for added leak insurance.

Fasten the sides with ¾" No. 8 flat head screws spaced about 2½" apart. If you wish you can substitute patent bronze or Monel nails for screws.

To mark the shape of the bottom plank, clamp and brace the plywood over the framework and pencil along the chines, bow and transom. Fit and fasten the bottom, using candlewicking to seal the joint. Then plane the edges flush with the sides.

When you've screwed on the rub strips, keel, keel batten and guards, you're ready to turn your dinghy right-side-up.

Finish Detail: Drive small nails through the side planks into the molds to hold the molds in place.

Then remove the setup stringers and fit the seats.

To fasten seat risers and supports, drive screws through the plywood sides into these members.

Take a "dry run" in your boat on the shop floor to position the rowlock blocks as you want them. •

Large-scale plans are available. Please consult your PLANS REFERENCE LISTING for the exact source and price. Refer to Plan Number 147.

Snapper

By Hal Kelly

This snappy hydro-kart is powered with a used 5 hp lawnmower engine.

HYDRO-KARTS have taken the boating world by storm, if you'll excuse the expression. They are safer than landlubber karts and they're also a lot more fun. You can sail one all afternoon around most any small body of water on a few quarts of fuel.

Snapper is designed as a low-cost hydro-kart (or aqua-kart, if you prefer). It is easy to build and has a four-cycle air-cooled lawn-mower engine as a power plant. A five-hp engine is ideal. You may be able to pick one up at a lawnmower shop for about $20. A new engine will cost about $75.

This little rig was designed to look like a fish with its mouth open (to gulp down fresh air for the air-cooled motor). To start her, just lift the hood cover, pull the recoil starter, snap the hood closed and away you go. My 8-year-old son has a ball with her. I have no fear for his safety. Snapper is flip-proof and if he should fall off, the safety throttle shuts the motor off. She is literally unsinkable because both side

PLYWOOD girders are nailed together so that both sides can be cut at single pass.

SMALL glue blocks are used to fasten ribs to main girders. Use four to each side.

compartments are sealed. With my 80-pound son aboard, she travels over 25 mph. With a 170-pound grownup she will do better than 20 mph. Planing on top of the water on this small hull gives you the feel of much more speed.

The hull, painted and covered with Fiberglas, will cost under $50. Time to build this outfit runs a bit over 50 hours. Using the best hardware plus a safety throttle, she will cost you a little over $100, exclusive of motor—certainly worth the time and money to build. Snapper weighs a bit over 150 pounds, motor and all, light enough to carry on top of your car. A somewhat similar store-bought model will cost around 400 bucks.

Before building Snapper go over the text, photos and drawings a few times. Make a building jig which is nothing more than two 2x4s set parallel to each other with the outside exactly 18 inches apart. They may be fastened to saw horses or any other rig that will give you a good working height.

The main girders are first. Draw the shape on quarter-inch plywood and cut both sides out at the same time. Don't forget the rib notches. One 4x8-ft sheet will do. The waste is used for transom, plywood gussets, fins, etc. Note that a small piece is left at the back of the main girders to facilitate clamping to the jig. This is cut off later.

Ribs: Draw each rib on paper (you really need draw only one-half of each, flipping the pattern for the other end). Draw to full size. Note that the bottom and sides of the transom and ribs Nos. 3 and 4 are the same shape; just the decking is changed. The transom frame is half-inch cedar. Cut all notches before gluing and nailing the transom to the frame. Use No. 16, ¾-in. Anchorfast nails; in fact, this is the only size nail used in the whole project. After the ribs are finished they are slipped into the notches in the main girders and fastened in place with glue blocks and nails.

After the transom is in place, sight from the transom to the bow from time to time to make sure each rib lines up with the transom. You might use a level for this but I find the eye is more

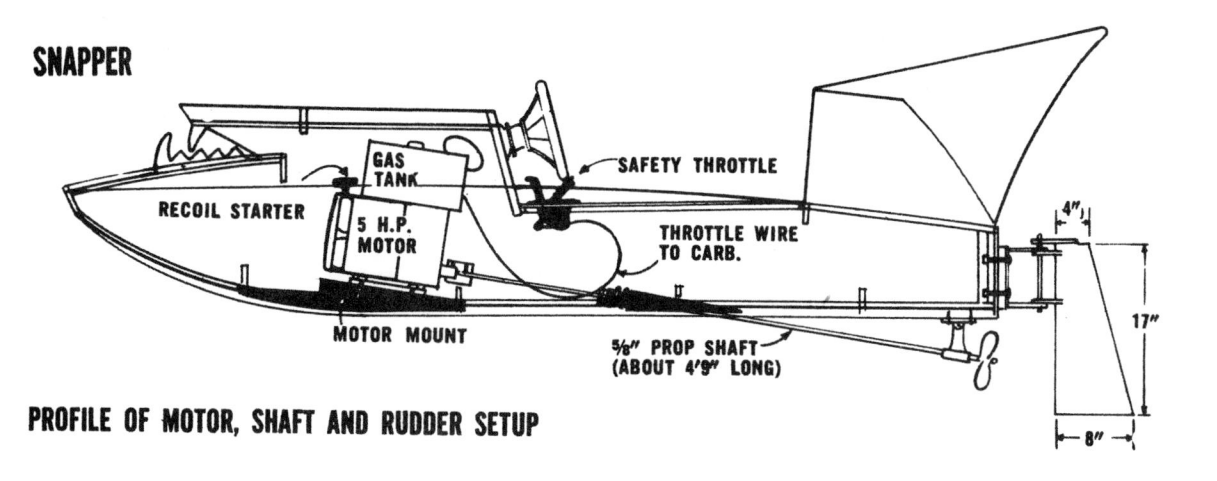

SNAPPER

PROFILE OF MOTOR, SHAFT AND RUDDER SETUP

CHECKING the bottom to make certain the planking rests evenly on all the battens.

A PLANING rasp is an ideal tool for fairing job. Note the motor mounts in place.

accurate because the jig or floor may be at a slight angle. The main girders are screwed to the deck beams from the inside. No. 7, 1¼-in. screws are used. Only two screw sizes are used, the other size is a No. 7, ¾-in. All screws are flat head, use only bronze, stainless steel or galvanized screws.

Keel: This is eight feet long, four inches wide and ¾ inches thick. It is cut to a width of two inches, starting forward of rib No. 2. This two-inch-wide section is cut down the center of its ¾-in. thickness with a band saw for about 28 inches from the bow. The keel is glued and fastened to the transom and all ribs with No. 7, 1¼-inch screws (two screws to each station). Glue is applied to the slit at the bow and the member is bent to shape. Small C-clamps are used to hold the bow section of the keel together until the glue is dried. The bow piece—half-inch thick cedar—is notched for the stem and then cut to shape. The main girders are glued and nailed to the bow piece. Next, the stem is glued and screwed to the notch in the bow piece.

The battens are now glued and fastened in place. The main girders are glued and nailed to the center battens. They also are screwed to all ribs and the transom, as well as to the outside battens. Use No. 7, 1¼-in. screws.

The sides are of cedar, half-inch thick. The five-inch width later is faired down to a little under four inches wide. Soak some rags in hot water and place them around the forward section of the sides to help with the bending. Start at the transom. Glue and screw the sides to each rib with two No. 7, 1¼-in. screws. Don't forget the motor mount, which is fastened to ribs Nos. 1 and 2. Check the power plant to see whether you have the correct placement for your engine.

Fairing: This is one phase of building you should not rush. Note that Snapper has a one-piece bottom that is rounded from chine to chine. Use quarter-inch-thick plywood across the bottom. Fair and round the battens and chines a bit so the plywood rests on all of them. Check with a long straightedge to make sure you don't have any hooks or rockers in the bottom, especially in the last four feet. Now rough in a hole for the shaft log.

Planking: The bottom is almost four feet wide, utilizing the full width of the 4x8-ft. plywood.

The one-piece bottom is the hardest task in building Snapper. However, it is really more time-consuming than anything else. Use screws for temporary fastening. Cut out a slit from the front up to the center about 30 inches long, fold one side down in place and trim for the cutout at the stem. Make a straight cut in the bottom at the center of the inside batten, about 24 inches long, then fold the outside section in place. Trim off the outside section until it makes a neat butt. This same procedure is used at the outside batten, also temporarily screwed in place. Do the same for the other side. Mark the shape of the outside of the boat on the underside of the bottom. At the same time mark off, from underneath, where all battens, the transom and the stem touch the bottom. Remove, trim all excess along outside.

Coat all battens, keel, chine, transom and bow pieces with glue. Note that the bottom is *not* fastened to the ribs. Now fasten the bottom in place. Temporary screws or nails will help to line up the bottom. Screws are best. When using nails on the outside battens, get a neighbor to hold a heavy weight under-

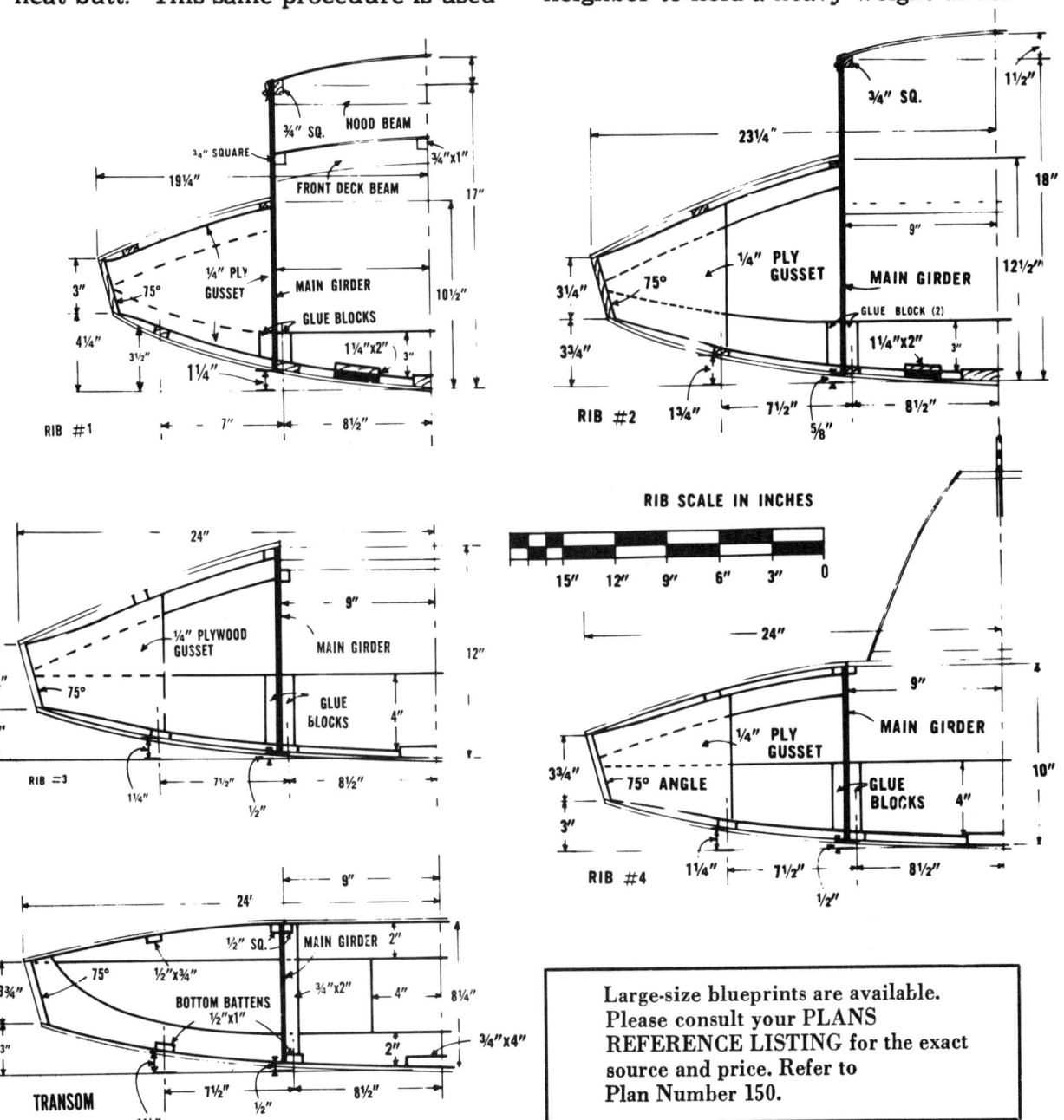

Large-size blueprints are available. Please consult your PLANS REFERENCE LISTING for the exact source and price. Refer to Plan Number 150.

THE MOTOR mount blocks are set at the appropriate angle and then screwed in place.

BOTTOM has received a coat of resin and cloth. Second resin coat is being applied.

neath the battens so the nails will pull the bottom snugly to the battens.

Now unclamp the hull from the jig and turn her right side up on the jig. Use some old rugs or rags as padding between the bottom and the jig. The deck battens are fastened in place with glue and No. 7 screws. The main girders are now glued and nailed to the inside battens. Fair the deck beams and sides in the same manner as the bottom. Cut off the section on the main girders you used to clamp to the jig. Before fastening the decking in place, add this safety factor: at the bow, forward of rib No. 1 under the decking, use a foam flotation kit made by Glass Plastics Corp. of Linden, N. J. Plug up the space between the rib and the bottom with a rag so this concoction will remain in the area where you want it. Then mix the foam. Use a little at a time if you are in doubt as to how much you will need. The mixture starts to foam almost immediately. If at first you don't fill the area you can always mix some more and add to fill. If it should overflow a bit, the excess can be cut off with a saw. Give the inside of the sealed compartments about three coats of varnish.

Decking: The quarter-inch-thick plywood is glued and nailed in place. Apply glue to transom, stem, all battens and sides. If you did a good job of fairing, the decking will rest firmly on the center batten.

Now for the finishing touches to the inside. The shaft log has a 12° angle. Thus, the angle blocks that are screwed to the motor beams are at 12° to the flat part of the bottom. They should taper from a sharp edge and be about 12 inches long. The shaft log is fastened between rib No. 3 and the keel with No. 7, ¾-in. screws. It is a good idea to use a seam compound between the log and the keel. The log and strut have a ⅝-in. hole for a ⅝-in. shaft. At a 12° angle, cut a ⅞-in. hole in the bottom. The hood and deck beams are now fastened in place. Use quarter-inch plywood for the little front deck, hood cover and sides of the back rest, to help keep this little outfit light. For the hood, a piano hinge is screwed to the sides and riveted to the hood cover. Small catches on the other side hold the cover in place.

The back rest with fin is next. This is made up separately and fastened to the quarter-inch plywood. Later the entire unit is fastened to the hull with eight screws. Fasten the footrests in place, using 1¼x3-in. mahogany. Carefully cut to the contour of the deck, glue and screw in place. Screw the main girder to the end of the foot rests, using long screws to the decking.

Fiberglasing: Bottoms up again! Carefully set Snapper at a comfortable working height. The bottom and sides are Fiberglased right up to the deck. If you Fiberglas the bottom you can eliminate some of this extra cost by using a good grade of exterior plywood instead of the more expensive marine grade. A 50-inch-wide cloth is used and the sides covered with scraps. The procedure is quite simple. The color is added to the resin. When finished, you have the bottom covered with a long-lasting material, plus built-in color, all in one application. The bottom first receives a coat of resin; then the cloth is laid in place. Then more resin is added over the cloth. A paint roller is the ideal tool for this part of the job. After

THE FITTING-OUT operation consists of installing the motor and the separate gas tank.

CLOSE-UP showing rudder construction and installation. Ready for shakedown cruise!

hardening, use a disk sander to grind off all the bumps (especially where the scraps on the sides overlap each other). Cut out and sand around the shaft hole. One more coat of resin is applied with a paint roller and you are finished. Working time is about 2½ hours at 1¼ hours each day. It would take you much longer to give the bottom three coats of paint, and paint takes longer to dry. I Fiberglas the bottoms of all my boats. On this little boat I believe it is necessary. I know my children will give Snapper a real workout. Years ago I found you could build things strong enough for grownups—but never for kids. The Fiberglas kit may be bought from Glass Plastics Corp., 1261 West Elizabeth Ave., Linden, N. J. for about $15.

While the hull is in this position, set up the strut. I used an adjustable strut, which I had to shorten. You will have to grind the bottom flat under this strut for a good snug fit. Make sure you have the shaft straight. You may have to do a bit of trimming on the bottom where the shaft comes out.

With the craft right side up, you are ready for finishing. The inside receives four coats of varnish. The decking, hood, seat, back rest and fin are primed with a coat of white Firzite. After sanding, the seat, hood, foot rests, back rest and fin are painted with two coats of bright red paint. The decking and "teeth" receive two coats of white paint.

Motor: You will find the 18-in. space between the main girders ample for most small four-cycle engines. Spend some time trimming the angle blocks on the motor beams so the motor lines up with the shaft. After the motor is lined up, bolt it to the angle blocks. On my particular motor the exhaust is at the side. I painted this hole to look like an eye and treated the opposite side similarly. Later I found out it was a good idea just to cut large holes for eyes. The effect is the same. It also permits a good air flow around the motor.

Transom handles are now attached, two to the back and two to the front. The steering wheel is a real racing wheel and so is the safety throttle, which shuts the motor off when released. Racing throttle, steering wheel and lifting handles may be bought from Keller Manufacturing Co., 18340 Ashworth Ave. North, Seattle, Wash. 98133. The rudder is made up of ten-gauge and quarter-inch steel. I had my local welder make it up for me (cost: about $5, including material and labor). The steering hookup is simple. Just run the cable around the drum a few times and cross through a pulley on each side attached to the rudder. Throttle wire runs from the carburetor, under the seat and over to the throttle.

Get some friends together and build a few of these karts. You can have a ball holding your own races. A small pond is suitable.

You will find that props are most important. I had the end of the shaft of my prop turned down to $\frac{9}{16}$-in. with a sheer pinhole to match an outboard racing prop.

After much testing and a few props I found that a Michigan 6x6-in. two-blade bronze propeller is about the best type. They cost about $12.

Once again—study the plans carefully, decide on a method of procedure that suits you best—then get to work. •

2220 • POWER BOATS

PAKEDO

By Donald H. Smith, SSCD

An ideal 18-ft. plywood outboard overnighter.

LAYING OUT stem components, right, before lamination and fastening with screws.

POWER BOATS • 2221

OVER THE PAST DECADE, the outboard cruiser seems to have pretty well established its popularity as a family boat with some real cruiser features. In the size range below twenty feet, these craft are generally light in weight, easily driven by a moderate amount of outboard engine horsepower. Pakedo was designed to fit into such a category; her construction is light and strong, featuring plywood planking over oak or mahogany framing. Conically developed hull lines with a minimum of severe bends have placed her well within the capabilities of any amateur back-yard boat builder. Pakedo's 17-foot 11-inch over-all length allows overnight accommodations for two persons in the cabin and two more out in the cockpit. This length combined with a beam just over seven feet will allow legal trailering in all states and she will be reasonably easy to handle in getting on or off a good brand of standard boat trailer. From a power and speed standpoint, Pakedo will cruise at a

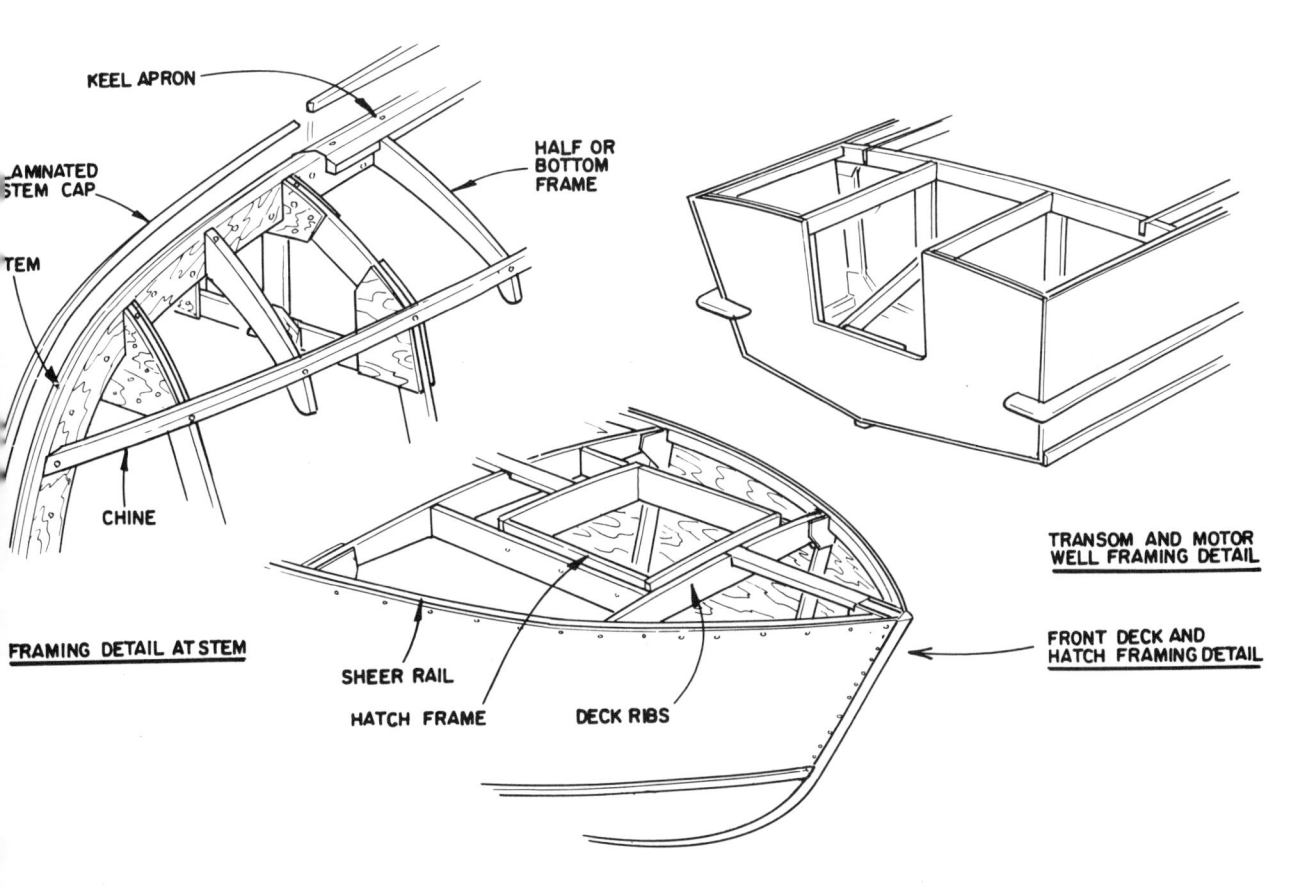

FRAMING DETAIL AT STEM

TRANSOM AND MOTOR WELL FRAMING DETAIL

FRONT DECK AND HATCH FRAMING DETAIL

PAKEDO is shown fully framed, ready for hull planking. Note building jig style.

WITH SIDE planking in place to stiffen the structure, bottom is ready to plank.

respectable 20 mph with a 40 to 50 hp engine. She has been clocked at 18 mph with 35 and 40 hp engines under relatively light loads.

Economy and simplicity are keynotes of Pakedo's design and she has lots of freeboard, ample beam, and topside flare. These characteristics render her a dry boat under normal sea conditions on the lakes, bays, and rivers for which she was designed. A small skeg reduces drift when running or maneuvering at low speeds and affords a degree of protection to the propeller.

The V-berths forward will comfortably sleep two six-footers and the galley will permit the installation of a small sink and marine stove. A galley cabinet will hold the stores and supplies as well as serving as an icebox if so desired and constructed. On the port side, a berth extension piece covers a marine toilet. This is rigged so that the plywood berth panel can be raised, swinging back against the coaming or inside of the hull. Space below the bunks is such as to allow storage of considerable amounts of gear. The roomy cockpit contains a deck area of about 36 square feet, big enough for a helmsman's folding seat and a couple of deck chairs. The outboard motor will be installed in a self-draining well as shown, to prevent following seas from coming aboard. A feature is included which is not always found on outboard cruisers of this size. This refers to the hatch in the forward deck which serves as a ventilator while under way but also provides access to or from the cabin in addition to the regular door opening. In any cabin boat, such a simple safety feature should be recommended or even required.

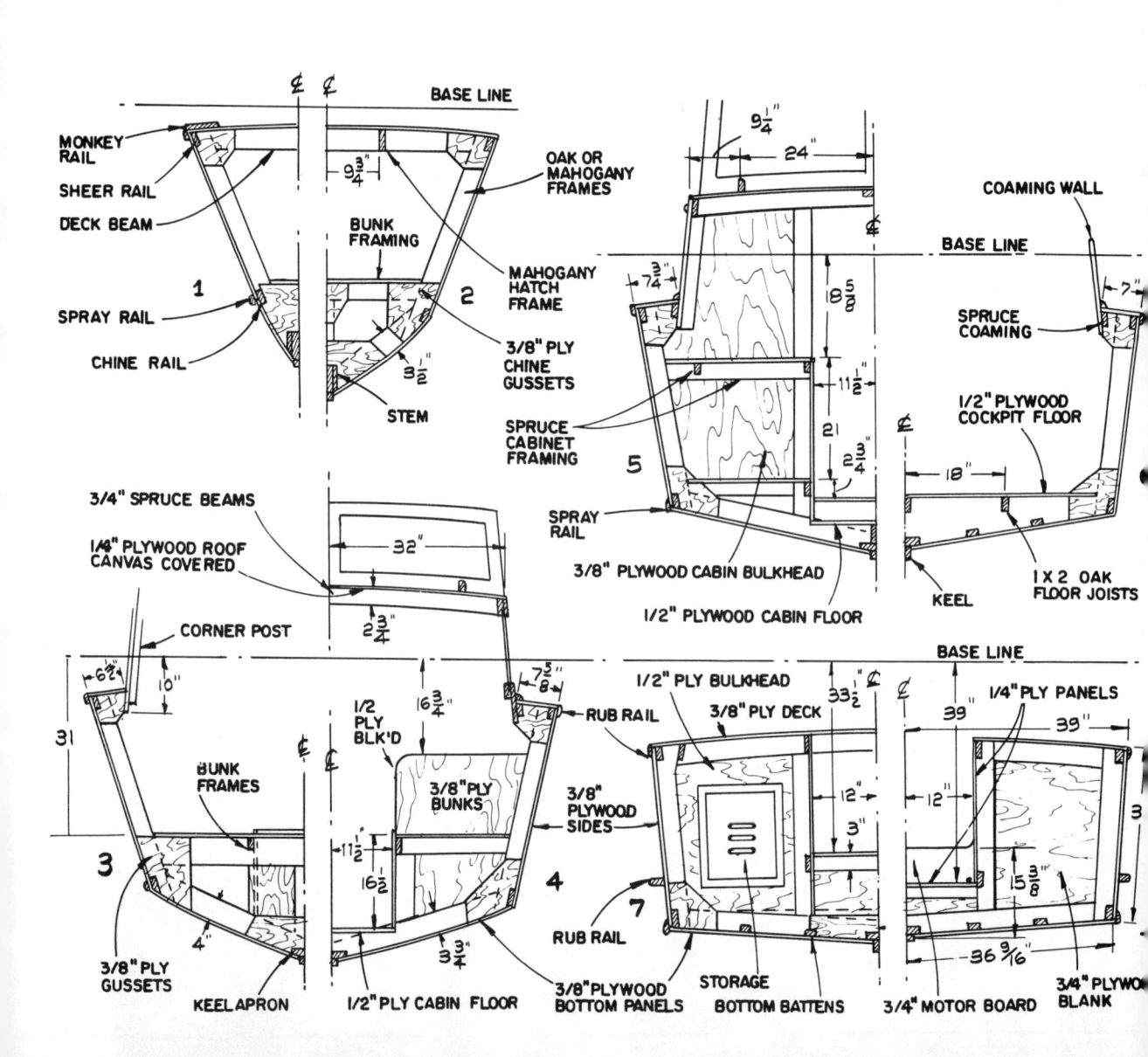

So much for general description. The actual construction of Pakedo can begin with the selection of a suitable floor area on which to lay down the full size lines. Once such an area is located, the complete lines drawings must be reconstructed from the offset table and all points connected by fair lines. Perhaps the easiest way to do this is to have one person read the offsets while another marks off the various points on corresponding station lines which will have been laid out perpendicularly to the base and center lines. By sweeping a ¾-inch pine batten through the points, fair curves for the sheer and chine can be drawn on the loft floor. The resulting body plan will permit the laying out of frame stock either directly over the full size drawing or by making patterns from the latter. In either case, the frames can be built up as shown on the sectional drawings.

When the frames have been assembled, they are ready to be set up for hull construction. It is recommended that a building jig be built prior to this operation. This can best be done by setting two 2x6-inch boards on edge, parallel to one another and separated by about 6 feet. At intervals corresponding to frame spacing, there should be connecting members of 1x4-inch stock. These will lie flat over the tops of the two longitudinal pieces and should be up to seven feet in length. The hull will, of course, be erected bottom side up. Therefore, the individual frames should have a cross spawl connecting the frame heels and these spawls may be set upon our jig at the proper stations. When the frames have been set up as described, they can be fastened to the keelson with 3-inch No. 12 flathead wood screws. Each frame must be plumb and straight prior to fastening. The stem, which can be built up at any time now, is to be let into the forward frames as shown, and secured to them and the keelson. The transom is to be raked at its proper angle and fastened to the keelson or keel apron. The chines and sheer clamps may be sprung into place after the frame and keel set up. These should be put in simultaneously working alternately on both sides of the hull until the members from each side are warped around to the stem. In this way, there will be no chance of springing the erected framework out of

COMPLETELY planked and ready for stem cap. Sides are one continuous length.

TURNING the hull over, ready to remove building jig and begin the interior work.

WITH THE forward deck and hatchway completed, the cabin installation may begin.

2224 • POWER BOATS

place. The final framing operation relates to the installation of the bottom battens which are let into the bottom frame members as depicted on the plans. It is suggested that all connecting surfaces and joints be made up with bedding compound or marine glue in addition to the size wood screws recommended for these areas of construction.

With the framing completed, the planking can begin. Prior to any planking, the entire frame assembly must be planed and shaped so that the faying or mating surfaces will allow the plywood to lie flat against them. When this is done, the plywood panels may be cut out from patterns or from direct measurement against the erected framework. All faying surfaces must be liberally coated with marine bedding compound before the application of the plywood planking. Following this, the plywood is pressed against the framing and clamped wherever possible while the screw fastenings are driven. It is best to work from the stern toward the stem in the screw fastening operation. When the planking is completed, final trimming will be the next step, followed by priming and painting of the hull. Then, with the help of about a half-dozen pairs of hands or a suitable block and tackle, the hull can be turned upright and either set into a preconstructed cradle or placed upon a boat trailer.

Next, the deck beams, flooring, coamings, and decking may be installed. Before going too far on the interior joinery, the inside of the hull should be completely painted. As various interior framing and related components are installed, it may be well to give them their required coats of paint or varnish at that time.

The cabin bulkheads, berth framing, berth tops and the like will best precede the installation of the cabin roof beams. This is a matter of convenience as well as providing natural light by which to complete the cabin interior work. When all deck beams, roof beams, and the hatchway are in place, then they should be coated, such as was the hull framing, prior to the application of the decking. •

LARGE SCALE BLUEPRINTS will greatly simplify construction of this boat, PAKEDO. Please consult your PLANS REFERENCE LISTING for exact source and price. Refer to Plan Number 108.

BILL OF MATERIALS

OAK OR MAHOGANY
 Keel apron—1 piece 1"x5"x14'
 Frame sides—3/4"x3"x42'
 Frame bottoms—3/4"x12"x33'
 Half frames—3/4"x6"x30'
 Chines—1"x2 1/2"x36'
 Bottom battens—3/4"x1 1/2"x40'
 Sheer clamps—3/4"x2"x40'
 Deck beams—3/4"x4"x20'
 King plank—3/4"x4"x4'

MAHOGANY
 Hatch framing—3/4"x6"x6'
 Cabin corner posts—3/4"x5"x5'
 Windshield framing—1" thick stock as per plans, make rabbets by laminating overlapped 1/2" thick members.
 Spray rail—1"x3"x14'
 Chine rail—5/8"x1 1/2"x36'
 Sheer rub rail—1"x1 1/4"x40'

PLYWOOD
 Hull planking—2 panels 3/8"x4'x20' marine
  2 panels 3/8"x4'x8'
  2 panels 3/8"x4'x10'
 Cabin sides, coaming—1 panel 1/2"x4'x14' mahogany
 Cabin front—1 panel 1/2"x2'x6' mahogany
 Decking—fore and aft, 2 panels 3/8"x4'x8' side, use leftovers from hull side planking
 Transoms—1 panel 3/4"x4'x14'
 Bulkhead—1 panel 3/8"x4'x12' marine
 Cabin roof—1 panel 1/4"x4'x12'
 Motor well—1 panel 1/4"x2'x6'
 Cabin floor— 1 panel 1/2"x2'x4'
 Cockpit sole (floor)—3 panels 1/2"x2'x6'
 Gussets— 3/8" marine as per plans, use scraps
 Interior paneling—bunks, cabinets etc., 1/4" to 3/4"

MISCELLANEOUS
 Stem—2"x10"x9' oak, mahogany or fir, core pieces
  1/2"x2'x6' marine plywood, covering pieces
 Keel or skeg—1 3/4"x6"x14' oak
 Roof beams—3/4"x3"x25' spruce or fir
 Roof support batten—3/4"x3"x5' spruce or fir
 Cabin clamp—3/4"x2 3/4"x7' spruce or fir
 Window slides—3/4"x2"x10' spruce or fir
 Floor stringers—1"x2" oak, mahogany or fir
 Interior framing—3/4" sided, fir or spruce stock. For pieces to be finished natural, use mahogany. Use scraps.

NOTE: All oak specified must be of Northern White variety and mahogany should be either a densely grained Philippine or Honduras species if obtainable. Spruce and fir will be clear, straight stock. All plywood must be of marine grade.

2226 • POWER LAWN MOWER

Real garden workhorse is this Jacobsen "GT" 14 HP tractor with 50-in. rotary mower attachment.

Lawn and Garden Power Equipment

POWER EQUIPMENT cuts your work drastically in caring for your lawn and garden. Many of the newer products are so designed that physical effort is reduced to a minimum. This growing array of power equipment is not only a worksaver —you'll also have more fun with less effort than you've ever experienced.

One type of equipment that is gaining more and more popularity is the lawn and garden tractor. Generally, these are defined as tractors with engines of 12 horsepower or less.

These small, four-wheel tractors mow the lawn, plow and cultivate a garden, sweep a lawn, haul debris, throw snow, and help with nearly every outdoor chore. They are built like small automobiles with geared transmissions, key operated electric starting switches, (there's a 12 volt battery in many), easy steering, gear shift levers, and foot brakes.

You can select a tractor depending on your present and future needs, the size of your lawn and garden, and your pocketbook. Many homeowners buy one to do the lawn mowing job in sit-down ease and comfort then add attachments. A tractor has a significant advantage over a riding mower—it can be used year 'round.

Snow removal is a "breeze" with a tractor-mounted snow thrower, or dozer

POWER LAWN MOWER • 2227

Gravely riding tractor gives 10 HP, features 50-in. mower, easily handles tough terrain.

blade. A tractor offers a wide variety of attachments for the garden. An eight-inch plow can dig deep into the earth to prepare a garden plot. This is equipped with an adjustable colter and depth-crank assembly. Or, you may prefer a rotary tiller, with its own three horsepower motor. The tractor acts as a guide or leader for the tiller and all power to do the actual tilling is supplied by the separate motor. Tilling width is generally 20 inches, which can be extended to 26 inches with extra tines. A 36-inch cultivator with six shovels and a disc harrow are also available to complete garden preparation and care.

One of the most popular attachments for a tractor owner is the trailer lawnsweeper used for whisking away leaves, grass clippings, twigs, and other lawn debris. This attachment eliminates old fashioned hand raking and cuts sweep-up time by as much as 90%. A good lawnsweeper will pick up most debris except the largest of broken tree branches.

For hauling and general cleanup, a five-bushel steel cart can be attached to the tractor. Dirt, gravel, firewood, and lawn debris are easily moved with this general purpose cart. There's also a sickle bar to cut heavy weed-and-grass infested areas in orchards, fields, or along fence rows.

For extremely large lawns, grass can be cut with a three-gang reel-type mower. This combination cuts nearly five feet of grass in one swath. It is similar to the type professional landscape gardeners use.

Unlike a single purpose machine, you don't store your garden tractor in the winter. When the fall cleanup is finished, you check either your snow thrower or snow dozer blade. Either one attaches to the front of the tractor. The first is a dual stage machine which means that snow is first ground up by a heavy-duty auger, then thrown as far as 40 feet by a separate impeller through an adjustable discharge chute. The dozer blade also finds many uses throughout the year in moving and leveling dirt and gravel.

Front engine rider from Toro delivers 8 HP and offers electric start with battery, 36-in. mower.

Since enough power is the key to making the attachments work, it is best to select a higher horsepower model if you plan to use the tractor for heavy work. Lower horsepower models do excellent jobs in lawn cutting, light snow removal, sweeping, and hauling, but the higher horsepower is needed for heavier jobs such as working the soil, heavy bulldozing, etc.

You can have all the horsepower needed, but if this isn't transmitted properly your attachments will not work as they should. Look for fully geared transmissions with several forward and one reverse speed. Check to see if the tractor also has a separate geared differential since it is the combination of these two that will transmit the motor's power to its fullest extent. Then look for conveniently grouped controls,

Homelite line boasts five garden tractors, three riding mowers, six walk-behind rotary mowers, two garden tillers, two snow throwers.

like a dashboard, and location of one or more control levers for attachments. Many models also have a combination clutch and brake pedal for transmission shaft braking and hill brake lock for positive control.

Cleaning the Lawn

Leading lawn experts agree that a clean lawn is a healthy lawn. Grass clippings, twigs, nuts, leaves, and other debris can accumulate rapidly to choke healthy grass and create a mold-producing thatch which can kill a lawn. A lawnsweeper quickly and efficiently removes lawn debris when used regularly. In the spring, summer, and fall, the operation of a lawnsweeper will build a healthier, more attractive lawn with a minimum of effort.

There are many different lawnsweeper models including hand, trailer, and self-propelled motorized units. One manufacturer has 14 different models in his line. Sizes are 26 and 31 inches wide and the hand-propelled models are constructed so you can push one without strain. Mechanical and convenience features have been improved so you find them equipped with accessories such as balers and wind aprons.

The lawnsweeper does its job by revolving brushes powered through gears in the large wheels. As the sweeper is pushed or pulled, the brushes hurl debris into a large canvas or steel hamper whose capacity may be from 5½ to ten bushels. This hamper is held by a tubular steel frame and is lifted out for dumping. This dumping is eliminated on one style designed for tractors or riding mowers. Both the back and bottom are steel plates which are hinged. As you ride, you can pull a rope attached to the back which simultaneously raises the bottom and opens the back for dumping.

The lawnsweeper's efficiency has improved so you can pick up more kinds of debris and sweep flat, hard surfaces such as patios, swimming pool aprons, and driveways. In the spring, use it to pick up dead grass, leaves, twigs, and even dog bones.

In the fall, a sweeper takes care of grass clippings and leaves. By sweeping every few days, your lawn is relieved of leaves which can damage the grass during the winter by forming an almost complete barrier to moisture and air. Compared to hand raking, you can sweep your lawn in about one-tenth the time.

Multi-Purpose Snow Throwers

A modern powerful dual-stage snow thrower is also a versatile homeowner's tool. Primarily designed to throw snow, it, too, has several attachments for use in other seasons.

All are self-propelled in 20, 24, 28, 32, and a giant 40-inch width. Again, your selection should be based on your particular needs and how much snow you'll have to remove from driveways, sidewalks, and other areas.

Each has dual stage action. In this, an auger crushes and delivers snow to a powerful ejector fan or impeller which

POWER LAWN MOWER • 2229

This powerful 12 HP Gravely tractor with a 26-in. snowblower attachment disposes of heavy snowfall.

AMF horizontal shaft reversing tiller has a 5 HP engine, 28-in. tilling width, adjustable handles.

does the actual throwing. Directional chutes let you throw snow through a 210° arc. Thus, if you don't want the snow to pile high, you can vary the pitch and arc to keep the snow in out-of-the-way areas.

To give you an idea of the speed of these units, they will throw snow at the rate of 300 to 350 shovels per minute or between 18 and 22 *tons* per hour. Motors range from three horsepower for a 20-inch unit to 10 horsepower for the 40-inch-wide style.

Again, like the garden tractors, there are automotive type transmissions to transmit maximum power. The auger and impeller can be independently controlled from the movement of the unit so, if you hit a deep drift, you can stop the movement while the auger and impeller dig in.

Similarly, you can stop the auger and impeller while moving from one area to another. Forward speeds are infinite to match snow conditions. Most can be equipped with electric starting which is useful on very cold mornings. The motor's starter is plugged into a standard electrical outlet, you flick a switch, and the motor starts.

All controls are grouped in a "dashboard" extending between the drive handles. This gives you fingertip control for throttle, remote chute control, and drive control lever.

The key to the year 'round versatility of the snow thrower is detachment of the impeller, auger, and chute from the power unit which includes the motor and controls. Only two screws need to be removed to separate the unit. Then you have the power unit ready to receive attachments.

One of these is an outdoor vacuum cleaner. Measuring 28 inches wide, it picks up, crushes, and packs all types of debris into a huge 12-cubic-foot bag through a rugged steel impeller spinning at 4800 rpm. There's a zipper opening at the rear of the bag to empty the debris. As compared with a lawnsweeper, it has more power and capacity.

Grass cutting can be accomplished with a 30-inch-wide reel-type mower attachment. Unlike garden tractors, all attachments for a snow thrower are mounted in front. So, with the grass cutter, you have a bigger-than-average self-propelled lawnmower. Cutting height is adjusted by raising or lowering the wheels.

Then, if you want to push dirt or snow, you can mount a 42-inch-wide dozer blade in place of the snow thrower. Remember, all power is coming from the rear to provide maximum push for the attachments. And, if you want to ride while using either the snow thrower or attachments, a sulky can be connected to the rear. You can also have a canvas cover, with plastic windows, to mount around the control handles and dashboard to protect you from winter winds.

Whatever your needs, your pocketbook, or the size of your lawn and garden, there's a motorized helper waiting to add more fun and comfort to keeping your grounds in tip-top shape.•

Power Motor Repair

by Richard Day

THE USE OF SMALL gasoline engines around the home has been running wide open for a number of years. You are doubtless responsible for one or more of these puny but peppy powerplants yourself. If you are, it will pay to treat it right so it can treat you right when it comes to grass cutting, leaf-raking, rototilling, snowblowing, sawing wood, generating electricity, mixing concrete, or cruising around the yard astride a shiny tractor.

Small gasoline engines do all of these things and more. Their extreme popularity is due to the fact that they're low in cost, light in weight, dependable, inexpensive to operate and completely portable. They're air-cooled to work anywhere, anytime.

As ideal as the small gas engine is for many home jobs, it can be ruined by a little inattention at the wrong time. For instance the oil level is supposed to be checked every time you use the engine (if it has oil in the crankcase not in the gas). Your car can be a quart low on oil, no sweat. But when one of these single-cylinder midgets gets a quart low on oil, that's it, baby. Many hold only a pint of oil.

So if you tend to the things the engine manufacturer outlines in the care-and-maintenance instructions that came with the engine, there isn't too much to worry about. The powerplant should stay running like new for a long time. This means easy, dependable starting, powerful running, idling without dying and smooth operation.

All gasoline engines operate either on the two-stroke cycle or four-stroke cycle principle. A two-cycle engine, as it is called for short, has a power impulse or explosion in the combustion chamber with every revolution. A four-cycle engine has a power impulse every other revolution. A two-cycle produces more power with less engine weight and is cheaper to build than a four-cycle engine. The four-cycle runs cooler, is quieter, smoother running and longer lasting. It's also more dependable. Fuel in a four-cycle engine need not be mixed with oil as in a two-cycle engine.

The engines used in automobiles are four-stroke cycle engines. Most outboard motors and the engines on many lightweight motorcycles are two-cycle.

In order to function, a gasoline engine must burn fuel, converting its heat into power out of the turning shaft. To accomplish this it does four distinct things: (1) takes in fuel mixed with air, (2) compresses the air-fuel mixture into something that will burn with gusto, (3) fires it off absorbing the power and (4) gets rid of burned gases before starting the series all over again. These four functions are called *intake, compression, power* and *exhaust.* Since the four-cycle engine has them all and keeps them distinctly separated, its operation is easier to understand.

The first stroke in a four-stroke cycle is the intake stroke. With the exhaust valve closed and the intake valve open, the piston moves down in the cylinder and draws the air-fuel mixture in.

Then the intake valve closes and the piston moves upward on the compression stroke compacting the air-fuel mixture into a small space between the top of the piston and the cylinder head. This space is the combustion chamber.

POWER MOTOR REPAIR • 2231

Clinton Engines Corp.
Small gasoline engines have developed into highly dependable, compact yet powerful machines for doing all sorts of outdoor work around the house.

The spark plug fires, igniting the mixture. The force of the rapidly expanding gases pushes the piston down on the power stroke.

Finally the exhaust valve opens, as the piston moves upward, and the spent gases are pushed out. This fourth stroke completes the cycle and it starts all over again with the intake stroke.

Two-Cycle Operation

In a two-cycle engine intake, compression, power and exhaust are completed in two strokes of the piston. On the upward stroke of the piston a partial vacuum is created in the crankcase. A rotary valve or reed valve lets the air-fuel mixture be drawn into the crankcase but won't let any out. The downward movement of the piston compresses the fuel charge that is trapped in the crankcase. Near the bottom of its stroke the piston clears the intake bypass port which connects the crankcase and the combustion chamber. Air-fuel mixture is blown into the cylinder. The piston also uncovers the exhaust port and the incoming charge helps to evacuate the spent charge. The top of the piston is shaped so that it directs the fresh charge toward the top of the cylinder minimizing mixing of new charge with old.

Then the piston starts up again. It compresses the mixture and the spark plug fires it, starting the piston down under power. The whole cycle is repeated with every revolution of the crankshaft.

The process of vaporizing or atomizing liquid fuel is called carburetion. The device for doing this is the carburetor. A small engine carburetor has a high-speed and a low-speed circuit. The high-speed circuit furnishes fuel efficiently at working speeds. It comes into play when the butterfly valve that controls engine speed is opened. Opening and closing of the butterfly is controlled by the throttle on your lawnmower, snow-blower or whatever. Air flowing rapidly into the engine runs through a constricted passageway called a venturi, inside the carburetor. Air rushing through the venturi sets up a vacuum just behind the smallest portion where the high-speed jet meters raw gasoline into the air stream. As the rushing air hits the gasoline, the latter is vaporized.

To operate the engine at idle speeds when the butterfly is closed, the low-speed or idle circuit takes over. At idle the partial vacuum created by the running engine gasping for air is concentrated behind the closed carburetor butterfly. A tiny fuel metering passageway leads from the gasoline supply in the carburetor to behind the butterfly. This feeds just enough fuel to mix with air leaking around the closed butterfly for running the engine slowly.

Carburetors have a needle valve for adjusting the amount of gasoline that is metered through the high-speed circuit. Some have a needle valve in the low-speed circuit, too.

To avoid a flat spot in engine performance between idle and high-speed running, an intermediate idle port is provided in some carbs to bridge the gap between the high-speed and low-speed circuits.

Float Bowl

Since a carburetor must keep enough fuel on hand at all times to supply gasoline for both the low- and high-speed circuits, a float bowl is provided. Fuel enters the float bowl by gravity from the tank. As the level of fuel in the bowl rises, it pushes the float up with it. When the float reaches the desired point it closes a needle valve and blocks off further flow of fuel. As fuel in the float bowl is drawn into the engine, the float lowers and permits more fuel to enter. The effect is one of keeping an even level of fuel in the float bowl at all times.

Some carburetors, particularly those on equipment such as chain saws that must operate not only right side up but on their sides, too, make use of a diaphragm instead of a float bowl to regulate fuel into the carburetor.

Float level is very critical. If it's off, the balance of the whole carburetor is likely to be off.

One more provision, a choke, is needed to start the engine at varying temperatures and with varying fuels. A choke is usually a butterfly valve in the air passageway at the entrance to the carburetor. When the choke valve is closed it reduces the air and increases the fuel being drawn into the engine. Even with low-vaporizing cold fuel and cold air the engine will get enough fuel to start easily when it's choked.

Both two- and four-cycle engines need something to produce a spark at the spark plug. Not only must this spark be strong enough to jump the spark·gap, it must occur at the right time to ignite the fuel-air mixture as the piston approaches the top of its stroke.

Most small gasoline engines depend on magnetos to furnish the spark. A magnet on the engine's flywheel passes by an armature and induces an electrical current in coils of wire around the armature. This is the magneto's primary circuit. The primary circuit electrical flow is stopped at the proper time by the opening of a pair of breaker points. This in turn creates a high-voltage electrical current in the secondary circuit and, snap, you have a spark. A condenser in the primary circuit keeps primary current from being wasted by arcing across the separating breaker points, in effect increasing the intensity of the spark.

With a dependable magneto to produce the spark, no batteries are needed to run a small engine. In an engine running at 3600 rpm the spark is created and correctly timed 60 times a second. A four-cycle engine needs only half that many sparks. But getting rid of the wasted spark that occurs at the end of each exhaust stroke would be too involved a production job. Besides it doesn't hurt anything. Better to waste it than an extra $10 or so in the cost of an engine that would make a spark only every other revolution.

Taking Care of Your Engine

The manufacturer of every small gasoline engine issues carefully prepared directions for the care and maintenance of that engine. Find the ones that came with your engine and follow them to the letter. They're the best instructions of all for

POWER MOTOR REPAIR • 2233

that engine. If you cannot find them, write to the manufacturer giving the model and serial number of the engine and ask for another booklet. Most will be able to supply one.

None of the regular service that small engines need is hard to give. Even a child can do some of it if he is shown how. The tasks pertain to keeping the engine well lubricated, providing it with clean air, a good spark properly timed, clean fuel and plenty of cooling air over its exterior surfaces. On a two-cycle engine there is the additional job of cleaning carbon away from the exhaust ports.

Most engine manufacturers recommend checking the oil level every day the engine is used. Because small engines don't hold much oil, it shouldn't be permitted to run low. Refill with the oil recommended by the manufacturer.

In four-cycle engines, oil should be changed after each 25 hours of running. Do it while the engine is hot. About once a season is the proper interval on a lawnmower. One thing sure—if the oil is dirty, change it. Too much changing can't hurt and it doesn't take that much oil. Too infrequent oil changing could harm the engine. Changing oil is better than changing engines.

Air-cooled engines are a lot rougher on a motor oil than auto engines that never get hotter than about 180°. An air-cooled engine can get quite hot. Because of this, engine parts must be built with greater clearances. More is required of the oil used. Use 30-weight oil rated for service MS. The designation on the can will read, "SAE 30, ML-MM-MS." Costlier oils designed for diesel engines and automobiles with hydraulic valve lifters should not be used. These are rated for service DG and DM.

For service at temperatures below 32° F. down to −10° use 10W oil with an MS service rating. For still colder weather use 5W oil with an MS rating.

The oil in two-cycle engines is mixed with the fuel. Sleeve-bearing engines usually get ¾ pint of oil per gallon of gas. Needle-bearing engines usually call for ½ pint of oil per gallon. The correct mixture usually is printed on the engine. Use SAE 30 high quality outboard motor oil or its equivalent in SAE 30 or SAE 40 automotive oil with a minimum MM or MS service rating. One-half pint is one cup household measure.

The easiest way to handle fuel mixture for a two-cycle engine is to set aside a separate can for it. Measure the oil into the can, carefully, then go to the service

Kohler Co.
Cutaway view shows the workings of a small gas engine which has many components similar to the automobile engine—but the engine is air cooled.

Briggs and Stratton

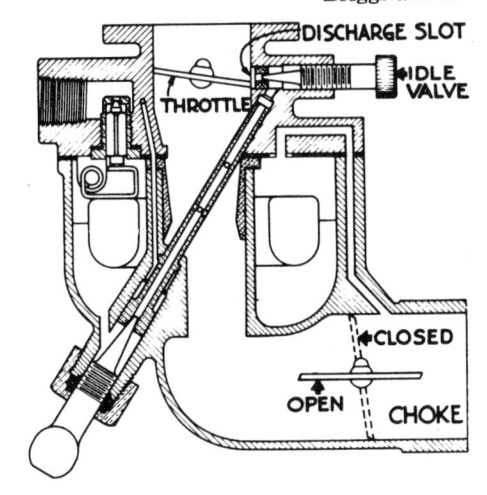

A cross section of air induction system shows air filters, carburetor, intake port and intake valve. Most small engines are equipped with governors to control top speed and give more power under load.
Kohler Co.

2234 • POWER MOTOR REPAIR

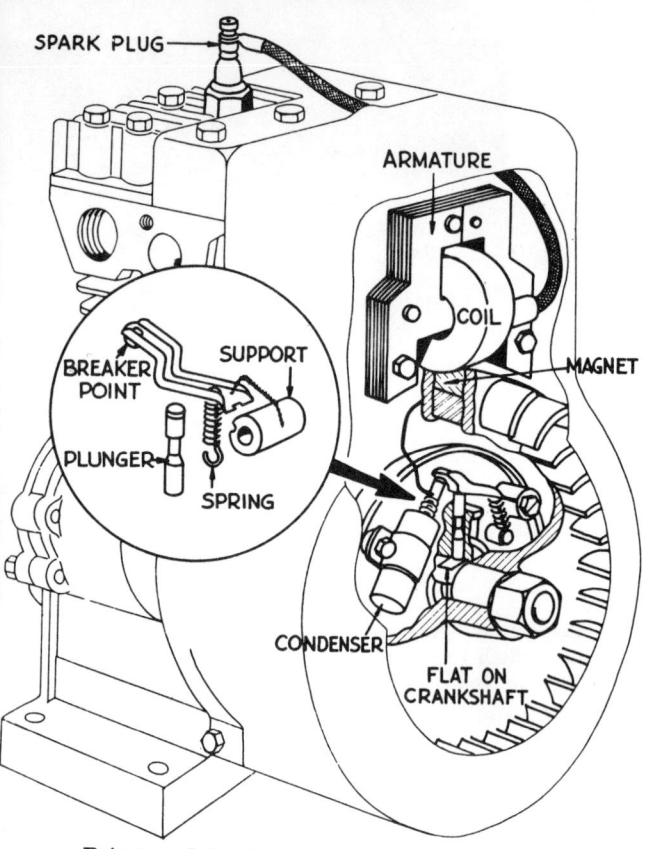

Briggs and Stratton

To clean a polyurethane foam filter first clean the filter element and metal parts in gasoline. After wringing out the foam, pour engine oil on it and squeeze the filter to distribute the oil.

station and have the gasoline added. Whenever you need two-cycle fuel, pour it from that container.

Fuel for two- and four-cycle engines should be a clean, fresh "regular" grade gasoline. Do not use "ethyl" gasoline or gas that's been stored over the winter. Get it fresh.

Some engines have fuel filters. These should be cleaned about every 100 hours of operation. Remove and clean the filter bowl in gasoline. If a filter element is used, swish the element in clean fuel, reinstall it and check for leakage.

Air Cleaner

Small engines sometimes operate under such dusty, dirty conditions they depend heavily on air filtering. As an operator you must do your part to see that the air cleaner is maintained properly.

There are different types of air cleaners. One uses an oiled metallic mesh to catch dust and dirt. Another passes the air over an oil sump. One is a porous ceramic element that catches dirt particles. The newer types of air cleaners feature either oil-soaked plastic foam or paper cartridges. The cartridge types resemble automotive air filters but they're smaller.

Clean the metallic mesh types by rinsing them out in gasoline, drying and re-oiling with engine oil.

An oil-bath air cleaner should be cleaned by dumping the dirty oil, rinsing out the sump and the filter material in kerosene and reassembling, adding new oil up to the level line.

Clean the oil-soaked foam types by taking the air cleaner apart and washing the foam pad in gasoline or detergent. Wrap the foam in cloth and squeeze it dry. Saturate the foam with engine oil and squeeze to remove the excess oil before reassembling.

Clean a porous ceramic element cleaner in gasoline and shake dry before replacing it on the engine.

The paper cartridge filters can be cleaned by brushing with a bristle brush and blowing a stream of air from inside the cartridge to the outside. Do not wet or soak this type of air cleaner. Eventual replacement is needed.

Air cleaners need servicing at least every 25 hours during normal operation. Under dusty conditions, clean them every few hours. The paper cartridge and ceramic elements tend to clog up quicker and need servicing more often.

Additional regular maintenance needed by a small gasoline engine is cleaning of

Remove grass, leaves and other debris to allow a free flow of air through the engine flywheel blower and over the cylinder's cooling fins. These air-cooled engines need all the air they can get.

After cleaning spark plug with a wire brush and solvent, scratch electrode with a hacksaw blade until it is bright. This will do more than anything else to restore the plug to good condition.

grass particles, leaves and dirt from around the flywheel housing. The engine depends on air blown by the vanes of the flywheel for keeping cool. Any air restrictions can cause burned valves, burned spark plugs and even a burned-out engine. Periodically, take off the blower housing and clean the flywheel's vanes and the cylinder's cooling fins. A light scraping with a screwdriver usually does the trick.

Ignition Maintenance

About every 100 hours of running, the spark plug should be removed, cleaned with a pen knife or wire brush and solvent and gapped. Set the gap to that called for by the engine maker. Often this is either .025 or .030 inches. Use a new spark plug if that is indicated by the condition of the old plug. Don't use an automobile spark plug. You may have trouble with it later on. Instead, get a special plug designed especially for small-engine use.

If a spark plug has heavy carbon deposits, burned electrodes or cracked insulation, replace it with a new one. A normal plug that can be cleaned and used has brown to grayish tan deposits and only slight electrode wear.

About once in 100 hours an engine's breaker points need inspecting and perhaps a good cleaning and adjusting. Usually they're located behind the flywheel. Take the flywheel off by removing the air shroud and flywheel nut. Watch out for a lefthand thread. Tap the shaft to dislodge the taper fit and lift off the flywheel. Then if there's a cover plate over the breaker points, take that off by removing the screws. If the point surfaces are pitted or burned, replace them with a new set.

Breaker point surfaces should meet squarely. If they don't, bend the stationary point support with a pair of pliers. See that the points open to the proper distance. This is usually specified at .020 inch. Use a thickness gauge to make the adjustment. Points that are pitted cannot be adjusted correctly.

A condenser rarely needs replacing. The one that is in service is more likely to be good than a new one. At least it has been tested and is known to work.

The hard life that small gasoline engines see makes them more in need of a carburetor adjustment than an auto engine. The adjustment should be made with the engine warmed up and with the air cleaner clean and in place. With the engine at normal operating speed turn the

2236 • POWER MOTOR REPAIR

Wide-gap plug trick is done with a spark plug on which gap has been widened to 3/16 inch. Ground the plug and turn engine over at cranking speed. If the plug sparks, then the magneto must be okay.

Use plastic electrical tape on flywheel to test magneto armature's air gap. Gap is okay if one layer of tape goes under armature without being scraped. But, two layers of the tape should rub.

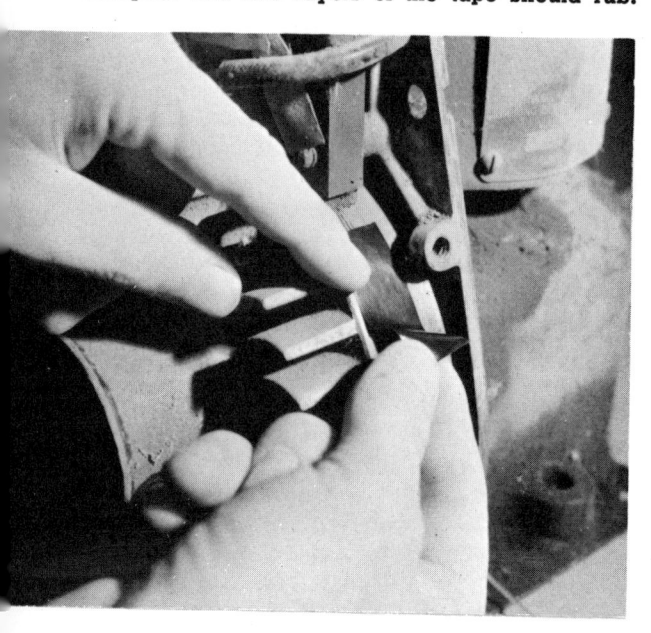

Briggs and Stratton

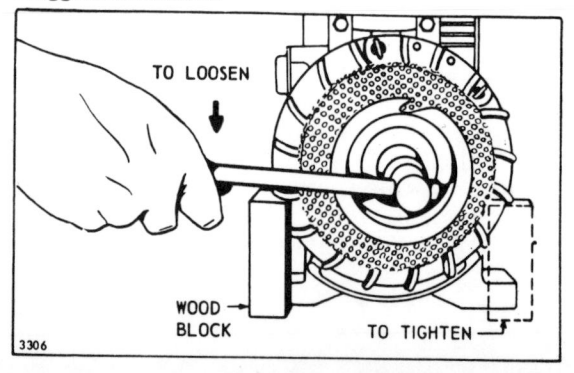

high-speed circuit needle valve inward (clockwise) until the engine starts to lose speed from the too-lean mixture. Then slowly turn it outward (counterclockwise) past the point of smoothest operation until the engine just begins to run unevenly. This mixture will give the best performance under load.

Idle Adjusting

To adjust the low-speed circuit, first adjust the throttle stop screw on the carburetor throttle valve until the proper idle speed, usually about 1750 rpm, is obtained. This may seem fast to those used to watching auto engines idle, but it's necessary. The higher idling speed ensures fast acceleration and proper cooling. On larger-horsepower engines the idle speed may be as low as 1000 rpm.

An engine with a centrifugal clutch connecting it to the load must idle at a speed low enough that the clutch is not activated.

On engines with a separate idle mixture adjusting screw, the needle valve should be turned in until the engine slows down and idles roughly. Then turn the screw out until the engine speeds up and idles smoothly at the desired speed. The throttle stop screw may need readjusting.

Since the high-speed and idle adjustments have some effect on each other, recheck the setting of the high-speed adjustment needle and make final adjustments, as necessary, to achieve the smoothest, most powerful operation.

If adjustments won't smooth out the engine and give it the power it should have, there may be other problems. These are covered later.

Two-cycle engine carburetors are adjusted with the engine under a load. With the engine running and loaded, turn the high-speed needle valve inward until the engine runs at its fastest speed. Then give it a one-eighth turn outward or until the engine begins to slow down. If this adjustment is correct, the engine will start easily and will pick up the load without stalling. The idle-speed needle, if there is one, is adjusted like that for a four-cycle engine.

The important thing to remember in making carburetor adjustments on a two-cycle engine is to favor a rich adjustment. This is because oil for lubrication is in the gasoline. When you lean out the fuel you lean out the oil too. An overrich mixture will not harm the engine except that it tends to foul out spark plugs. An overlean mixture can ruin the engine. Favor richness.

Some of the newer Briggs and Stratton engines are equipped with a simplified choke control that is also a throttle control, enabling you to choke the engine from operating position. Called *Choke-A-Matic*, if the system gets out of adjustment, it can cause hard starting or failure of the engine to stop when the remote control is placed in the stop position. The problem is most likely a misalignment between the engine controls and the remote controls on the powered equipment.

To check the *Choke-A-Matic* remote control adjustment remove the air cleaner and move the control lever to "choke" position. The carburetor choke should be fully closed. Next, move the control lever to "stop". The control lever on the carburetor should then make contact with the stop switch. Adjustments are made by loosening the control cable attachment near the carburetor and sliding the cable one way or the other. Retighten when the position is where it should be.

Troubleshooting

Nothing is more maddening than a single-cylinder engine that won't start or won't run right when it does. Unless it's an electric-start job, you kill yourself, not the battery, by cranking it. You can't call the motor club for a push. All you can do is keep trying, trying, trying. But what if it keeps refusing, refusing, refusing? You've got troubles.

When an engine isn't running right, it is not necessary to be reminded that something is wrong. You know it. The first step toward solving the trouble is to find out what it is. Having a set procedure can help a lot. Here are four basic steps to help you diagnose the trouble. The steps cover (1) magneto output, (2) compression, (3) fuel and (4) spark plug.

Check magneto output first, using the old wide-gap-spark-plug trick. It's one the pro's follow. Clean an old, but good, spark plug and widen the gap to between 5/32 and 3/16 inch. Fasten the engine's high-tension lead to the spark plug and ground the plug to the engine. Crank the engine over and see whether there is a spark. It takes about as much juice for the spark to jump such a wide-gap plug at normal air pressure as it does to jump a normally gapped plug under compression in the cylinder. If there's a spark, you can assume the magneto is okay.

If there is no spark, check the breaker points as previously described. Also see that none of the wires inside the magneto are shorted or grounded.

To remove the flywheel, leave the flywheel retaining nut flush with the end of the crankshaft and tap sharply with a lead or plastic-faced hammer, meanwhile pushing the flywheel out with one hand.

Breaker-point surfaces should meet squarely. If they don't, the stationary breaker point mounting should be bent with pliers, if necessary, to align points with each other. Don't bend movable point.

Briggs and Stratton

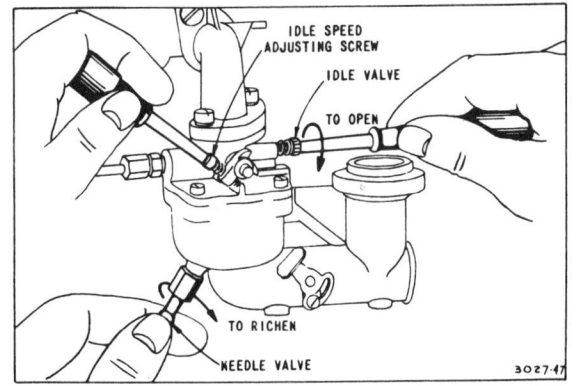

Check the air gap between magneto armature and flywheel. Normally this is specified at .007 to .017 inches.

Check the air gap this easy way. Put a piece of black electrical tape on the flywheel in the area of the magneto. Turn the flywheel with the tape on it past the magneto armature. If the armature cuts into the tape the air gap is too small. Now put another piece of tape on top of the first one and turn the flywheel again. This time the armature should score the tape. If it doesn't, the air gap is too wide.

As a last resort to get a magneto sparking again, try replacing the condenser.

Compression

Good compression in a one-cylinder engine is important because there are no other cylinders to help carry a bad one along. A loss of compression causes a corresponding loss of power, along with hard or impossible starting.

The standard compression gauge method of checking compression, that works so well in automobile engines, isn't too satisfactory for checking small engines. A better way is to give the engine a quick spin, by hand, backward against the compression. It should rebound sharply rather than mush past the compression point.

If the compression is below what it should be, maybe the valves need work, the head gasket between the cylinder head and cylinder block is leaking or the piston rings and cylinder need reworking. If you tackle any of this, get a copy of the service manual covering the engine. It often gives full directions on this type of service.

Third in diagnosing engine trouble is fuel supply. If the carburetor is equipped with a bowl drain valve, press that and let a little fuel run out. Check it for signs of water or other foreign elements. If any are present the carburetor, fuel line, fuel filter and tank may need a good cleaning.

TROUBLESHOOTING THE SMALL ENGINE

Won't start or hard to start
  Faulty ignition
    Check stopping device
    Check spark plug
    Check breaker points
    Check for grounded leads
    Check condenser, coil, magnets
  Faulty fuel system
    Out of fuel
    Gas not reaching carb
      Shut-off valve closed
      Dirt, gum or water in line or carb
      Stale fuel in tank
    Carb not adjusted
      Too lean, starved for fuel
      Too rich, engine flooded
      Choke not closing fully
      Throttle not opening fully
  Low or no compression
    Blown head gasket
    Damaged or worn cylinder
    Valve problems
  Not cranking fast enough
    Impulse starter spring weak or broken
    Too much drag on driven equipment
  Carbon blocking exhaust ports (two-cycle)
  Reed valve broken (two-cycle)
  Loose blade (vertical-shaft engines)

Engine misfires
  Spark plug gap too wide
  Wrong carb setting or lack of fuel
  Wrong type spark plug
  Improper timing
  Valve sticking
  Loose high-tension wire

  Stopping device not positively on
  Weak or irregular spark—check magneto

Engine surges or runs unevenly
  Clogged fuel line
  Water in fuel
  Improper fuel mixture
  Loose ignition connections
  Air leaks into manifold or carburetor
  Gas cap vent plugged
  Carb float level too low
  Carb out of adjustment
  Governor or throttle parts binding

Overheating
  Dirty air intake screen, shroud or fins
  Improper fuel mix (two-cycle)
  Low on oil (four-cycle)
  Fuel mixture too lean
  Improper ignition timing
  Engine overloaded
  Too tight valve tappet clearance
  Running too fast, too slow
  Engine dirty
  Too much carbon in combustion chamber
  Obstructed exhaust

Engine will not idle
  Incorrect carb idle adjustment
  Carburetor clogged
  Spark plug gap too close
  Leaking carb or manifold gaskets

Backfiring
  Fuel mixture too lean
  Improper ignition timing
  Valve sticking

POWER MOTOR REPAIR • 2239

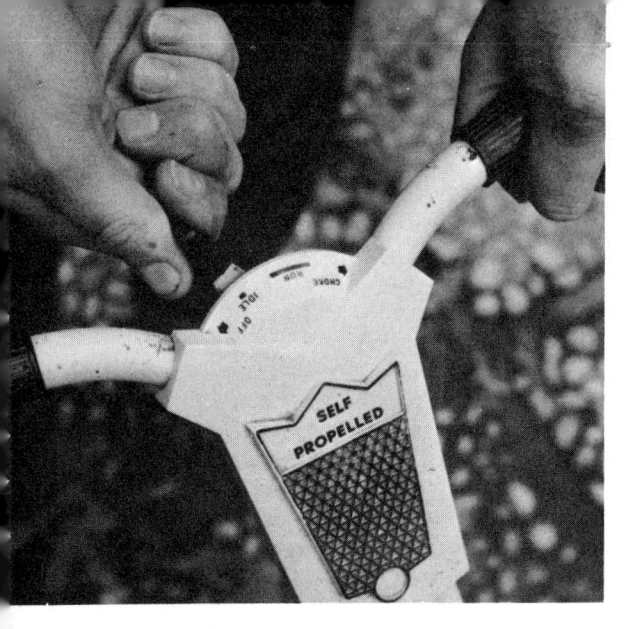

If Choke-A-Matic control gets out of adjustment the choke, idle and shut-off will not function. Problem is easily fixed by adjusting cable backward or forward where it mounts onto engine.

Scraping carbon build-up away from exhaust ports with a screwdriver should be done regularly on a two-cycle engine. Avoid gouging into piston by turning crankshaft so piston is clear of opening.

If there is no bowl drain, remove the air filter, choke the engine fully and try to start it a few times. Then look in the throat of the carburetor to see if raw gasoline has been drawn into the carburetor by choking. If it has not, disconnect the fuel line at the carburetor and see if fuel runs out. If it does, the trouble is most likely in the carburetor. Follow the instructions in the engine manual on carb service.

Some engines are equipped with fuel pumps. These should be checked to see that they're pumping.

Spark Plug

During an engine diagnosis the spark plug should not be overlooked. In no-start problems, on a two-cycle engine, a fouled plug is most often the cause. It sometimes pays to keep an extra spark plug cleaned and ready to install on a balky two-cycle.

The check that can be made on a spark plug is entirely visual. Look for carbon buildup, burned electrodes and incorrect gap.

A careful examination of the spark plug after removing it can give an indication of what is going on inside the engine. Dry, fluffy black deposits may result from overrich carburetion or excessive choking. A clogged air cleaner can restrict the air flow enough to cause overrichness. Poor ignition output can reduce voltage and cause misfiring. Too much idling and slow engine speeds under light loads can keep plug temperatures so low that normal combustion deposits are not burned off. If this is the case, use a higher heat range spark plug for a replacement.

Wet, oily deposits, with a minor amount of electrode erosion, may be caused by oil that is pumping past worn piston rings. Breaking in a new or overhauled engine may produce this condition, too. Usually such plugs can be cleaned and reinstalled. While a higher heat range plug may minimize the oil deposits, an engine overhaul may be necessary to get satisfactory service in severe cases.

Burned electrodes or blistered insulator nose and badly eroded electrodes are indications of spark plug overheating. Improper spark timing or low octane fuel can cause detonation and overheating. Leaves, or grass, in the way of the cooling air may cause overheated spark plugs. Lean air-fuel mixtures are an additional cause. These causes and sustained high-speed heavy-load service produce high temperatures in an engine that require the use of lower heat-range plugs.

By making the four checks you can find what part of the engine needs attention. If the steps outlined are followed—not necessarily in that order—a lot of time can be saved by working only on the part of the engine that needs it.

If you keep your small gasoline engines properly maintained they will be ready when needed to keep your house and grounds maintained. •

ALL ABOUT FIREPLACES

In modern homes the fireplace is an aesthetic adornment, and its function as a heating device has become of secondary importance. In general, the efficiency of a fireplace is low, so that its use has been limited to emergencies or to provide its cheery atmosphere.

The efficiency of an ordinary fireplace is only about 10-15%. Therefore, unless firewood is plentiful and cheap, the cost of use of a fireplace may be extremely high. The efficiency of a prefabricated fireplace that provides a means for circulating room air over the back and side heating surfaces is considerably higher than that of an ordinary fireplace. The addition of a circulator fan to a prefabricated circulating fireplace may be justified.

Gas-fired logs in which the flue gases are vented up the chimney, are inefficient burners of gas compared to boilers or furnaces. An electric log, which is nothing more than an electric light designed to resemble a fireplace, will be no more wasteful of electric energy than an ordinary light bulb, as long as the chimney is closed or blocked. If the flue is left open as an exhaust vent, it should be closed as soon as the need for venting is accomplished.

When the fireplace is located in the same room as the room thermostat for the central heating system, the heat supplied by the fireplace will tend to keep the room warm enough so that the thermostat does not call for heat. The remainder of the house will then be cooler than normal, resulting in a saving from the underheating of the rooms not exposed to the fireplace.

The fire in the fireplace gives off most of its heat by radiation from the flames, the hot coals, and the surface of the back of the fireplace. However, a large amount of heated air is drawn up the chimney and vented to the outdoors, and this is a waste of thermal energy. After the fire had died down, the warm room air will continue to escape up the chimney. Since the fireplace will continue to release combustion gases as long as the embers are warm, and the damper can not be closed until the fire is dead, some means must be found to close the front of the fireplace.

Attractive covers made of tempered glass are available for this purpose. The glass doors can be closed even with the fire still active. A low fire can be left to die out without attention, and the fireplace can be closed in the morning. The use of a cover made from a fire-resistant material, such as pressed asbestos-board is also possible. After the fire has died down, and the embers are completely cold, the flue damper should be closed.

When the fireplace chimney is located on the inside wall, part of the heat absorbed by the chimney is recovered by the house. However, if the chimney is located on an outside wall, so that three sides of the chimney are exposed to the outdoors, very little heat from the chimney is retained.

NEWSPAPER LOGS

If old newspapers are not being recycled, they should be considered for use in the fireplace. Papers are folded in half and stacked until they are about one inch thick. They are then tightly rolled to make a simulated log. Metal plant ties or plain pliable wires are wrapped around the bundle so that the "log" does not fly open when the outer layer is exposed to the flame.

It is possible to burn cartons, wood crates, mill ends, and other materials in a fireplace, but these should be handled with care because of the possibility of overfiring. The main drawback to the use of various kinds of waste material is that constant firing is required and the fire can not be left unattended.

As a safety measure, when prolonged use is made of the fireplace, combustible materials should not be close to the rear surface of the fireplace, since the heat transmitted through the back of the fireplace and chimney can char wood or blister the painted surface of any object touching the back wall.

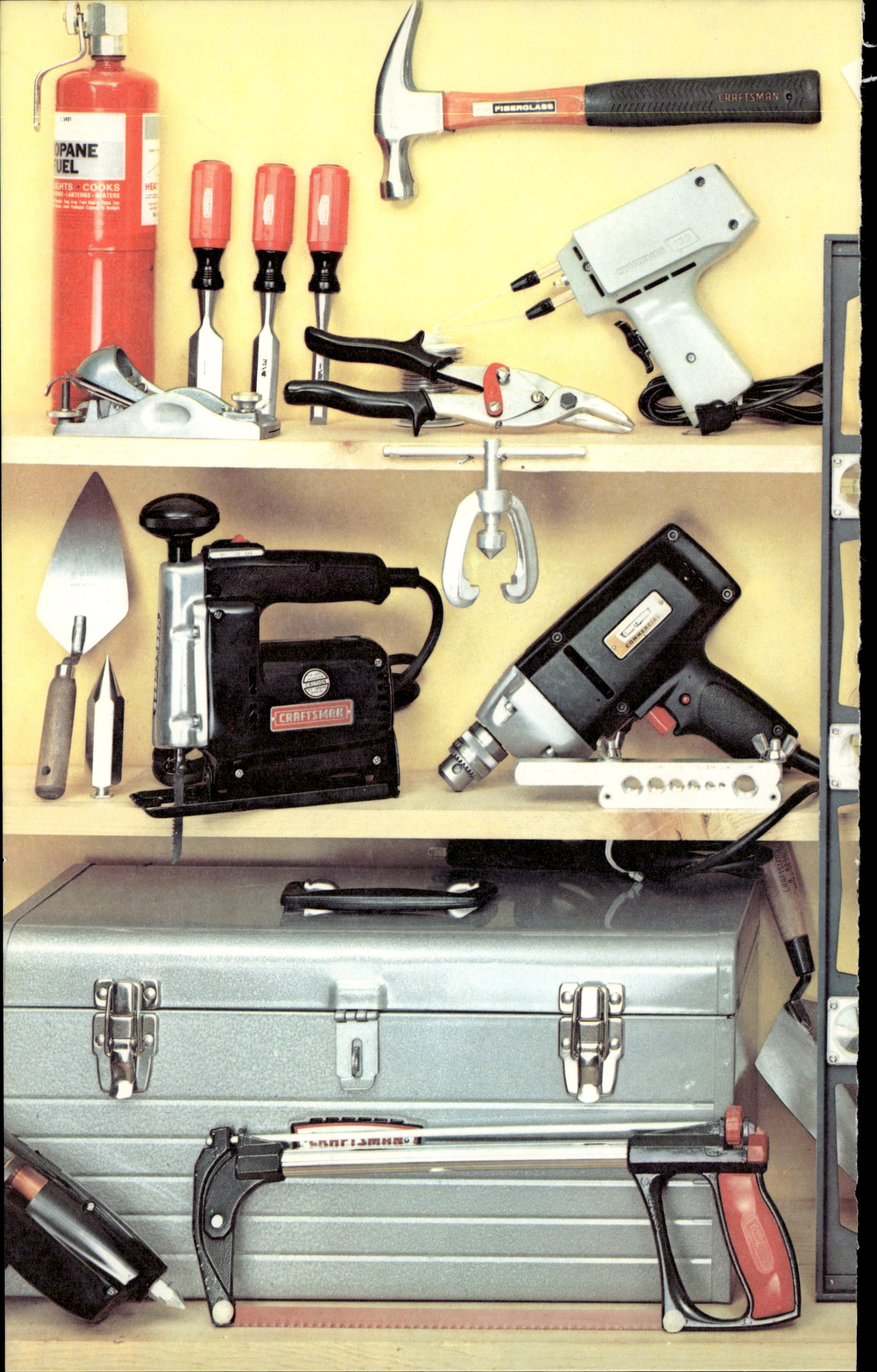
FIBERGLASS
CRAFTSMAN
CRAFTSMAN